SCHOOLCRAFT COLLEGE LIBRARY

W9-ADM-005

WITHDRAWN

BEEN A HEAVY LIFE

CRITICAL PERSPECTIVES IN CRIMINOLOGY

Series Editor
Bruce A. Arrigo,
University of North Carolina, Charlotte

*A list of books in the series
appears at the end of this book.*

Lois Presser

BEEN A HEAVY LIFE
STORIES OF VIOLENT MEN

UNIVERSITY OF ILLINOIS PRESS

Urbana and Chicago

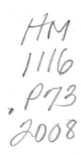

HM
1116
.P73
2008

© 2008 by the Board of Trustees
of the University of Illinois
All rights reserved
Manufactured in the United States of America
1 2 3 4 5 C P 5 4 3 2 1
∞ This book is printed on acid-free paper.

Library of Congress Cataloging-in-Publication Data
Presser, Lois.
Been a heavy life : stories of violent men / Lois Presser.
p.   cm. — (Critical perspectives in criminology)
Includes bibliographical references and index.
ISBN-10: 0-252-03358-2 (cloth : alk. paper)
ISBN-13: 978-0-252-03358-2 (cloth : alk. paper)
ISBN-10: 0-252-07558-7 (pbk. : alk. paper)
ISBN-13: 978-0-252-07558-2 (pbk. : alk. paper)
1. Violence in men.
2. Abusive men.
3. Criminal behavior.
I. Title.
HM1116.P73   2008
305.38'962—dc22   2008006459

In loving memory of Helen Presser,
who set an example of compassion.

Contents

Foreword

BRUCE A. ARRIGO

Ethnographic studies of "dangerous men" have generally taken us behind bars. Erving Goffman's (1961) arresting critique of the confinement setting as a generative milieu for the exercise of power helped to spawn a series of monograph-length works recounting life, death, and survival behind prison walls (e.g., Jacobs 1978; Sykes 1971; Toch 1977). A second wave of penological analysis, still concerned with "everyday experience" behind bars, challenged the correctional system as an extension of the state's regulatory ambit. For example, Irwin's (1970, 1985) studies of the felon and the jail respectively ushered in a new era of incisive commentary. Crime control as industry was understood to function as a gulag (Christie 1993), and the American corrections project generally was recognized as one of doing harm (Clear 1994).

More recent studies have continued the "insider" tradition of penological inquiry. To illustrate, investigations documenting the life of confined convicts (e.g., Hassine 2007; Santos 2006) form part of what now is termed "convict criminology" (Ross and Richards 2002), in which the full effects of society's mass imprisonment binge are made abundantly clear (Garland 2004). Among other things, we have sacrificed racial minorities (Mauer 2006), women (Bloom, Owen, and Covington 2003), the mentally disabled (Haney 2006), juveniles (Bortner and Williams 1997), families (Mauer and Chesney-Lind 2003) and even economically depressed neighborhoods (Clear 2007) at the altar of a politically ensconced corrections agenda.

The harm that offenders did or might do in the future remains the official but widely accepted justification for mass incapacitation. The flaws of mass incapacitation are forgiven so long as offenders cannot or do not "make good" (Maruna 2001). Cynically or not, we expect offenders to reclaim their lives, and they strive to do the same. Theirs is perhaps the more complex effort, for it includes resisting the terms in which "reclaiming one's life" have been circumscribed (Bosworth 1999). Resistance takes place behind but also, significantly, beyond metal bars and electronic fences—in stories and vocabularies for storying personhood, manhood, harm, violence. It is at this juncture that we confront the brilliant new volume, *Been a Heavy Life: Stories of Violent Men,* by Lois Presser.

As the author herself notes, it is not enough to document the stories of convicts. We must understand how these stories are assembled in the social and institutional world, to grasp both the offenders' struggles and the operation of the political economy of criminalization and criminal justice. We must recognize the socially mediated construction of personhood—of who the "convict" is—through a methodology that builds on the insights of labeling theory (e.g., H. Becker 1963; Lemert 1967), symbolic interactionism (Cooley 1902; Mead 1934; see also Blumer 1969; Stryker 1980), neutralization studies (e.g., Maruna and Copes 2005), and discourse analysis (Arrigo, Milovanovic, and Schehr 2005; Holstein and Gubrium 2000). This is an approach that stresses the value of reflexivity (Bourdieu and Wacquant 1992) and the co-production of historically specific meanings (Henry and Milovanovic 1996).

In her thoughtfully researched, skillfully interpreted, and thoroughly engaging study, Presser gives us this much needed view of the violent offender's narrated, situated identity. Embedded in these narratives are statements about the possibility of being a good self. Perhaps most illuminating is the discussion of the reformist tale (chapter 5 and the "good" self), the stability account (chapter 6 and the never "bad" self), the elastic narrative (chapter 7 and selfhood as "creative integration"), and the heroic story (chapter 8 and internal and external morality struggles). Each of these analytic descriptions provides considerable breadth and depth to the theoretical and methodological foundations of this book. Presser understands that narrative is inevitably influenced by others, including by the researcher. It is tied to narration, hence context. And, in this respect, perhaps her work is consistent with the somewhat auto-ethnographic accounts of Liebow (1967), Griffin (1960), and Rhodes (2004). To be clear, this orientation only magnifies the texturing of Presser's inquiry and the eloquence of her insights.

In the final chapter, the author revisits her persuasive thesis that "violent men" are ever under construction, discursively and practically—by those men who do violence *and* by those who profit from their control. Given the power of (belief in) narrative, heroic stories in which prospects for change and possibilities of redemption are seeded in the struggle to overcome (Nietzsche 1968) may be criminogenic.

But how shall we characterize the struggle to remain human, all too human, despite marginalizing and alienating characterizations, if not in heroic terms (Nietzsche 2006)? In the realm of penology—especially behind the walls of silence that contain and engulf the offender's structures of suffering—humanity requires sound policy, sensible practice, and steadfast activism. This is the agenda to which Presser purposefully redirects our collective attentions, inviting us to rethink those conditions that oppress and deny the humanness of us all. To do otherwise imprisons the self, whether physically confined as such or, equally as profound, psychologically held captive. This is the deplorable state of our "freedom"—a state in which we, regrettably, erect nothing more than debilitating mechanisms of escape from society, from others, and, ultimately, from ourselves (Fromm 1994). Presser's volume is a fascinating assessment of how convicts (and society more generally) can indeed overcome such devastating suffering.

Acknowledgments

A great many people made this book possible. My helpers are dear friends and teachers: Bruce Arrigo, Deidre Ashton, Julia Chu, Todd Clear, Marilyn Croman, Reuben Danzing, Rob Danzig, Russel Durst, Eric Fieldman, Bernadette Fiore, Emily Gaarder, Elaine Gunnison, Cyndi Hamilton, Brooke Judkins, Miriam Levering, David Lundgren, Bernice Mahler, Shadd Maruna, Paul Mazerolle, Kumiko Mitarai, Judy Montville, Caroline Nicholl, Sharyn Roach Anleu, Michelle Rosen, Joyce Sacco, Suhith Wickrema, and Anthony Zitrin. They include my financial supporter, the Office of Research and Advanced Studies at the University of Cincinnati, and my intellectual partners in the Department of Sociology at the University of Tennessee.

Joey Presser was a constant source of encouragement and sometimes emergency assistance. Ami, Laura Retyi-Gazda, my friends in Frontrunners of Cincinnati, and my allies in the March for Justice of Cincinnati, made life in Cincinnati worthwhile. Administrators and staff of four different agencies generously allowed my work to interfere with theirs.

Thanks to Ed Latessa for his kindness. Thanks to Pat Van Voorhis, John Wooldredge, and Frank Cullen for modeling integrity and excellence in research. Thanks to Lorraine Mazerolle for her boundless intellectual curiosity and insight. Thanks to Robert McConaughy for his empathy and wisdom. I am especially grateful to my three parents, who live in my heart. My father Alex Presser, my natural mother Hilda Winnick Presser, and my adoptive mother Helen Terowsky Presser valued people and education and influenced me to do the same. Finally, the book stands on the stories of twenty-seven men, for whom I wish peace.

SELF AND STORY

"Who are you?" is a question with a long answer or a short answer.
— Louise Erdrich, "The Butcher's Wife," 2001

Complex personhood means that the stories people tell about themselves, about their troubles, about their social worlds, and about their society's problems are entangled and weave between what is immediately available as a story and what their imaginations are reaching toward.
— Avery F. Gordon, *Ghostly Matters: Haunting and the Sociological Imagination,* 1997

In this book, I report on the talk of men who murdered, raped, and assaulted others. I focus on how these men spoke of *who they are.* During in-depth interviews with twenty-seven men in and out of correctional institutions, in halfway houses, and on death row, I heard depictions of the self as morally decent and as engaged in a heroic struggle of some sort. It is crucial that we understand such talk. Violence is excused and justified through talk about the self in relation to others: for example, by saying that the victim has wronged one in the past (Sykes and Matza 1957). Furthermore, one who has done harm may desist in the future by constructing a self that is capable of being good (Maruna 2001). In other words, the way people identify themselves makes harmful action (like all action) possible; in changing how they identify themselves, people are less likely to do harm.

Talk of violence by perpetrators of violence has been probed before, mainly for the purpose of understanding causes (Athens 1997; J. Gilligan 1997; Hearn 1998; Toch 1969; Vetlesen 2005). From these investigations, we have learned how actors' *interpretations* of harmful action and the situation for harmful action influence the action. Scholars have listened to *what* violent men have said about their violence: for example, that it is good (Toch 1993) or restorative (Alvarez 1997), it establishes justice (J. Gilligan 1997), or creates a better society (Alvarez 1997). I listen to *how* they say it, and particularly to how they situate their violent actions within a longer life story—a self-story. The whole self-story—the entire interpretive context for one's violent behavior—bears on the violence (Maruna and Copes 2005, 253).[1]

People are not, of course, exactly who they say they are. Yet, neither are they who easily recorded "facts" such as criminal convictions—or even crimes they admit to having committed—say they are. (See table 1 in chapter 4 for "facts" about the men I interviewed.) Personhood, as Avery Gordon puts it, is complex. Our selves, including our preferred selves, are always still in the making. And so, I view even my interviews with these "violent men" as sites of identity construction. *Here* (but not only here) is where violent selves were made and unmade. This book both describes the life stories of violent male offenders and examines how these stories were collaboratively constructed. At the end of the book I suggest a theory of violence based on stories and the "heavy life" circumstances that underwrite them.

Narratives and Identities

What I call a *narrative* is more precisely an oral self-narrative, a spoken rendering of one's personal experience as an agent in the world (Rosenwald and Ochberg 1992). Narrative in this sense is sometimes called a life story or life history (Linde 1993). But a narrative is not a report on one's entire life so far. Rather, a narrative may attend to a specific period of one's life or to a single episode. Importantly, a narrative always draws selectively upon lived experience (Gergen and Gergen 1988; Polonoff 1987).[2]

Narratives (self-narratives) have an evaluative point to make about the self. A description of the amount of water in my glass is not a narrative because it makes no evaluative point. But if I embed my description in a statement about how hard I am working—so hard that I take no time out to fill the glass, though I am thirsty—then it is part of a narrative. This narrative is a rendering of my experience of working hard.

What I call *identity* is one's sense of who one is. Scholarly approaches to identity are varied. One may be seen as "having" various categorical identities, which are akin to roles in society, such as daughter or student (G. Stone 1962; R. Turner 1976). Or, one's identity lies in the *meaning* that these roles hold for the individual. For example, Stryker and Craft (1982) observe that it is "not enough to know that a person appropriates a role label—say, male—as part of self; it is essential to ask what being a male 'means' to the person" (164; see also Burke 1991). Besides social roles and their meanings, identity is said to involve personal attributes (e.g., honest, shy) (C. Gordon 1968; Kinch 1963; Kuhn and McPartland 1954). Chad Gordon (1968) notes that "the ordinary member of the society conceives of himself [sic] in terms of both categories and attributes simultaneously" (117). Accordingly, identity is that which we share with other people *and* that which distinguishes us from other people (Jenkins 2004). Some identity theorists define these as social identity versus personal identity (Goffman 1963a; Tajfel 1981; J. Turner 1999; see Jenkins 2004 for a critique). Social identity calls upon one's perceived membership in a group; personal identity calls upon individual differences from the group (J. Turner 1999, 12).

In each of these conceptions of identity, the self cannot be known without reference to other people. That insight is important to this book, which conceptualizes the researcher as one referent (and therefore the interview as a meaningful forum) for identity expression. But I wish to emphasize a conception of identity that moves beyond static positions altogether. In contrast to categorical *or* trait-based conceptions of identity is a dynamic, *storied* one that emphasizes our becoming. It locates identity "in overlapping networks of relations that shift over time and space" (Somers 1994, 607). A diverse group of scholars espouses this storied notion of identity, including sociologists (e.g., Somers 1994), sociolinguists (e.g., Linde 1993; O'Connor 2000), psychologists (e.g., J. Bruner 1990; Gergen and Gergen 1986, 1988; Polkinghorne 1988; Sarbin 1986), and philosophers (Kerby 1991).

According to this view, identity is not communicable in single terms but rather in past, present, and future tenses. The stuff of identity is lived social experience—the subjective past and present—as well as the desired future. Consider these features in Tim's narrative.[3] Tim had committed rape and attempted homicide. "Been a heavy life [*laugh*] man—some weird stuff. I been involved in some of them dumb things, man. Heart-rending for me. You know, well—it's not so bad anymore 'cause I've pretty well come to grips on things an' I got a lot of things under control. An' I've had time to think about things, analyze things an' uh, just sorta reevaluate my priorities. You know, a lot of things. An' my value system's totally different than it had been." Tim's identity cannot be summed up in a few choice words. It demands fuller qualitative expression. Specifically, it demands narrative form: a discursive structuring of experiences such that they are *connected* both logically and temporally (Gergen and Gergen 1986; Linde 1993; Somers 1994). Tim's identity encompasses more than what he currently believes himself to be. It also encompasses what he has been. And it anticipates a *future* self—one guided by "totally different" values than he has lived by before.

Social group affiliations and traits do enter into this more dynamic conception of identity. For example, Tim told me that he raped a woman once but that he is "not a rapist." Repeatedly, over the course of four interviews, Tim stressed his struggle to escape the label of rapist, in part by appealing to traits that "rapists" purportedly lack. Yet Tim's identity, I contend, is not simply that of a "non-rapist." First, to state and to conceive that one is a non-rapist (or rapist) makes no sense disassociated from past events and future goals. Further, rape was just one of many actions Tim took in his life, and rapist is just one label he has adopted, albeit unwillingly. Tim's identity materializes in a tale of trying to reconcile socially ascribed labels (e.g., that of rapist) and all that they mean (e.g., bad) with other affiliations and traits—those valued and those not—as he encounters new experiences and new people. This is a formidable project but an important and a universal one.

We strive toward self-continuity in the face of observed variation in the self over the life course and across situations (Guerra 1993; Lecky 1945; Schwartz and Stryker 1970). Narrative helps us in that project "to tie together the more disparate strands of our lives, of our history" (Kerby 1991, 105). The intimate tie between identity and narrative is conceptualized especially well by Polkinghorne (1988): "We achieve our personal identities and self-concept through the use of the narrative configuration, and make our existence into a whole by understanding it as an expression of a single unfolding and developing story. We are in the middle of our stories and cannot be sure how they will end; we are constantly having to revise the plot as new events are added to our lives. Self, then, is not a static thing or a substance, but a configuring of personal events into an historical unity which includes not only what one has been but also anticipations of what one will be" (150). Specific linguistic characteristics of narrative are enlisted in establishing a cohesive self (Linde 1993; McAdams 1999). McAdams (1999) explains, "By scripting one's life in such a way that different characters or subselves take on different roles and attributes, the I is able to express the multiplicity of selfhood within a single story of the self. In this way, especially integrative life stories solve the perennial identity problem . . . of the self's need to be many things and one thing at the same time" (486). In narrative it is common to have multiple selves. These correspond to different phases of or happenings in one's life. Narrative chronicles different events, up to and including, often explicitly, the event of narration. There is some disagreement about whether narrative order always reflects the order of actual events, or whether narrative order may upset the "actual" order in favor of the present logic—or plot—attributed to those events. Labov and Waletzky (1967), who advanced a popular model of narrative structure, state the former view: "The basic narrative units that we wish to isolate are defined by the fact that they recapitulate experience in the same order as the original events" (20–21). Linde (1993) concurs: "Temporal continuity of the self is built into the very fabric of narrative, since the defining characteristic of the narrative is its reliance on the principle of narrative order" (106–7).

An alternative perspective, articulated by poststructuralist literary scholars, holds that chronological order takes a backseat to logic. Roland Barthes (1977) suggests that narrative "ceaselessly substitutes meaning for the straightforward copy of the events recounted. . . . Thus is established a kind of logical time that has very little connection with real time" (119). Barbara Herrnstein Smith (1981) points out that our knowledge of actual past events, no less than that of fictional events, is highly impressionistic. Therefore there is reason to question "the notion of a set and sequence of events altogether prior and independent of the discourse through which they are narrated" (179). If recollected experience has no single and precise chronological order, then neither does narrative. Psychologists Gergen and Gergen (1988) also stress that ways of structuring narrative are virtually limitless; only cultural standards constrain them. It is merely conventional, though by no means necessary, for contemporary stories to order events as they supposedly occurred.

Boden (1990) resolves this disagreement by noting that the "sequential production [of stories] mimics though does not mirror the sequence of events being captured" (260). Likewise, Polkinghorne (1988) states that narrative "pays special attention" to the sequence of events remembered, but is fundamentally oriented toward a plot (36). In all of these perspectives, the emplotment of events—what they *mean* as a whole—is central. Even Labov and Waletzky's (1967) model assigns a primary role to the "evaluation" of a narrative, which "establishes the importance or point of the narrative" (32).

The plot of a personal narrative encapsulates our reasons for our experiences and actions. Social scientists join scholars from the humanities in associating narrative with *explanation* for deeds done. Literary theorist Albert Stone (1982) calls autobiography "the activity of explaining oneself by telling one's story" (10), and philosopher Paul Ricoeur (1984) states: "To identify an agent and to recognize this agent's motives are complementary operations"

(55). In their classic article, sociologists Scott and Lyman (1968) argue that identity takes shape when we verbally *account for* our behavior. They define accounts in terms of deviance, as "linguistic forms that are offered for untoward action" (47). "Every account is a manifestation of the underlying negotiation of identities" (59). Psychologists Schlenker, Weigold, and Doherty (1991) concur that "identity is constructed via the layering of judgments that emerge from being accountable for events" (110).

By giving accounts acceptable to our audience, we might improve our social status. Thus, when a person is labeled as deviant in some way, narratives help him or her renegotiate that label, in part by complicating and historicizing "who he or she *really* is" in the eyes of others and thus ultimately in his or her own eyes. Thus we demand that critics let us tell "the whole story." For instance, according to Scott and Lyman (1968), "Those labeled as mentally ill may relieve themselves of the worst consequences of that label by recognizing before their psychiatrists the truth value of the label, by reconstructing their past to explain how they came to deviate from normal patterns, and by gradually coming to give acceptable accounts of their behavior" (54). Likewise, Benson (1985) found that white-collar offenders gave varied accounts of their crimes in order to "defeat the process of identity transformation" that comes with criminal justice processing (598). That process of identity transformation—ritualized by "status degradation ceremonies" (Garfinkel 1956)—would present the perpetrator stereotypically or "as all of one piece" (Benson 1985, 600). The narrated identity communicates instead a more complex and distinctive character that has unfolded over time and has the potential for further change. The evolution of one's deviance from identifiable causes positions us as less deviant than an ascribed label suggests.

The potential for narrative to attenuate one's supposed deviance lies also in the "consciousness of narrativity" (Polonoff 1987, 53). Narrative itself presupposes a moral self in the narrating present. Linde (1993) explains: "The act of narration itself creates a split between the narrator and the protagonist. It allows the narrator to stand apart from and comment on the actions of the protagonist. Even if the two have the same name and are connected in time, as is the case in first-person narrative, the reflexivity created by the act of narration means that the speaker is always moral, even if the protagonist of the narrative is not" (123). Simply by narrating, the moral deviant separates him- or herself from past wrongdoing. Jerome Bruner (1990) notes that narrators generally "come off best," whether the "protagonist" of the narrative is vilified or praised (96). One's narrative is a vehicle, and the setting in which it is told is a forum, for taking a moral stance.

The Stories Violent Men Tell: My Influences and Objectives

The identities and consequently the narratives of violent qua "serious" offenders hold particular interest because their behavior has been deemed *immoral*. By definition, within any society, serious crime warrants explanation—an "account" (Scott and Lyman 1968). Criminologists and laypersons alike pose the question: Why? Questions about causes of violent behavior inevitably turn to answers about who the violent person is and how he or she became that way. In other words, violent behavior commonly demands a story about its perpetrator.

Given academic and popular concern with causes of violent behavior, it is not surprising to find that the bulk of research on offender identities and offender narratives treats them as independent variables in theories that try to predict criminal behavior (or its desistance). I review this research, though my own study enables me to illuminate the social construction of offender identities and narratives, and not their potential influence on criminal behavior. Nonetheless my study is relevant to a theory of behavior. I take the position that one's behavior is a function of narratives about one's behavior (Mills 1940). Narratives about oneself as an agent shape behavior now and in the future (Maruna 2001).

In addition, the criminological literature on offender identities and offender narratives provides insight into popular and academic "metanarratives" about violent criminals—specifically about what they say and think of themselves. Contemporary criminology also theorizes social conditions that may lead to crime. The criminological knowledge base therefore creates background expectations that my research participants and I hold and that framed our conversations.

The argument that identities are fashioned through social processes is not new (Berger and Luckmann 1966). Most sociologists take for granted the "social construction of reality." The argument is less often backed by close observation of identities being shaped in interaction with other people. In particular, it mostly remains to be seen how the identities of problematic persons (Loseke 2003) get constructed and reconstructed in social encounters.

As compared with studies of property offenders, there have been few ethnographic studies of *any* nature of *violent* offenders. Those that have been done are oriented toward specific crime events (e.g., Toch 1993). Sociological research on offenders' *talk* is likewise generally event-oriented (e.g., Cressey 1953; Mills 1940; Scott and Lyman 1968; Sykes and Matza 1957; see Maruna and Copes 2005 for discussion). For example, Scott and Lyman (1968) focus on accounting for conduct deemed unacceptable, with either excuses—"socially approved vocabularies for mitigating or relieving responsibility" (47)—or justifications, where one accepts responsibility for an action but denies that the action is bad. Sykes and Matza (1957) likewise define neutralizations as akin to "defenses to crimes" (666). Accounts of whole lives have been neglected. The turn to violence (and the turn away from violence) must be processual (Athens 1997); as Alvarez puts it concerning participation in Nazi genocide, it "did not merely involve a single internal readjustment" (169). The need for studies that consider whole lives as constructed by the actor is noted by Sampson and Laub (1993): "Qualitative data derived from systematic open-ended questions or narrative life histories are crucial in uncovering the social processes underlying stability and change in criminal and deviant behavior" (251; see also Ulmer and Spencer 1999). This book fills these empirical gaps. The narrators in my sample gave not only accounts of their violent and nonviolent offenses but also overarching accounts of their lives. Following suit, the focus of the book is the complete life story and not stories of individual deviant events.

There is a methodological gap the book fills as well. I view the interview as a social transaction, with key similarities to any other social transaction (Kuhn 1962). Because the interview is a social transaction, the narrative that emerges from the interview, and therefore narrated identities "collected" by interviewers, are social products (Chanfrault-Duchet 2000; Gadd 2004; Holstein and Gubrium 1995, 2000; Ives 1980; Miles and Crush 1993; Mishler 1986a, 1986b, 1992; Wiersma 1988). I am myself a contributor to or "co-producer" of the narrative data. As they spoke, the men in my study were already incorporating the interview—all that it involved and signified—into their narratives. The fact of the interview and specifics of the interview exchange were significant experiences for them. The interview shaped their life stories.

Those who study narratives, no less than students of more conventional topics, have tended to be carefully passive during the interview. For example, Willott, Griffin, and Torrance (2001), in reporting a discussion held with four incarcerated white-collar offenders, note that the interviewer present "kept her contributions to a minimum" (448): "Within the constraints of a recorded interview, therefore, we believe that the discourse sampled was as reasonably close to what might be expected in naturally occurring conversation." The research setting is not "natural"—it is atypical, but it *is* a social setting. The researcher is a social actor. As Fontana and Frey (2000) point out, the interviewer has a demeanor and ways of interacting with the research participant "whether the interviewer is just being 'a nice person' or is following a format" (660). In 1958, Dean and Whyte pointed out that the "interview situation must be seen as just one of many situations in which an informant may reveal subjective data in different ways" (35). Yet decades later, Mishler (1986a) reported that "with few exceptions, effects on the form and content of a respondent's story of the research interview as the context in which it is told have received little attention" (245). Even more recently, ethnographer Lisa Maher (1997) stated: "A truly reflexive approach to fieldwork involves talking about how we create these worlds—about how the 'there' we study does not exist prior to, and independent of, the shared worlds we create with our informants. Such approaches remain rare" (213). Critical theorists have done much to call attention to the pervasiveness of researcher bias (see Norum 2000) but not to the practical, contingent ways in which qualitative data are co-produced by researcher and participant.

I explore both the substance and the process of narrative construction of "violent offenders." First, I consider the narratives themselves and identify patterns in the men's stories. Second, I demonstrate how identities are constructed through talk. I identify precise instances of the co-production of the men's stories.

What Do Narratives *Really* Represent?

Narratives hold substantial promise as tools for understanding a wide range of social phenomena (Sarbin 1986). They are undergoing a "revival" in the social sciences (McCall and Wittner 1990). Still, narrative data pose some knotty problems that can be summed up with the question: What do they really represent?

In their most basic conception, narratives are records or descriptions of human behavior. For example, oral historians and anthropologists have used narratives in order to understand a group of people about which outsiders know little (see, e.g., Ives 1980). Journalists count on such narratives to cover "the news." The assumption here is that a narrative documents, though it is not equivalent to, what actually happened or is happening in someone's social world.

Narratives are also, perhaps predominantly, used to illuminate how people see (or saw) their world. Here the narrative is appreciated as a certain *rendering* of what is happening or has happened. Ethnographic or field researchers collect and analyze narrative data for the express purpose of understanding people's interpretations of their world. Interpretations are significant to researchers because people act based on their perceptions of things that concern them—the so-called Thomas Theorem (Thomas and Thomas 1928). People do not respond to things as they "really" are. As Burgess (1966) noted concerning the validity of the life history of young Stanley, analyzed by Shaw (1930) in *The Jack-Roller,* "In human affairs it is not the absolute truth about an event that concerns us but the way in which persons react to that event" (189). For sociologists who use narrative data primarily, their interpretive nature is their main draw.

A key difference between these two formulations of the narrative—as historical record versus interpretive statement—is the latter's emphasis on subjectivity. In scholarly practice, this difference has mainly been considered unproblematic. Accounts of the past are usually recognized as being "subjective" to varying degrees. That is, these accounts are processed by individual minds and therefore at a remove from the actual past. Investigators interested in historical events *qua* events conduct checks on "validity" by amassing and comparing multiple narratives as well as "hard data" or documentary proof—for example, physical evidence of atrocities (Dean and Whyte 1958; Minow 1998; Scheper-Hughes 1992). They then present common themes. More often, however, narratives are seen to provide the human context of historical events, which gives the latter meaning.

Critical theorists, most notably feminist and other scholars from historically marginalized groups, have taken issue with the idea that one can narrate from a neutral, value-free position (see D. Smith 1987). Following the view that subjectivity is never eradicable, they substitute more reflexive analyses of their own. There they reveal the stakes that the investigator has in the data. The data are shown to reflect a political reality of which the investigator is a part. These critics embrace the subjectivity of all narratives by exposing the research itself as a narrative—a story that the scholar is telling within a particular historical context.

I adopt a "post-positivist" perspective on narratives that takes the assertion, that all documentation/knowledge is partial, even further. According to this perspective, narrative is seen as *constitutive* of reality—not as its representation.[4] Increasingly, this theme is sounded in mostly conceptual writings. Gergen and Gergen (1988) propose that "we live by stories—both in the telling and the doing of self" (18). Somers (1994) observes that "social life is itself *storied* and . . . narrative is an *ontological condition of social life*" (613–14; emphases in original). Polkinghorne (1988) points out that our existence "adheres according to protocols that are literary or narrative in character" (64). We cognitively structure events in our lives according to some narrated plot, even as we experience them; we do not (merely) structure them later

(Polkinghorne 1988, 68). Furthermore, we live out those plots that are made available to us in particular social, historical, and cultural moments.

The post-positivist stance is founded on a recognition of the preeminent role of language in guiding what we take to be "the real." Pure "perception" is never revealed because human beings think *through* linguistic articulation. Mary Gergen (1992) explains: "When we tell one another our deepest secrets we use a public language. The nuances of consciousness, emotions both subtle and profound, inner yearnings, the whispering of conscience—all of these are created in the matrix of this language. The words form and deform around us as we speak and listen. . . . Our cultures provide models not only for the contents of what we say but also for the forms. We use these forms unwittingly; they create the means by which we interpret our lives. We know ourselves via the mediating forms of our cultures, through telling, and through listening" (128). Linguistic categories, provided by the dominant culture as well as by specific subcultures, shape how we understand our experience (K. Gergen 1971; Merleau-Ponty 1978; Polkinghorne 1988; Taylor 1985; Whorf 1956). To use a topical example, vocabulary for talking about crime ("Was it *justified?*" "Was there a *rational* motive?") configures our reactions to crime (Henry and Milovanovic 1996; Matza 1964; Mills 1940; Sykes and Matza 1957). We interpret our experiences in the only way we can as human beings—symbolically and, specifically, linguistically (Taylor 1985). Phenomenologists (e.g., Husserl 1964; Merleau-Ponty 1978; Schutz 1967), hermeneutic philosophers (e.g., Ricoeur 1984, 1985; Taylor 1985), contemporary linguists (e.g., Benveniste 1971), and others embrace this idea (see also Maynard and Whalen's [1995] review). Yet contemporary social scientists have rather cautiously taken it up, evidenced in Van Maanen's (1995) sardonic comments: "As virtually all ethnographers now realize (however much they may complain), language has been promoted in the intellectual scheme of things. Language is now auditioning for an a priori role in the social and material world, a role that carries constitutional force—bringing facts into consciousness and therefore being. No longer then is something like culture or, for that matter, atoms and quarks thought to come first while our understandings, models, or representations of culture, atoms, or quarks come second. Rather, our representations may well come first, allowing us to selectively see what we have described" (14).

What is true for representations of "culture, atoms, or quarks"—that they shape their objects—is all the more true for representations of the "object" that is the self. Self-representation is unique because what is being represented—the self—is concurrently doing the representing. Polonoff (1987) explains: "Our knowledge of the self, though often tantalizingly similar to other kinds of knowledge, is never entirely the same, for the representations one forms of oneself are part of the very self one seeks to represent" (45). In Mead's (1934) terms, the self is both a subject and (to itself) an object (136–37). But these remarks on the special nature of the self as a thing featured in a narrative, or in any other text, do not take away from the general point that a text shapes any object to which it addresses itself.

Perhaps one still wishes to maintain that there exists some internal notion of things (e.g., one's notion of one's self) more or less beyond social influence. We are nonetheless unable to access it. First, upon contemplating one's life experiences (say, prompted by a researcher), one finds they are always already changed by the contemplation. As Polonoff (1987) notes: "Even the private consultation with recollection issues in a kind of narration in which temporal gaps are elided and the continuous succession of experiences is organized as movement to and from significant episodes or markers" (47). In other words, even personal reflection undergoes selective representation, and thus social influence. For what are those significant episodes or markers if not those deemed as such by persons and institutions of a particular cultural-historical context? Mead theorized that individuals recall what is publicly deemed appropriate to recall, and thus the present always shapes what we call "the past" (Maines, Sugrue, and Katovich 1983). Our recollections must be intelligible within our cultural environment. Gergen and Gergen (1988) agree: "Memory is not so much an individual as it is a social process" (20).

Second, and especially germane to this study, research (or any other kind of inquiry) itself exerts influence. This is recognized in the physical sciences as much as in the social sciences. In 1927, physicist Werner Heisenberg articulated his "uncertainty principle," according to which the actual velocity and position of an electron can never be known in a given moment because the light needed to observe the electron alters them. Similarly, the social scientist affects the research participant's expressed thought. As Pool (1957) observed on the topic of survey methodology: "The rule is that the social milieu in which communication takes place modifies not only what a person dares to say but even what he thinks he chooses to say. And these variations in expression cannot be viewed as mere deviations from some underlying 'true' opinion, for there is no neutral, non-social, uninfluenced situation to provide that baseline" (192). Previously I made the point that an important sociological understanding of identity is attainable through the study of narratives. I have just argued that identity cannot be studied any other way.[5]

Of course, identity and narrative *have* been studied separately, with important consequences. *Expression* of identity has been overlooked as a main source of influence on identity.[6] Studies have been designed as if the *way* informants are instructed to express themselves does not significantly shape findings. These include tests of "labeling theory," in which deviant identities play a prominent causal role. I return to this critique in chapter 2.

It is in the nature of a narrative to make something about the narrator *known* to other people. To convey a particular viewpoint is to portray one-self as one who has that viewpoint. In this way, a narrative is an important resource for managing the impression or "face" that the narrator is making (Goffman 1959). To the extent that it is such a resource, a narrative does not simply *represent* the narrator's perspective. It is a public *presentation* of a per-spective. Laypersons tend to view offenders as especially duplicitous people (see Shover 1996, 190–91). Indeed, from some theoretical positions it is in the nature of criminality to be deceitful and manipulative (e.g., Samenow 1984). Practically speaking, offenders face tangible incentives for portraying themselves as guilty and/or remorseful (Minow 1998). Thus, when subjects are offenders, a particularistic notion that narrative is "for show" pertains. Yet impression management is a universal activity, not limited to the so-called deviants among us. As Matza (1969) observes: "Presenting a front, putting people on, and telling prepared sad tales are features of social life, deviant or unconventional" (38).

When we speak, we—and not just others—are "in" the audience. Through linguistic expression we make ourselves known, to others *and* to ourselves (Foote 1951; Kerby 1991). In short, one's identity is shaped both by the ways we make self-conception understandable to ourselves and to others, and by public "appearances." It is problematic to suggest that one holds a more authentic perspective internally than externally, as that perspective gets expressed.

Organization of the Book

My investigation of the "stories of violent men" is laid out in ten chapters. Chapter 1 was introductory. Chapter 2 reviews the literature pertinent to narrated identities among violent offenders. Because of the interdisciplinary nature of the study, its theoretical background is terrifically broad, including insights from sociology, criminology, philosophy, psychology, linguistics, an-thropology, and cultural studies. I limit my review to sociological and crimi-nological perspectives concerned with deviant identities and narratives.

In chapter 3 I review theoretical approaches to "research effects" on what research participants say. What my research participants said to me is the focus of the remainder of the book. These later chapters share how the men established themselves as morally decent and even heroic. I discerned two basic structures stressing *reform*—actually, a return to moral decency—or constant moral decency—*stability*—as well as a hybrid or *elastic* structure that combined talk about self-reform *and* self-stability.[7]

In chapter 4 I provide details of my research methods. Information on methods is usually reserved for an appendix of a book such as this, being seen as detachable from the theoretical and empirical aspects of the study. Not so in this case, where the research itself is under investigation as a setting for the construction of violent men's stories.

The findings of my study are shared beginning with chapter 5. I discuss "reform narratives" in that chapter, "stability narratives" in chapter 6, and "elastic narratives" in chapter 7.

Chapter 8 examines how the men conceived of their lives as heroic struggles against some omnipresent challenge or challengers, internal or external. The nature of these struggles is examined. Chapter 9 is a discussion of how the narratives were situated within the interview. The interview and I were resources that the men used to present certain selves. The situated-ness of the narratives in the interview amounts to what I call the "co-production" of narrated identities.

Themes in the men's stories were *gendered:* they were framed as manly endeavors. Whereas gender is emphasized in investigations of female offending, criminologists pay scant attention to the male-gendered nature of male violence (J. Allen 1989; Naffine 1997). I apply just this sort of gender lens as I discern masculinity in the stories *and* in the interviews—as something accomplished *with* me (West and Zimmerman 1987).

Finally, chapter 10 offers summary remarks about my findings and highlights the theoretical, methodological, and practical/policy significance of the findings. I outline a theory of narrative and harmful action. It is my contention that narratives of violent selves are the groundwork for all violence. One of my research participants, Arnell, made a similar point: "I was tellin' people before I even left the prison—they asked me 'What you gonna do when—you go home?' 'Maw, I'm gonna sell drugs an' get high an' do stick-ups an' stuff like that.' So, when you keep telling yourself that, you believe it and that's what you *do*." Arnell here applies a labeling perspective to construct himself as decent *now*. He resists a criminal self-image for the sake of desisting from criminal behavior. In articulating his resistance, he establishes himself as a moral evaluator who struggles *against* crime. This book brings to light such identity negotiations.

2

OFFENDER IDENTITIES, OFFENDER NARRATIVES

To just say "Well I'm a criminal," that's not a very positive, assertive thing to say about yourself. You know, you start believin' that stuff, and then the next thing you know you're doin' what *criminals* do.
— Tim

How do offenders identify themselves to investigators? What immediate, contextual factors affect their claims of being this or that sort of person? And what do sociological and criminological theories predict about offender identities and narratives and contextual effects on them?

Sociologists agree on two basic *premises* concerning offender identities and offender narratives: that is, identities and narratives regarding one's non-normative behavior as it is defined in a given society (H. Becker 1963, 9). It is assumed that:

1. Offender identities are socially constructed
2. Offender narratives are socially constructed

I myself have built these premises into my working definitions of identities and narratives and I see them as starting points for sociological inquiry about identities and narratives. Empirical work need not and should not test their veracity; they are "true" by our definition. On the other hand, specific *processes* by which offender identities and narratives are socially constructed can be verified. In fact, such processes demand better clarification: this is my present task.

In addition, criminologists—who are specifically concerned with criminal behavior—advance two theoretical propositions about offender identities and offender narratives. These *propositions* are the basis for empirical testing:

3. Offender identities promote offending behavior
4. Offender narratives promote offending behavior

This chapter provides a review of literature pertaining to these four statements (two premises and two propositions).

My research is not a test of propositions 3 and 4, nor is it a test of any other propositions. It is an inductive work. For this study, propositions 3 and 4 are not important to the extent that they are true or "valid." They are important because they, along with propositions derived from other criminological theories, shape offenders' self-stories. Theories are embedded in our cultural discourse. The men in my sample used prevailing criminological explanations during the interview to account for their criminal behavior; I did the same. These stories, or propositions, were collaboratively built into our discussions about who the men *are*. The propositions themselves are social constructs.

Offender Identities Are Socially Constructed

To speak of the social construction of offender identities implies at least two streams of influence from other people—influence on identity/identification generally, and influence on what we deem to be offending or characteristic of offenders. The dominant sociological perspective known as symbolic interactionism theorized the former, whereas the labeling perspective, inspired by symbolic interactionism, theorized the latter.

Symbolic Interactionism

Perhaps the core idea of symbolic interactionism is that people act on the basis of the meanings that they assign to "things." These meanings are not inherent in things but rather are derived from social interaction (Manis and Meltzer 1978). The self is one of those things about which meanings are socially derived. "The self is no more immune to re-examination from new perspectives than any other object" (Strauss 1997, 35).

Cooley and Mead, two of the most important founders of symbolic interactionism, were concerned with how the self is formed through social interaction. Cooley (1902) theorized that our sense of self is shaped by what we suppose others think of us. Borrowing from the economist Adam Smith (who used the idea to describe buyer-seller relations), Cooley called this "the looking-glass self." Mead (1934) echoed this theme of perspective taking: "We appear as selves in our conduct insofar as we ourselves take the attitude that others take toward us. We take the role of what may be called the 'generalized' other. And in doing this we appear as social objects, as selves" (270).

In fact, Mead radicalized Cooley's ideas on role taking by arguing that the self itself—and not just a "sense" of self—was constituted by that process. David Miller (1973) explains: "Although Cooley's ideas were very suggestive to Mead, Mead was not satisfied with what had to be presupposed if Cooley's theory was true. In brief, Cooley started with selves, each of which was, in principle at least, complete in itself, and he then tried to show how one self can take the attitude of another, or how one self can get outside itself and look at itself from the perspective of the other. Mead was profoundly impressed with Cooley's theory of social behavior—how the behavior and attitudes of others condition our own behavior. And, starting with social behavior, Mead was successful in showing that language and selves emerge from it" (xx). Thus we see this tension in symbolic interactionism, from its earliest statements, between Cooley's privileging of individual being and Mead's arguments for decentering the individual.

Whereas Cooley stressed the function of the imagination—again, individualizing—in forging the self, Mead pointed out that immediate interactions as well as interactions one has had with significant others are the psychosocial contexts for adopting other people's attitudes toward us. Contemporary criminologist Lonnie Athens (1994) elaborates on Mead's work by stressing soliloquy or self-talk as the dynamic behind all thought—when communicating with others or when alone. It is through soliloquizing that one (1) fully constitutes one's self, including one's thoughts and feelings, and (2) becomes aware of oneself. Soliloquies are always social events. Athens (1994) states: "When soliloquizing we always converse with an interlocutor, even though it may deceivingly appear as if we are only speaking to ourselves" (525). One converses with various interlocutors from the past and the immediate present.

Although symbolic interactionists agree that the individual constitutes him- or herself through social interaction, there is some question about how fluid or stable identity is (Athens 1994). Various "identity theorists" propose that one's identity is constructed through adjustment to some stable social reality or at least a *sense* of social reality as stable (see Fine 1993a). For one thing, one's daily existence is circumscribed by available social roles. Roles—foundations for identity in "identity theory" (Stryker 1980)—refer to the "kinds of people it is possible to be in a given society" (Stryker and Statham 1985, 323). If roles represent other people's expectations of who one is, they may be said to exist *prior* to interaction (e.g., Stryker and Statham 1985). On the other hand, Blumer (1969) emphasizes the flexible development of roles and other elements of "social structure" *through* interaction (75). Likewise, Jenkins (2004) suggests that "identity can only be understood as process, as 'being' or 'becoming'" (5).

Cognitive-psychological perspectives suggest that people actively seek and assimilate information that conforms to some existing identity. Summarizing research on this broad phenomenon, Gecas and Burke (1995) note that "the self is not simply a passive sponge that soaks up information from the environment; rather, it is an active agent engaged in various self-serving processes" (51). Social interaction offers only a field of possibilities. The meaning that environmental feedback, roles, and so forth hold for the individual is always involved. Thus is the individual's agency located in his or her active interpretation about who or what one is, was, and may be. For symbolic interactionists, such interpretation is always interactive, involving face-to-face encounters, shared symbols, or both. It follows that conceiving of oneself as an offender (or as anything else) is a social enterprise. Labeling theories evolved from symbolic interactionism to explain deviance.

From Symbolic Interactionism to Labeling Theory

For labeling theorists[1], what is true for identities in general is true for offender (or, more broadly, deviant) identities in particular. That is, deviant identities have their origins in the social world. Deviance is always an interactive process that ontologically begins with the identification of certain individuals as offender (H. Becker 1963; Kitsuse 1962). Labeling theories fuse symbolic interactionism with conflict theory's central claim that behavior seen as threatening dominant group interests is labeled offender (Melossi 1985; Paternoster and Iovanni 1989). Early delinquent behavior—Lemert's (1967) "primary deviance"—is held to be pervasive. Social reactions to such behavior supposedly increase the likelihood of hardening of the delinquent lifestyle (Schur 1971) and, subsequently, "secondary deviance."

The offender label is internalized from some salient social environment of which one is a part. Both informal (e.g., family, peer group) and formal environments (e.g., the juvenile justice system) are said to confer the offender label, which then gets internalized as an offender identity (H. Becker 1963; Kitsuse 1962; Schur 1971; Tannenbaum 1938). According to Howard Becker (1963): "When a person makes a definite move into an organized group—or when he realizes and accepts the fact that he has already done so—it has a powerful impact on his conception of himself. . . . Membership in such a group solidifies a deviant identity" (37–38).

For labeling theorists, the various processes by which offender identities are produced are reciprocal over time (Stryker and Statham 1985). An example is the process linking labeling and offender identity through group affiliation. Offender labeling promotes offender identities through affiliation with other offenders, *and* offender identities in time lead to *greater* affiliation with other offenders, which further increases the likelihood of being labeled an offender (H. Becker 1963).

Offender Identities Promote Offending Behavior

The idea that our sense of self guides our actions is fundamental in the identity literature. The idea that an *offender's* sense of self guides his or her offending is an extension important for criminology.

Social-Psychological and Structural Mechanisms

With the proposition that offender identities promote offending behavior, symbolic interactionism achieved its best-known place within texts of criminological theory: this despite protestations by labeling theorists that they are not primarily concerned with the etiology of offending behavior (e.g., H. Becker 1963, 179; Lemert 1974; Schur 1971). It is hypothesized that the nature of one's identity and not just, say, the value (positive or negative) associated with one's identity, influences specific action (Stryker and Craft 1982, 179; Thomas and Bishop 1984, 1232–33). How exactly does a certain identity lead to identity-related action?

The symbolic interactionist perspective on the self itself makes a foundational argument. The self is led to act in ways consistent with identity: that is, consistent with what specific actions *mean* for the self (Blumer 1969; Rosenberg and Kaplan 1982; Schwartz and Stryker 1970; Stryker and Craft 1982). This argument is buttressed by evidence of a self-fulfilling prophecy, wherein other peoples' expectations influence behavioral conformity to those expectations (see Leary 1995; Markus and Cross 1990). Others' expectations are realized through labeling, or what Strauss (1997) calls "status-forcing" (79). Adoption of a certain identity is said to mediate between labeling and behavior consistent with both the label and the identity.

Certain mechanisms have been cited to explain this self-fulfilling prophecy. First, structural events are said to mediate between a certain identity and action consistent with it. As discussed previously, a deviant label leads one to associate with others who have been similarly labeled (Braithwaite 1989; Goffman 1963a; Tannenbaum 1938). In the face of rejection by "normals," there is comfort in banding together with a community of other outsiders.

In addition, an offender label makes particular structural opportunities and roles unavailable (H. Becker 1963). There are many instances of civic participation denied the officially designated ex-offender, particularly the ex-felon; these include voting rights, public offices, and various occupational licenses (Olivares, Burton, and Cullen 1996). Having one's life options constrained purportedly leads one back to a life of crime. Ideas about the crime-causing role of "strain," consisting in blocked opportunity, are relevant here (Agnew 1992; Merton 1938).

Just as offender group affiliation may fortify the offender identity that motivated it, so apparently do one's offending behaviors congeal the offender identity that motivated these behaviors (Caspi, Bem, and Elder 1989, 389). People seem to internalize their self-presentations (Blumstein 1991; Leary 1995). Various psychological mechanisms explain such internalization. There is a social learning explanation. If one presents oneself in a way that leads to reinforcement, one is more likely to repeat that presentation, abandoning at some point the belief that it is merely a presentation (Leary 1995). Alternatively, Bem's (1967) self-perception theory suggests that people infer what they are really like by observing their own behavior. Thus a provisional identity leads to certain behavior, which then solidifies the identity.

Another way of thinking about identity processes promoting offending is through their reversal. The question here is: Do offending behavior patterns change when an offender identity is *discarded?* If so, how? Ebaugh (1988) and Herman (1993) have examined how ex-nuns and ex-psychiatric patients, respectively, "become exes." Herman (1993) reports that "ex-patients were successful in transforming their offender aspects of self when (or if) (a) they began to think of themselves in terms of current, nonoffender roles and began to project such an image to others and (b) others began to relate to them in terms of those *new* roles" (324; emphasis in original). Braithwaite's (1989) reintegrative shaming theory predicts that criminal behavior patterns may be interrupted if communities condemn crime but then reintegrate offenders as potential law-abiders: that is, granting them a role as "essentially like us."

Research findings relating offender identity to offending behavior have been inconsistent at best. This is not the main concern of interactionist scholars, for whom "a totally determinant explanatory model of social interaction is not possible" (Stryker and Statham 1985, 322). If concern with prediction is not typical of interactionist scholars, neither are the research designs for testing interactionist-labeling theory. Studies have largely neglected the basic framework around which labeling effects were originally conceived. Paternoster and Iovanni (1989) note: "For the most part, empirical tests of labeling propositions have been conducted with grossly misrepresented hypotheses that are more caricature than characteristic of the theory" (360). As suggested, labeling theorists specify *probabilistic* effects of identity on behavior (H. Becker 1963, 181). Behavior is always subject to human choice and thus ultimately indeterminate. As Strauss (1997) puts it, "Rules govern the interaction, but not entirely the outcomes" (86). Bowing to the indeterminacy of the identity-action relationship, recent adaptations of labeling theory specify more or less complex mechanisms by which labeling leads to behavior in line with the label. These suggest alternate pathways that the labeled person follows depending on relationship to those who affix the label; how one is treated after labeling (Braithwaite 1989) and the extent to which one believes that the labeling/sanction is legitimate (Sherman 1993).

In addition, labeling affects other life events and decisions, which then affect offending. The impact of labeling on behavior would seem to operate through indirect rather than direct effects (Matsueda 1992; Paternoster and Iovanni 1989; Sampson and Laub 1993). "Labeling" is a matrix of efforts to classify others, self, and the actions of others and the self. It must be conceptualized as a process and not as a discrete event (Lindesmith 1981).

"Doing" Identity through Crime

In applying structured action theory to the study of crime, Messerschmidt (1993, 1997, 2000) proposes a less linear variation on the idea that offending behavior is a function of identity. Rather than arguing that criminal identity *leads to* criminal behavior, Messerschmidt argues that criminal behavior is itself an accomplishment of particular identities whose meanings are socially and historically circumscribed. Criminal behavior is like any other behavior in this regard. As West and Zimmerman (1987) maintain: "Any social encounter can be pressed into service in the interests of doing gender" (138). Much of Messerschmidt's work has focused on the accomplishment of *masculine* identity via crime, his theory serving to explain the disproportionate participation of males in criminal activity. Messerschmidt shows how violence is perceived as an available resource for "doing" masculinity where other resources (given the social relevancies of age, class, race, and physical stature) are perceived as unavailable. In effect, *normatively* sanctioned identities—

such as masculine identity for men—engender offending behavior in the context of various kinds of structural deprivation.[2]

Shover's (1996) study of persistent male property offenders suggests that the phenomenological rewards of offending ("life as party") include its role in crafting a certain identity. Demonstrably "successful crime commission reinforces a sense of personal competence and occupational success" (Shover 1996, 103). Shover writes: "Prospective actions are evaluated not only in terms of the amount of trouble they may bring but also for what success at them would suggest to others about one's identity or character. These matters can be extremely important, particularly for men whose investments in legitimate identities and lines of action are shallow and unrewarding" (109).

The idea that crime is an achievement of certain social identities echoes Albert Cohen's (1955) classic work on boys in gangs, for whom delinquent action confirms their "essential masculinity" (140), as well as more psychologically oriented theories of violence: for example, those of Toch (1969) and Bandura (1973). Toch (1969) developed a typology of individual dispositions to violence. Though not an interactionist per se, Toch is alert to the representational character of offending, including what it means for one's identity. He deems it vital to "explore the meaning of violence for the person who had engaged in it" (13). Protection of one's image, as fearless, manly, and so forth, was determined to be a primary impetus to violence among the repeated violent offenders whom Toch and his staff interviewed (135). Violence is, in effect, identity work when the "confrontation that finally takes place is between two symbols rather than between two real people" (Toch 1969, 121). An identity that lauds violence as heroic spurs more violent confrontation.[3] According to Toch, "Having acquired reputations, some heroes feel that they must live up to these reputations. They must feed them through new heroic acts, which they have to seek out" (203).

Bandura's (1973) theory is a broad sweep of the myriad ways in which aggression is learned socially. He observes that *symbolic* reinforcers are influential for humans' learning of aggressive behavior patterns (Bandura 1973, 47). Aggression may be reinforced by identity and by a sense of one's masculinity (ibid., 256). He contends that the social rewards of aggressive behavior work most effectively through the granting of self-rewards, including desired identities. This idea has implications for behavior modification: "Some of the most drastic changes in behavior are achieved in large part by modifying a person's basis for self-evaluation" (49).

In each of these perspectives, crime is at least in part a character display. Its accomplishment signifies socially valued personas.

Offender Narratives Are Socially Constructed

Analyses of the social construction of offender narratives may be distinguished, for expository reasons, into those concerned with whole life stories (my main concern) and those concerned with particular offender actions, or parts of potentially fuller life stories. The latter have focused on explanations offered for one's deviance.

I will not discuss the extensive literature on the social construction of narratives generally. That review would have to span the literature from entire disciplines and specialties within disciplines, including sociolinguistics, discourse analysis, conversation analysis, and cultural anthropology. These deal with the way narratives are patterned by conventions of speech, particular story genres and other themes in the culture, and the like. My review in this chapter is focused on the narratives that individuals tell concerning their offending behavior.

Life Stories

Athens (1994) notes that our "soliloquies change endlessly with our experiences: what we say to ourselves invariably changes according to the nature of the social experience that we are undergoing" (530). He adds that social experiences of the past, which remain with us in the form of "phantom communities," impact the present soliloquy (and thus identity) as well. For the violent offenders Athens (1997) has spent much of his career researching, offender narratives have origins in early experiences with significant others, including brutalization and intimidation. The construction of soliloquy is, for Athens, a function of experiences with other people over the life course. But what about how those experiences are culturally framed—the contextualization of subjectivity itself? Athens's theory does not account for macro level influences on life stories.

There is a cultural-historical context for representing experience that affects the ways in which we *experience* and *talk about* our experiences (J. Bruner 1990). Narrators draw on "a common stock of narrative formulations" (Atkinson and Silverman 1997, 316). Particular life events, and reasons for them, get accepted as normal in a certain cultural environment. Such a supply of events and reasons for events constitutes what Linde (1993) calls a coherence system, which "represents a system of beliefs and relations between beliefs" (Linde 1993, 163). A coherence system is derived from more expert systems of knowledge (e.g., criminology). "One does not have to believe in these systems, even if one uses them, but the existence of such a system in the language and the culture makes certain kinds of thoughts, beliefs, attitudes, and actions extremely easy to formulate and makes others almost impossible to think or convey" (ibid., 216). When a coherence system is recognizable, "we may be surprised by the sorts of things the speaker cites as reasons, but we can understand why they count as reasons" (175).

Agar and Hobbs (1982) employ a concept similar to coherence system, which they call a cognitive world, and Chanfrault-Duchet (2000) makes the same point in terms of a social representation. She writes: "To be relevant, a life-story must refer to the expected features of life course as viewed through the current social representations" (66). The form of a life story bears the imprint of social expectations about what a life is or should be (see E. Bruner 1986, 142–43).

Larger systems of meaning are always at work in interpersonal communication, for "although the coherence of a given narrative in a given conversation is the creation of the participants in that conversation, they have a cultural supply of expected events in a life course, commonly recognized causes, and shared possible explanations from which to construct individual coherences" (Linde 1993, 19). In short, one's narrative is constrained by the need to be culturally recognizable. I might tell you about my growing interest in salsa dancing followed by my signing up for lessons in salsa dancing. A narrative told in the reverse order, with lessons first, *then* interest would be somewhat unrecognizable and thus suspect. Polonoff (1987) states that an "externally coherent" narrative "must conform in some degree both with the versions that others in the culture form of themselves and with the versions that others form of him. A high degree of variance from these other accepted versions constitutes prima facie grounds for declaring his story to be wrong" (50). Besides dominant cultural templates, life narratives may follow subcultural forms, such as the forms promoted by particular social movements and belief systems (Denzin 1987; Harding 1992; Hayes 2000; Maruna 2001; Zajdow 1999). For instance, the recovery narratives characteristic of "twelve-step" rhetoric impinge on the talk of the majority of my research participants.

Explanations for Deviant Actions

Much has been made of how offenders verbally account for their deviance, and how these specific narratives are situated within a particular social and historical context. Mills (1940) argues that motives—important components of narratives that explain action (see Kerby 1991, 90)—are relatively stable social constructs. The words themselves are "out there" in society, already linked with particular actions. Motives "do not denote any elements 'in' individuals. They stand for anticipated situational consequences of questioned conduct" (Mills 1940, 905). The socialization of children includes inculcation into the society's motives: "Along with rules and norms of action for various situations, we learn vocabularies of motives appropriate to them" (ibid., 909). For example, Mills (1940) offers as contemporary urban American vocabularies of motive those related to things "individualistic, sexual, hedonistic, and pecuniary" (ibid., 910).

Matza (1964) similarly stresses the linguistic basis for vindicating oneself, and sees the location of elements of offender narrative *in* society. He focuses on the jurisprudential language of a particular societal institution: the juvenile justice system. He compares the language that young people use to neutralize their delinquent conduct with statutes of juvenile law. For example, the law typically excuses a violator of criminal responsibility if either self-defense, insanity, or accident are indicated. The delinquent expands on mainstream legal logic, for example: "The legal and delinquent views of self-defense are similar but different. The legal view may be summarized in the following directives: You must never take the offensive; in most situations you must take the coward's path, if possible; at home, however, you may stand your ground. The view of the subcultural delinquent may also be summarized: You may always take the offensive though not without some sense of proportion; ordinarily, you may take the coward's path, stand your ground, or take the offensive, basing your decision on a cool assessment of the situation; at home, however, you are ill advised to take the coward's path" (79). The delinquent code expands on not just the spirit but also the language of the linguistic code, according to Matza. He concludes that the "law contains the seeds of its own neutralization" (61).

Scott and Lyman (1968) describe the process of accounting for deviance as largely situational. Those accounts that they call excuses exploit *collective* understandings about what may absolve people of full responsibility—for example, biological (e.g., sexual) drives (49): "Such commonplaces as 'men are like that' are shorthand phrases invoking belief in sex-linked traits that allegedly govern behavior beyond the will of the actor. Precisely because the body and its biological behavior are always present but not always accounted for in science or society, invocation of the body and its processes is available as an excuse." If that biological drive narrative had no social currency, it would not be invoked or, if invoked, it would be rejected.

Benson (1985) considers how white-collar offenders use socially acceptable justifications and excuses. He interviewed thirty such offenders and found that accounts given for their conduct varied with offense type. For example, income tax violators in Benson's sample tended to stress error or altruism toward employees, while embezzlers tended to frame the offense as an aberrant moment in their careers. In general, "accounting strategies and offenses correlate" (599).

Whereas Matza (1964) and Benson (1985) link individual narratives with larger systems of institutional meaning, they do not examine constructivist processes in action. Such examination requires the kind of situated investigation that ethnomethodologists are known to conduct.

Taking an ethnomethodological (specifically conversation analytic) approach to the practical accomplishment of social life, Molotch and Boden (1985) demonstrate how accounts delivered by one conversant are shaped by what the other conversant says. They analyzed linguistic devices with which Senator Edward Gurney, an investigator in the Watergate hearings, succeeded in framing as illegitimate the testimony of John Dean, counsel to President Nixon. One such device is summarized as follows (Molotch and Boden 1985): "Gurney offers only questions that seem to require 'simple facts' as their answers. In this way, Dean's incapacity to respond with simple, literal reporting of White House events can discredit the substance of his testimony. Even though Dean was as central to the Nixon cover-up activities as any person in the White House, Gurney attempts to show him as unable to meet the formal criterion of competent account giving" (276). Molotch and Boden's study shows talk to be a venue for exercising power. This is so only partly because Gurney was controlling the investigation and Dean was made to follow his lead. Gurney used specific tactics for making Dean articulate an apparent offender account about his political activities. The contingent nature of the construction of offender narratives is a topic ripe for close empirical examination. The proposition that offender narratives promote offending suggests that we have much to gain from such study.

Offender Narratives Promote Offending Behavior

Criminologists have long used offender narratives to reveal what happened in the offender's lived experience, and what meaning the offender has made of that experience. We have far less often probed narratives *themselves* for their role in promoting offending. To do so requires a post-positivist approach that privileges language over "actual" social phenomena. Concepts *related* to narratives, such as neutralizations and interpretations, have seen greater use in explanations of crime. But Maruna's (2001) theory of desistance posits narratives as central in interrupting "criminal careers."

Techniques of Neutralization

Sykes and Matza (1957) is the best-known statement of discursive effects on deviance itself. They propose that juvenile delinquents use certain "techniques of neutralization" or ways of talking about their delinquent behavior, such as denial that it was truly harmful, to release themselves from moral prohibitions against the behavior. They further suggest that neutralizations increase the likelihood of offending in the future (see Akers 1998, 112). Paying a debt to Sykes and Matza, others have described specific neutralizations used for specific kinds of crime, such as marijuana smoking (H. Becker 1963), contract killing (Levi 1981), white-collar offending (Benson 1985), and the Nazi Holocaust (Alvarez 1997). From all of these perspectives, verbalizations about one's offending behavior play a key role in maintaining the behavior.

Sykes and Matza's scheme has alternately been called (1) a control theory, by those who see neutralizations as loosening the social controls that otherwise restrain people from offending (see Hirschi 1969, 24); and (2) a social learning theory, by those who see neutralizations as social definitions favorable to criminal behavior (e.g., Matsueda 1997, 435). A debate has sprung up concerning which theory truly "owns" the techniques of neutralization (Matsueda 1997). The debate may be seen more generally in terms of the question: Is the verbal device merely associated with behavior that one is otherwise motivated to engage in, or is the verbal device the motivating or enabling force itself (see Akers 1998, 112; Benson 1985, 587–88; Cressey 1953, 94–95; Maruna 2001, 41)? The question itself assumes the analyst's ability to both (1) isolate social processes (e.g., of interpretation and action) from social context, and (2) isolate causes from effects. From the perspective of symbolic interactionism, the analyst's ability is limited in both ways.

It bears noting again that interactionist scholars largely consider initial deviance to be omnipresent and therefore not an important question for social theory (see Lemert 1967; Matza and Sykes 1961). They tolerate their inability to pinpoint behavioral origins because they do not find these to be problematic.

Interpretations of Crime

An interpretation of one's past criminal behavior—regardless of whether it is formulated to absolve oneself—may be seen as part of a narrative.[4] The proposition that offender narratives conduce to deviance is a focal point for Athens (1997) and Katz (1988a).[5] Both scholars locate the instigators of offending behavior in how offenders *interpret* the immediate circumstances surrounding the potential criminal act. To bring order to the discussion, I have categorized the theories of Athens and Katz as primarily concerned with offender narratives. Actually, for both, identity and narrative (interpretation) are of a piece, working in concert.

According to Athens (1997), a "physically defensive interpretation" of a situation—to choose one type—may lead to violence when one concludes that the potential victim poses a threat, either to oneself or to one's loved ones. A subsequent interpretation, a "restraining judgment," may nonetheless stop the violent action before it starts. All of these interpretations are shaped by self-images (identities) that themselves consist in the kind of "generalized other" one has. For example, persons who hold "violent self-images have an *unmitigated violent generalized other*—an other providing them with pronounced and categorical *moral* support for acting violently toward other people" (99). Interpretation seems to be a facet of self-image—its enactment—in Athens's (1997) scheme: "Thus the type of self-image that people hold is intimately connected to both the *range* and *character* of the situations that they will interpret as calling for violent action, underscoring that their self-images are congruent rather than incongruent with their interpretations" (98–99).

Katz (1988a) suggests that the criminal offender, like everyone else, acts in ways that are mindful of "the narrative possibilities" of the action (302). In acting, one is scripting a moral tale of one sort or another. The tale posits its protagonist as a particular sort of person. For "the badass"—one of the archetypical criminals Katz names—the "logic of domination is to mean nothing more or less than meanness" (100). For those drawn to the "sneaky thrills" of covert property crimes, there is "a secret, internal desire to be offender" (58). "The person's situational involvement in sneaky property crimes begins with a *sensual concentration on the boundary between the self as known from within and as seen from without*" (ibid.; emphasis in original). Katz explains that aggressors "are engaged in a transcendent project to exploit the ultimate symbolic value of force to show that one 'means it'" (321).

Athens and Katz are specifically concerned with the interpretive project of offending for offenders. In this they share common ground with certain experts in correctional treatment who have embraced the idea that what offenders *think* is the site of criminality, and thus the recommended site of rehabilitation. Identifiable "irrational beliefs" (Ellis 1973) or "thinking errors"—fifty-two of them, according to Yochelson and Samenow (1976)—lead to offending behavior. An example of a criminal thinking error is "a flawed definition of success and the time it takes to succeed" (Van Voorhis, Braswell, and Lester 2000, 174). Such thinking errors may be thought of as offender narratives, except that rehabilitation scholars are prone to viewing thinking errors as internal, psychic phenomena, not necessarily having been narrated. Interestingly, it is in the treatment setting (e.g., group work) where the erroneous thoughts supposedly *must* get expressed or narrated for the sake of effective intervention (Ellis 1973; Samenow 1984; Yochelson and Samenow 1976).

Narratives of Desisters

Maruna (2001) provides a variation on both (1) the proposition that offender narratives promote deviance, and (2) desistance research to date, which has tended to overlook interpretive processes along offender careers (Ulmer and Spencer 1999). Based on qualitative interviews with matched samples of desisting and persisting property offenders in England, Maruna found that "the self-narratives of the desisting sample feature a number of key plot devices with striking regularity" (87). In general, the desisters described a prior lack of agency: that is, circumstances led them to offending. The narrated present stands in contrast. The desisters "portray themselves very much in control of their current and future life direction. This change in personal agency is frequently attributed to empowerment from some outside source" (13). Maruna (2001) calls the narratives of desisters "redemption scripts" marked by "tragic optimism" (11): "Essentially, desisting interviewees have constructed a meaningful story to redeem themselves" (55). Degenerate lives give way to stories in which they give back to society. Maruna counters the idea, directing some correctional treatment interventions, that offenders should be completely honest about their pasts in order to change. For those in Maruna's sample, immodest and selective narratives facilitated exit from deviance. Maruna's findings are consistent with studies of how twelve-step programs purport to work, by "storying" one's reform (Denzin 1987; Swora 2002; Zajdow 1999).

Summary

This chapter has canvassed the literature on two major theses—that offender identities and narratives are socially constructed, and that offender identities and narratives affect offending behavior. The former thesis is foundational to my research project. The latter thesis establishes the practical import of studies of offenders' self-construction. In addition, as I will show, the men I interviewed referenced theories of criminal behavior based on labels and self-understanding. Offenders are purveyors of criminological perspectives positing subjectivity as conducive to misconduct.

Offender identities and narratives are constructed during interactions between people—face-to-face interactions and those that transpire through other forms of symbolic communication. Mead decentered the individual subject that Cooley alleged to be "behind" identity and language. Still, sociologists—including students of crime and deviance—have held fast to the idea that individuals look inward for the words and forms with which they talk about themselves and their actions, even if those words and forms originate in the social world. My study suggests the more sociological perspective. Narratives and identities are, by their nature, constantly changing (Stryker and Craft 1982, 169–70). More radically, they are processed *through* articulation (Athens 1994; Goffman 1963b; Jenkins 2004). It follows that *offender* narratives and identities are situationally constructed. The offender persona is edified potentially anywhere and everywhere. If understandings of oneself change as soon as one expresses them, then research itself affects what is being researched. No doubt, the prospect of such effects is highly unsettling to the notion that one may collect snippets of a reality that exists "out there."

Later in the book I will analyze how the men I interviewed constructed stories of self, and how they did so using the situational resources afforded by the interviews. The next chapter will explore how other scholars have treated so-called research effects.

THINKING ABOUT RESEARCH EFFECTS

> What social science is properly about is the human variety, which consists of all the social worlds in which men have lived, are living, and might live.
>
> —C. Wright Mills, *The Sociological Imagination,* 1959

> Even when we feel ourselves simply spectators, we are also participants.
>
> —Louise M. Rosenblatt, *The Reader, the Text, the Poem,* 1978

Are researchers ever really spectators to the activities that they study? The image of researchers on the outside looking in is prevalent in most literature on methodology for social research. But it troubled me because, trained to see the social all around me, I thought social influence should extend to my research interviews. The narrative data I "collected" should, to some extent at least, be a product of the interview and not a sole-authored work of the narrator.

In this chapter I describe how I came to investigate the situated production—call it co-production—of narrative data in the research settings in which they were voiced. I then discuss various methodological approaches to research effects on data and potential problems with recognizing oneself and one's study "in" one's data.

When "I" Entered the Study

When concrete plans for this study were first laid early in 1999, I had a non-specific interest in the self-narratives of violent men: a raw fascination with what they would say about themselves when prompted to talk about who they are. I also had a desire to air their stories as something of a political act, like qualitative researchers before me (see Norum 2000; Sullivan 1998). Contemporary criminal justice processes tend to construct offenders as "less than fully human" (Harris 1991, 90). I hoped that my research would counter that construction (Delgado 1989). I would engage offenders in storytelling, that most human of activities.

At a pivotal point in my analysis, I began to see the narratives as conditioned by the research interview. Review of the methodological literature brought me to fairly recent writings on reflexivity. In this literature, reflexivity implies that one's observations are always affected by researcher characteristics and perspectives and by social processes engaged by research (see Hammersley and Atkinson 1995, 16). A reflexive scholar is one who reveals her own standpoint and often her own voice in the research. These days it is quite common to read something about the position that the researcher takes on her subject matter. Some reflexivity is demanded by contemporary scientific norms.

As my analysis proceeded the ways in which the interview seemed to have "entered" the narratives became more apparent. For example, I saw that social appearances and roles were not merely setting the stage for the interview, or being talked about during the interview, or coloring the narratives by some quantifiable measure (more on this momentarily). They were, rather, under construction during the interview. The more that I followed this notion, the more my attention, and particularly my reading of the data, turned to contextual effects on the data. Glaser and Strauss (1967) refer to theoretical explanations "grounded in" one's data. Here was a *methodological* turn grounded in my data.

Traditional Perspectives

Of the various realities that social scientists are said to have excluded from their studies (Belknap 2001; C. Gilligan 1982; A. Gordon 1997; Harding 1987; Henry and Milovanovic 1996; Richardson 1995; Ross and Richards 2002), the one I am immediately concerned with is that of the researcher as social actor. It is not the case that the social scientist has been rendered *invisible* in her research. Rather, the necessarily elastic, indeterminate, and evolving character of social interaction between researcher and study participant has been denied.[1] Research effects (also called "reactivity") have been conceived as phenomena that should and can be controlled (Bachman and Schutt 2001).

At least three dominant approaches to research effects may be distinguished. First, *naturalistic studies* involve total immersion of an ethnographer in the culture of those under study. The ethnographer's prior ideologies are supposedly eclipsed by those of her research participants (Hammersley and Atkinson 1995, 16). This process of "going native" is in fact considered a hazard of being too comfortable in the culture of those one is studying (Maxfield and Babbie 2001, 281). Objectivity may be compromised. Nonetheless, once the researcher is accepted as something of a member of the culture being investigated, the behavior of the true members (research participants) also supposedly becomes uninhibited in her presence (see Marquart 2001, 42). The researcher has been assimilated and this effectively eliminates the effect she has on her participants.

Second, and far more commonly (inasmuch as participant-observation is uncommon), research effects are considered to be *biases* that "creep into" a study at numerous points. Often biases are treated as unavoidable: for example, the consequence of relating to research participants in a polite manner. Cicourel (1964) calls for exploiting biases that "facilitate the flow of information and communication so long as we are aware of their use and effects and thereby have some control over them by knowing how to correct them later" (92). He continues, "The impression we must avoid is that all factors producing error can be eliminated" (101). Cicourel's statement makes plain the view of these research effects as problematic. Pool (1957) critiques such a view of research effects. He writes: "We have treated them as a nuisance. We have used the words 'bias' or 'error' in most of our descriptions of them and have acted as though the goal was somehow to get rid of interpersonal effects so as to get at the truth which would be there if the interpersonal character of the interview didn't interfere" (193).

Standardized procedures for sampling, collecting, and analyzing data are designed to remedy biases. Thus, for example, the wording of survey questions should be neutral, with the understanding that the "meaning of someone's response to a question depends in large part on the wording of the question" (Maxfield and Babbie 2001, 251). Fontana and Frey (2000, 649–50) describe typical instructions for so-called structured interviewing:

- Never get involved in long explanations of the study; use the standard explanation provided by the supervisor.
- Never deviate from the study introduction, sequence of questions, or question wording.
- Never let another person interrupt the interview; do not let another

person answer for the respondent or offer his or her opinions on the question.

- Never suggest an answer or agree or disagree with an answer. Do not give the respondent any idea of your personal views on the topic of the question or the survey.
- Never interpret the meaning of a question; just repeat the question and give instructions or clarifications that are provided in training or by the supervisors.
- Never improvise, such as by adding answer categories or making wording changes.

Through the use of such standard procedural guidelines, one supposedly obtains responses reflective of true opinions, which are assumed to exist prior to the intervention of the survey researcher. As much as narratives and identities are appreciated as being social phenomena, research on both has largely maintained this conception of a priori narratives and identities, which the research merely uncovers (e.g., Burke and Franzoi 1988; Willott et al. 2001).

It would seem that survey methods using cross-sectional data are handicapped at the outset in their ability to study what people (including selves) and relationships mean in the moment of action. Given a view of identity, in particular, as evolving and episodically structured, retrospective self-report measures of identity are problematic. Surveys seem never to "show up" on time for "the continuous joinings and leavings of social life" (Stryker and Craft 1982, 176).

A third dominant approach to research effects is characteristic of *experiments*. While experimental researchers *control* a host of research effects, they carefully *exploit* others. Attempting to hold all else constant, they purposely impose selected stimuli on research participants. Experiments in behavioral psychology are designed to observe whether a particular action on the part of the investigator or a particular aspect of the research setting provokes change in a particular behavior of participants. Relevant to my study of narratives is Greenspoon's (1955) experiment in which participants' verbalizations were seen to vary when research staff said "mm-hmm" at appropriate times.

Substantive differences aside, these three approaches share a view of the researcher's influence as *finite* and *recursive*. They envision a stimulus-response sequence that begins with researcher input and ends with participant output. This is most plainly demonstrated in survey and experimental research, where agency is reserved for the researcher. Relative to field studies, surveys and experiments place heavy restrictions on those responses that count as data. Moreover, these studies are conceived as a "time-out" from social life, although it is hoped that study findings will generalize *to* social life.

Reflexivity

Feminist theorists have caused scholars to think seriously about their research, especially research producing "grand theories," as part of a system of oppression wherein "others" get defined and/or (often as part of the same phenomenon) their experiences overlooked. For these theorists, scholarship is no "time-out" from social life. It is a microcosm of the social world and it perpetuates that world, for good or for bad. From this belief came a "reflexive" perspective on research effects.

The "reflexive ethnographer does not simply report 'facts' or 'truths' but actively constructs interpretations of his or her experiences in the field and then questions how those interpretations came about" (Hertz 1997, viii). Reflexivity is grounded in an epistemological stance that takes all knowledge to be historically and culturally situated (D. Smith 1987). That stance is concerned to show how power relations have been cloaked within a supposedly neutral scientific discourse. For example, the behavior of females has appeared inferior to that of males inasmuch as the gendered perspective of the (traditionally male) expert is not acknowledged (C. Gilligan 1982; D. Smith 1987).

Those who endorse a reflexive approach have attempted to "write [themselves] into the analysis" (Gilgun and McLeod 1999, 185; see also Arendell 1997; Armitage 1983; Frankenberg 1993; Manning 1995; Norum 2000). They disclose where they stand in relation to both research questions and research participants. Sandra Harding (1987) clarifies this approach in recommending a so-called feminist methodology: "The best feminist analysis goes beyond . . . innovations in subject matter in a crucial way: it insists that the inquirer her/himself be placed in the same critical plane as the overt subject matter, thereby recovering the entire research process for scrutiny in the results of research. That is, the class, race, culture, and gender assumptions, beliefs, and behaviors of the researcher her/himself must be placed within the frame of the picture that she/he attempts to paint. . . . Thus the researcher appears to us not as an invisible, anonymous voice of authority, but as a real, historical individual with concrete, specific desires and interests" (9).

This kind of analysis tends to integrate observations about whomever or whatever is intentionally being studied with the researcher's personal but structurally situated responses to her findings. The researcher acknowledges—stresses, even—her subjectivity. This surely represents a departure from the aforementioned traditional approaches. The researcher's analysis is appreciated as being shaped by her experience of the world. Still, what research participants say is not generally considered as shaped by the researcher, with a general exception being that participants may speak more candidly knowing that the researcher is doing so (see Frankenberg 1993, 35) or is validating his/her experiences (Gadd 2004, 397). The researcher and the participant are not necessarily cast as social interactants, *creating data* together.

Symbolic Interactionists on Research Effects

Interactionists focus attention on "the special mutuality of immediate social interaction" (Goffman 1963a, 16). One would expect them to have made unique advances in the constitution of meanings—including meanings about the self—*through* research communication.

Yet researchers inspired by symbolic interactionism have generally not gone much further than non-interactionist researchers to access the interaction between researcher and participant. First, methodological guidelines for studying interactionist processes hardly diverge from the traditional approaches to bias (e.g., Herman 1994). Second, social influences on participants are those defined as such by the researchers. In their classic work, Kuhn and McPartland (1954) presented the Twenty Statements Test, in which they instruct participants responding to the question "Who am I?" to answer "as if you were giving the answers to yourself, not to somebody else." They call this "an endeavor to obtain from [the participant] *general* self-attitudes rather than simply ones which might be idiosyncratic to the test situation or those which might be uniquely held toward himself in his relation to the test administrator" (72, emphasis in original). On the other hand, they view the self as "an interiorization of one's positions in social systems" (ibid.). Apparently the testing situation does not constitute such a social system.

Another example is Holbert and Unnithan's (1990) survey of prison inmates, from which they related inmates' self-perceptions to their "immediate situations." These researchers imposed a definition of the immediate situation as the inmates' experience of the justice system, such as whether one's instant (current) sentence was determinate (fixed by law) or indeterminate; the number of previous incarcerations; and participation in counseling (measured dichotomously, as participation/no participation). The experience of completing a survey was not seen as part of the "immediate situation."

However, there is a chorus of alternative interactionist voices. Katz (1988b) contends that it is the unique methodological strength of interaction-guided qualitative research that the investigator potentially recognizes and exploits *relationships* she has with research participants. Katz (ibid.) recommends that field researchers use research effects in order to glean insight, instead of hoping that they will go away: "Member behavior that has been shaped in response to the researcher's methods is not necessarily more problematic as substantive data than behavior shaped in any other interaction. Field researchers have missed this point. Common topics in the literature on participant observation concern whether members are lying, being superficial, or showing racial deference to the researcher. There is no fundamental difference between these problems of interpretation and those about whether members are lying, being superficial, or showing racial deference to each other" (139). Katz observes that qualitative researchers are significant others to research participants, who "cast [researchers] into identities rich with indigenous meaning" (138).

Ickes and Gonzalez (1996) argue that "some of the most central and fundamental processes of social knowing operate only within the intersubjective context in which they naturally occur" (288) and bemoan the predominance of research in social psychology using "subjectivist, single-subject paradigms to study what are more appropriately construed as intersubjective phenomena" (289). They encourage researchers to study research participants in dyads or groups. Still, they do not see the researcher as a member of those dyads or groups.

McCall and Wittner (1990) are more enterprising about the researcher's role and work, urging symbolic interactionists to innovate: "Symbolic interactionists have at least as much to learn from the greater willingness of life historians in anthropology and literature to take their project to its logical conclusion by trying to develop new forms of analysis and presentation that support rather than undermine their own meanings and intentions. What does it mean for our work to speak of subjects and agency if our analysis functions as the authoritative voice, controlling subjects' speech and interpreting it for the audience?" (85). McCall and Wittner take issue with the researcher's dominant voice and thus the meanings that the researcher gives to things, in interactionist studies. Their concern resembles those of critical theorists who wish to see the power dynamics of science made candid by the investigator. They do not take issue with meaning-making as something a person does on his or her own. They retain the codification of individuals having and (thanks to ethnography) telling their "own" stories. If the self is a social invention—as Mead said—what of *stories* about the self? Their development during interaction with researchers should seem obvious to symbolic interactionists.

Maynard and Whalen (1995) state: "In social psychology, symbolic interactionists have been most concerned with language" (150). Yet Boden (1990) observes that symbolic interactionists have rarely studied language directly: "The very words 'language' and 'meaning'—particularly the latter—seem to conjure up symbolic interactionism for most American sociologists. . . . There are times, however, when the importance of language to meaning seems more slogan than practice within the field, and language becomes one of those taken-for-granted features of interactionist research. . . . Rarely are language and meaning per se objects of symbolic interactionist enquiry; rather they typically serve as resources out of which the essentially shared and social nature of society is conjured" (245). With interactionist researchers neglecting linguistic processes of communication, it is no wonder that they have hardly considered the influence of their own communication in research situations.

Behind this seeming neglect among interactionists of communication and its workings in the research setting, there is a considered rejection of postmodern thought, particularly its questioning of the ethnographer's ability to uncover her informant's subjective world (see Prus 1996, chap. 7). It is true that there are epistemological problems in conceiving of data as co-produced. For one thing, it problematizes the idea that researchers (or at least ethnographers, hence Prus's objection) can be detached from their subject matter. If the researcher's approach is assimilated into what is being researched, the space needed for investigation grows alarmingly small. That is a problem I cannot resolve here, or anywhere. However, I would briefly note that the "postmodern" deconstruction of knowledge, including knowledge about the self, is merely an extension of the interactionist's skepticism of positivistic research and its premises, and not an altogether different concern (see Gecas and Burke 1995, 58).

The Co-production of Data

Critiquing what I call a reflexive position, Atkinson and Silverman (1997) comment on how recent qualitative sociological work presumes to liberate the authentic voices of informants. Even among critical scholars, there is an abiding faith in the independent existence of personal narratives. The reflexive scholar problematizes the ideological grounds of the study but, nonetheless, maintains that these are extricable from the study results.

For example, regarding whether or not she should have confronted the men in her sample—divorced fathers—on their sexist views, Arendell (1997) determines: "This would have *confounded further* the interactional dynamics" of the interviews (364; emphasis added). Arendell adroitly details the accomplishment of gender during interviews, thus positing the interview site as a social domain. However, she maintains a traditional distinction between research process and research topic: "Gender identity was a crucial issue in the telling of their divorce stories *and* gender was both displayed and accomplished during our contacts" (347). Atkinson and Silverman's (1997) observation about the neglect of the *creation* of selfhood *through interviews* applies here. Arendell (1997) does not consider how the men created themselves as divorced fathers in the interviews. She attends to decontextualized stories about being a divorced father; along the way she observes research-situated gender construction.

There are the values and beliefs of the researcher and there are those of the researched. The trend toward reflexivity has bid us to include both. Yet investigators have seldom made the connection by focusing on their nexus.[2] I agree with Williams (1999), who notes that "a form of subjectivity that combines both researcher and researched is probably necessary in order for social scientists to understand social reality" (11). Chanfrault-Duchet (2000) goes so far as to *define* the life story as an artifact of social-scientific and tape-recorded research: "The oral situation makes the speech act a narrative interaction demanding the physical presence of a narrator (informant) and a narratee (researcher), so that the narrative is the product of co-enunciation and co-construction processes. The life-story as an object is then at first the interaction as recorded on the tape or its written version: the transcription" (62).

Studies of actual co-production of self-narratives are scarce. Chanfrault-Duchet (2000) offers one good example. Her analysis of the narratives of three women focuses on the channeling of shared ideas about possible "life courses" for women and possible ways of defying them: for example, through formal education. In sharing the narrative of a furniture maker, Mishler (1992) states: "It reflects my active participation—how I let him know that his 'story' made sense, how and when I asked him to fill in 'missing' pieces, as well as how I failed to ask for further information. These effects are not a function of my idiosyncratic interviewing style but are inherent to all interview situations" (Mishler 1992, 35).

Far more than empirical precedent, there is theoretical support for studying co-production processes. Psychologist Jerome Bruner (1990) observes that "'the-story-of-a-life' as told to a particular person is in some deep sense a joint product of the teller and the told" (124). Schiffrin (1996) writes: "The identities that we display and that others act upon during sociolinguistic interviews, and during the narratives told during such interviews, are no less situated than those whose relevance emerges during other activities" (200). Edward Bruner (1986) refers to anthropological ethnographies as "coauthored"—"not simply because informants contribute data to the text, but because . . . ethnographer and informant come to share the same narratives" (148). Sociologists Atkinson and Coffey (2002) propose that researchers "appreciate that interviews are occasions in which are enacted particular kinds of narratives and in which 'informants' construct themselves and others as particular kinds of moral agents" (808).

The study of co-production closely parallels a major contemporary trend in literary studies, toward viewing texts (e.g., novels, poems) as joint products of writer and reader. Polkinghorne (1988) calls this view "reception theory." The author is involved with would-be, imagined readers in creating a text. Later, each reader works out meaning from the text (Iser 1978, 1989; Rosenblatt 1978). Of course, there are many readers and thus many readings; meanings are always multiple. My study is indebted to this development. There is the obvious connection between literary artifacts and the life stories I have collected. But the kind of data involved is not as important as the fact of *engaging* with the data, even as one is "collecting" it. Rosenblatt (1978) writes: "No matter how impersonal and objective, no matter how descriptive and technical, historical or critical interests may seem, the raw data, so to speak, must be individual personal encounters with texts" (174–75). This perspective leads me to answer the question with which I started this chapter. I maintain that researchers are never just spectators to the activities that they study. This fact can be ignored or it can be put to use to cover new, in my case sociological, ground.

I did not only ask the men in my sample "who they are." I am embedded in their answers. The findings of my research are situated in the concrete encounters I had with the men. Wieder (1977) states that ethnomethodology "both involves a substantive area of study, and . . . the use of a specific attitude or posture" (1), the latter being an interest in *how* things get done. The typical subject matter of ethnomethodologists is the practical accomplishment of everyday reality, including everyday understandings and practices (Garfinkel 1967). Given my concern with both the "what" or substance *as well as* the "how" (Holstein and Gubrium 2000) or assembling of identity, my contribution is more theoretical than ethnomethodologists are inclined to be (see R. Watson 1992). Rather, my study is "ethnomethodologically informed"

(Fontana and Frey 2000). It is concerned with the practical accomplishment of social life and particularly with identities (see also Holstein and Gubrium 2000, 88).

Among ethnomethodologists, Lynch (1991a, 1991b) is notable for his concern with the social world of scientific *research*. He states: "If 'there is no time out from society,' then measurements of things are measurements in, of, and as social practices" (1991b, 98). Lynch and his colleagues have studied the coding of data for quantitative analysis. My study differs from their work in two ways. First, I am working with qualitative data solicited through open-ended questions, closer to Wieder's (1974) study of a California halfway house for parolees, although I did not also closely *observe* a social setting as he did. My interview format allowed for extensive (though not unlimited) elaboration by my research participants (cf. Suchman and Jordan 1990). Second, I am not here considering my coding of these data, though that would make for an interesting and possibly important study. I am considering, rather, how the data—narratives—were constructed during the interviews. My theoretical concern is with data collection, not data processing. But I am problematizing the words *data* and *collection,* which together are used to refer to already-formed matter. Borrowing from Lynch, my study exposes data as "things" formed through always-interactive research activity.

Conversation analysis is informed by ethnomethodology but is specifically concerned with talk.[3] Analysts hear talk (literally, for their data are recordings) as social action. Talk orders social life: it is considered "the working mechanism of social life itself" (Gubrium and Holstein 2000, 494). At the same time, talk is socially ordered: it is a cooperative achievement, even when one person dominates as the speaker. Conversation analysts have something to say about narrative, which is seen to be part of ordinary talk and not a discrete activity or entity. Boden (1990) observes that stories are "not 'just' tales but active and interactive productions which . . . reveal collaborative qualities of verbal and nonverbal displays of participation both by speaker and recipient" (260). That sort of insight is key to my argument that narratives are situated in the research interviews in which they are told.

There may be topics—pieces of social reality—that are more or less interpretable without including the immediate situation in the analysis. For reasons previously discussed in chapter 1, it is doubtful that the narrated self counts as such a topic.

Varied disciplines and perspectives support the idea that data are co-produced. For all its scholarly intuitiveness, though, the idea is not without its problems.

Problems with Co-production

In conceptualizing herself as co-producer of the data, the researcher must, it would seem, attend to herself while also attending to the research participant. More accurately, she must attend to the communicative domains she shares with the participant (e.g., discussion, achieved understanding, etc.). This makes unusual demands on powers of concentration, especially if data are recorded through note taking rather than with a recorder. Since I knew that most of my interviews were being tape recorded, I could avoid thinking about the dialogue I was having with my participants *in situ* (see Cicourel 1964, 102).

Less concretely, it is hard for researchers to be reflexive because to do so obviously involves self-appraisal. When one finally publicizes the research, self-revelation is involved as well. No wonder, then, that research of which the research process is itself the focus has been called "confessional ethnography" (Van Maanen 1995, 8). These activities have the researcher exposing more of herself—and more of her conduct during the study—than is typical in the social sciences. They heighten her emotional vulnerability and her vulnerability to criticism as well (Fine 1993a). My phrasing of questions and my responses to participants' answers do not always place me in a flattering light as a researcher, from dominant scientific perspectives.

There is a different sort of danger: that the researcher will present herself in an especially positive or at least an especially important light. She has allowed herself this opportunity to present herself as never before; why not seize it for self-promotion? I do not believe that this is a danger unique to self-appraisal in research. In fact, scholarly self-aggrandizement is probably a greater threat when we are poised as all-knowing beings hovering above the data.

I believe that my influence on research participants (and by that I mean to include the influence of the study) is merely one influence, exemplary of social influence generally (Katz 1988b, 137–39). First, patterns of social behavior—roles, identities, or anything else—are obviously *not* reinvented from one encounter to the next. Individuals "will come into any microsituation with a past history of encounters in other microsituations, and these make up the ingredients of what will happen in that particular situation" (Collins 1987, 197). Any influence the researcher might have is usually no match for those chains of interactions that participants have experienced to date. To take one example, in detailing how motherhood is constructed among impoverished women on the Alto do Cruzeiro of Brazil, anthropologist Scheper-Hughes (1992) recognizes her own influence on their thinking patterns: "Although psychodynamic self-analysis is obviously not a native practice among the people of the Alto, as a result, in part, of the style of questioning and the close and intense scrutiny that I have introduced into their lives, some *moradores* [residents] have begun to think in personally self-reflexive ways, for better or worse. Xoxa, the young teenage daughter of Biu, started working with me in 1987, beginning from a state of original and blissful naïveté. Three years later she was an introspective young woman who enjoyed thinking aloud with me about 'why' things were the way they were in her own life and family, among her neighbors, and in the community at large" (447). Allowing for her own influence, Scheper-Hughes nonetheless clearly shows that it competes with a myriad of political, economic, social, and cultural influences on the women's belief systems about selves and lives.

In a very different sort of anthropological study, Agar and Hobbs (1982) consider the life story of one drug addict as influenced by his experience as a member of a street culture, his knowledge of "straight" culture, *and* his experience in "the interview cognitive world" (9). This last influence is the least prominent but it is still discernible. These two examples support my own sense that neither the interview nor I necessarily hold a special place in the lives of my participants.[4] As Schuman (1982) states in reference to surveys, "systematic influence due to interviewer characteristics is both limited and delimitable" (24).

Second, individuals are still active authors of their own life stories, and thus shapers of their own identities. This is the case in part because the interview format required me to minimize my talk, and simply "hear" what the narrator would tell. Hence Chanfrault-Duchet (2000) states: "The researcher has to fade out in order to play the discursive role of narratee (and thus loses control of the interaction)" (64).

More generally, situational factors are always strategically, though perhaps not consciously, selected for use in the telling of "who one is." Gecas and Burke (1995) summarize research pointing to "the active, selective, and protective nature of the self in its relationship to various social environments" (53). We tend to select those environments and cognitively attend to features of environments that promote a unified sense of self (Lecky 1945; Markus and Cross 1990). My research participants selected features of the interview that would support a certain identity. Chance occurrences during the interview—an interruption by another person, my own "casual" remark about something, a new discovery about me—were pressed into the service of identity affirmation. They became examples of what the narrator was "already" saying or "already" meant to say.

Third, the interview is one—and only one—forum for social processes (see Cicourel 1964, 90). My decision to focus on *research* effects is, importantly, opportunistic. Individuals are continually forming identities. Blumstein (1991) observes: "The process of identity negotiations should be viewed as ubiquitous because there are identity implications . . . in even the most insignificant nuances of communication" (300). Identity negotiations may be ubiquitous, but the interview was available to me for empirical observation. Other social settings were and are not so readily available. Just as my presence is a resource in my participants' identity work, the interview exchanges are resources for my *investigation* of identity work.

Whereas I have located myself in the data, the analysis centers on my participants' words and actions to the virtual exclusion of my own. I am a secondary character (see Tedlock 1991, 81). I recognize that *my* talk is an enactment of my own identity, that *my* talk is also conditioned by what my research participants say and do. I play a role both in the field (Fine 1993b; Reinharz 1997) and now in the writing up of results (Mills 1959, 219). These facts are mainly not of interest to me. My words and actions are analyzed only insofar as they influence those of my participants, by creating opportunities for making certain self-claims. Compare this with the analysis/writing of Gilgun and McLeod (1999), who studied sex offenders: "We chose to present 'close ups' of some of our emotional reactions to the [violent] acts that we struggled to understand, along with our representations of our informants and our more 'detached' analyses" (173). I do not go as far as these scholars do to convey my reactions and struggles; I do not present "parallel stories" as Norum (2000) does so bravely. This was the choice I made: to focus on the selves of violent men and not on *my* self.

Summary

The exchange between researcher and research subject has not traditionally been assessed as social interaction and, therefore, as *necessarily* shaping data. In the naturalistic field study, the investigator's influence on the data is said ultimately to disappear. Most positivistic research, including experiments and quantitative analyses of survey data, codifies research effects as biases, which can and should be contained for the sake of studying the phenomena of interest. Finally, feminist and other critical scholars conceptualize and report their findings *reflexively.* The focus of this last group is on values, which cannot and ought not be kept out of the research.

Symbolic interactionism offers a paradigm for understanding communication as constitutive of meanings about the self and about society. My analysis brings the interactionist paradigm to bear on the contextualization of the narrative data in the research interview. In attending to the dynamism that is self-identification through storytelling, the analysis promises to illuminate the making and the unmaking of "violent men" in the interview exchange.

4

RESEARCH METHODS WHEN RESEARCH IS BEING RESEARCHED

Early on I was helped in my methodological decision making by the conventions of qualitative sociology. Some very general tools for working can be taken for granted. For example, the qualitative sociologist typically uses nonprobability sampling. If the researcher intends to conduct interviews, the interview format tends to be open-ended. The analysis usually emphasizes the perspectives of those whom one is studying, but also incorporates one's own perspectives into analysis and documentation, the latter being the reflexive position described in chapter 3.

At the design stage, then, I had the welcome feeling that my research methods were for the most part handed down to me. This impression turned out to be illusory, as I had few guidelines to follow when it came to analyzing the interview's shaping influence on the narratives of my participants. I encountered few precedents for a methodological process that would yield a close and deep examination of the "how" of talk, and not just the "what" (Holstein and Gubrium 2000). I constructed my own process (Presser 2005). Thus, this chapter follows a trajectory from fairly derivative to more creative decision making.

Accessing Violent Men

My research participants were referred to me by agencies and organizations working with convicts, ex-convicts, and homeless people. Thirteen men were from Harrison, New Jersey (near New York City); ten were from Cincinnati; two were from New York City; one was from Philadelphia; and one was on death row during the research, in a state withheld to disguise his identity.[1] Participation was voluntary, but only one potential research participant declined to participate. I also presented tape recording as optional, but all of my participants consented to being tape recorded.

All of my research participants were males seventeen years of age and older who had been convicted of committing at least one violent crime *or*—though never convicted—reported *committing* at least one violent crime. Most of the participants (twenty-five of the twenty-seven) were in fact convicted of a violent crime: this comes as no surprise, since I had asked my contacts to refer me to men with such a conviction history. I reasoned that being *labeled* violent might cause some havoc to one's identity. But two of the men referred to me had not, after all, been so convicted. Table 1 provides select sample information: pseudonym, age at first interview, race (racio-ethnic group, based on self-report), and violent offenses based on self-reports and official records. In parentheses are self-reported crimes of which subjects were not convicted. Multiple counts of a charge are not noted.

My working definition of *violent crime* was an act intended to cause *and* causing harm to another person. The violent crimes committed by my research participants were assault, robbery, rape, and/or murder. Many of the men had committed more than one of these offenses. Some men told me that they had committed additional violent crimes unbeknownst to law enforcement officials. Only two of my research participants denied having committed the violent charges of which they were convicted. Several more men disputed offense specifics and not the fact that they had violated another person.[2]

Originally, I wanted to expand the taken-for-granted meanings of violence by including persons who were responsible for harming people in their capacity as professional decision makers. Such persons, if they are called "offenders" at all, are commonly called white-collar offenders. My early efforts to include them failed. Though I tapped a fairly wide network of acquaintances and friends working in criminal justice, law, and business, I was unable to find persons willing to be interviewed, conceivably because of outstanding civil

Table 1. Research Participants

Name	Age	Race	Violent offenses
Arnell	29	Black	Aggravated manslaughter/armed robbery; (assault)
Clarence	35	Black	(Aggravated assault); (assault)
Cyrus	57	Black	Homicide; robbery; (assault)
Dwight	41	Black	Rape; assault; robbery; (aggravated assault)
Harry	41	Black/white	Domestic assault; child abuse; (attempted homicide)
Hector	54	Black	(Assault); (child abuse)
James	39	Black	(Assault)
Joe-Ray	22	Black	Aggravated assault; robbery
John	33	White	Felonious assault of police officer
José	22	Latino	Armed robbery; (assault)
Kevin	37	White	Homicide/armed robbery
Larry	39	White	Aggravated manslaughter; (assault); (domestic assault)
Lyle	17	Black/Latino	Armed robbery
Marco	18	Latino	Robbery; (assault)
Max	46	Latino	Aggravated manslaughter; aggravated assault
Nelson	33	Asian	Armed robbery
Oren	25	Black	Aggravated manslaughter
Peter	38	White	Vehicular homicide
Ralph	34	Black	Robbery; rape; burglary
Reuben	22	Black	(Assault)
Shawn	39	White	Attempted rape/assault; (rape); (domestic assault)
Steve	45	White	Domestic assault
Tim	47	White	Aggravated assault; rape; (domestic assault); (attempted homicide)
Tré	23	White	Manslaughter
Vaughan	57	Black	Homicide
Wayne	33	White	Felonious assault of police officer; domestic assault; (assault)
William	21	Black	Robbery

liability risks. Consequently, my sample consists of offenders traditionally defined as violent, with direct bodily harm a basic aspect of that definition.

The decision to sample men exclusively was made early on. It was influenced by scholarly work on masculine identity construction and violent offending (Connell 1995; Gilgun and McLeod 1999; Messerschmidt 1993, 2000). I was also inspired by the feminist call (J. Allen 1989; Naffine 1997) to understand crime for its sex specificity: simply, men perpetrate most violent crimes (U.S. Department of Justice 1999).

Data Collection Procedures

My primary data were tape recordings of interviews that I conducted from April 1999 through August 2001. All but one of my research participants was interviewed on one to four separate occasions. Any one interview tended to last from one to three hours. The majority of the interviews were held on the premises of the organizations through which the men were referred: that is, a community-based correctional facility, a halfway house, a probation agency, and a homeless shelter. These interviews were held in rooms that were vacant except for the interview participants, with doors closed. Interviews with two men (a one-and-only interview with Shawn and a follow-up interview with Tim) who were living in the community were held at coffee shops that were fairly crowded and noisy. Four additional interviews were held on a college campus (classroom, conference room, or office). All nine interviews with Kevin were conducted over the phone, while he was on death row.

Most of my encounters with the research participants were dyadic, meaning that they included only the participant and myself. Two participants were interviewed with others present. One encounter, with James, occurred in a group (class) setting. It was not nominally an interview at all but rather a class on restorative justice for which I was the instructor and James was the invited guest speaker.[3] Wayne, a deaf man, was interviewed three times in the presence (that is, with the assistance) of a sign language interpreter.

Ethnographic interviews are typically open-ended and "iterative" (Rubin and Rubin 1995), meaning that questions largely emerge from the interviews themselves. Still, I posed a limited number of standard questions to stimulate discussion about one's self-perceptions in the past and present and about one's violence. These included: "Would you tell me about your life?" and "What do you think caused your violent behavior?" The open-ended nature of questioning encourages research participants to say what they want to *as* they want to. But Mishler (1986a, 235) points out that interviews do not necessarily lead to *narratives:* "There is a cumulative suppression of stories through the several stages of a typical study: interviewers cut off accounts that might develop into stories, they do not record them when they appear, and analysts either discard them as too difficult to interpret or select pieces that will fit their coding systems." Mishler adds that the "general stance of an interviewer as an attentive listener and how the interviewer responds to a response" largely determine whether the interview will produce a narrative (ibid.). My own manner was usually that of an interested listener open to all that the speaker had to say.

Whereas I was attentive to "untruths" (e.g., denials of guilt despite other evidence of guilt) I was not inclined to validate what my research participants told me against other data, such as official records. Self-presentation was

being studied; historical events were not. I obtained scant official information about the men, other than information about a past violent conviction.
I did, however, note those discrepancies between official and self-reported
information that somehow became known to me. As Harter (1996) puts it:
"The particular, underlying reasons for such discrepancies may be far more
interesting and may ultimately tell us more about the self" (29).

I did all my own transcribing, a task I was glad for as the study progressed
and I grew more sensitive to research effects on data as well as the significance
of verbal construction. An interview transcript is always the transcriber's
representation (Ives 1980, 94). Perspectives enter the transcribing process via
apparently routine decisions: say, how to transcribe the speaker's dialect. Early
on in the study, my perfectionism and not epistemological considerations led
me to record "exact" wording, accents, modulation, coughs, laughs, pauses,
and the like. In little time I found theoretical justification for treating all
aspects of conversation as having a discursive function (e.g., Schegloff 1982).
Eventually I came to believe that the "debris" in offenders' stories reflects
socially situated identity challenges (McKendy 2006).

I took field notes on notebook paper before, during, and after the interviews. I transcribed these, attaching them to the transcripts of interviews
that corresponded temporally to the notes. The field notes consist of informal observations about the research participant, the interview, and myself.
In addition to field notes, I had notes based on infrequent phone contacts
with participants (e.g., to check on how they were doing after our interview). All data on my contacts with Kevin, a death row inmate, are based on
telephone and mail contacts. A small number of participants gave me their
original autobiographical writings, which I have examined to gain insight
about self-presentations. These include, remarkably, a published book by
Vaughan (Booker and Phillips 1994).

In that one's life story is ever under construction, it might be said that I
have only obtained a *sample* of the life stories of each research participant.
I would agree, adding that a sample of their stories provides adequate information about how they articulate who they are (see Linde 1993, 51). Still,
there is the question of representativeness. The qualitative researcher seems
to hold a great deal of power in her sampling of stories without any formal
system of accounting for how representative they are. What keeps me from
selecting only those participants, observations, and stories that support the
claims I want to make? Katz (1988b, 141–42) wisely answers that the theoretical significance of qualitative data is usually unclear during data collection:
"In the field I often wonder whether I should be elated or depressed for my
theory in response to the course an interview or observation is taking. . . . A

fieldworker inclined to ignore disconfirming data and record only confirming data often could not easily make the discrimination." This is so partly because analysis of qualitative data, like that of quantitative data, requires a great deal of concerted effort. Whereas analysis is going on even during data collection (H. Becker 1958), it is in very primitive form at that time. As was Katz's experience, it was only in my final stages of analysis when I began to "know" what claims I would be making.

Besides, the close relationships that the researcher has with her research participants and her readers regulate the reporting of results. Katz (1988b) observes that the relationships forged with participants engender in the researcher a felt obligation to be as true as possible to what they meant to say. In addition, one's readers serve a control function. Misreporting to them would be "laborious," since each "quote or episode would have to be edited carefully so that it might avoid contradiction elsewhere in the analytic framework" (ibid., 142).

Getting to the Story

How did we—research participant and I—"get to" the life story that was my research interest? Each of us has multiple "life stories." Our lives are "about" a myriad of things (Gergen and Gergen 1988). Many factors shape the life story we will tell and how we will tell it. Local factors shaping our life story include the immediate circumstances of the storytelling, the audience, and our own present concerns.

Change and struggle are said to be universal themes of life stories (Gergen and Gergen 1988). The men I interviewed stressed change and struggle in regard to their illegal activities. This focus on crime is not surprising. I introduced myself as a student of crime and offenders. I told the men that I was interested in their experiences with the criminal justice system. Several of my questions communicated that interest as well. Thus I had an early influence on the stories they told. But I am not solely responsible for this focus. The men were at a point in their lives where deviance and conformity were central issues. When I first interviewed the majority of the men, they were either under correctional supervision or recently released from correctional supervision. Their most recent conviction loomed large in their lives, both in and beyond the interview. But the sense of being deviant was likely aroused in the presence of a new socially "normal" person (Goffman 1963b).

On first meeting a research participant, I began the interview with a review of the informed consent form. After hitting the record button on the tape recorder, I typically made "small talk" about myself, the research participant, and/or the immediate situation. An example of such small talk is my remark to Peter, "Looks like you have a picture of an alien on your—um—on your ID [*laughing*]. Is that true?"

Next, I did one of two things. I asked where the narrator was from or what his current circumstances were, but never at this point about the instant offense per se. A common question was "How long have you been here?" Alternatively, I encouraged the research participant to tell me whatever he wanted to about his life. Sometimes when I did so, the research participant countered that he needed some idea of what I wished to know in particular. In those cases I resorted to asking about his background or current circumstances.

Some men took a while to start relating about themselves without my asking questions. Usually in these cases I asked what they had done to bring them to the immediate situation or facility. I stated these early references to the men's crimes in terms of criminal charges. I never named the men as perpetrators. Here are opening exchanges with Lyle:

> *Lo:*[4] How long have you been here?
> *Lyle:* Almost five months.
> *Lo:* And before that where were you?
> *Lyle:* Rosedale.
> *Lo:* How long were you there?
> *Lyle:* Uh. Like—almost a year.
> *Lo:* What kind of—uh—charge?

Whatever my opening, at some early point the men usually gave short statements about their criminal histories. Tim began: "I got a long criminal record." James announced: "My name is James Smith. I'm thirty-nine. Uh, I'm a seven-time convicted felon." These statements conveyed categorical identities. They preceded a much fuller chronicling of life events. Whereas the initial introductions were mostly similar, usually referring to one's record, the chronicle of events was far more idiosyncratic. The chronicles were framed in terms of who the narrator has been over time.

Harry, whose life story stressed that many of his crimes were beyond his direct control, stated how long he has been at the halfway house and then said: "So I've seen a lot of people come and go, you know. But, uh, as far as my own drug abuse and that type of thing, my drug abuse started at the age of thirteen. Um, I was sexually molested by my mother at *four* years old." Steve discussed having come to Cincinnati from Detroit as a teenager: "I grew up down there. I left when I was fifteen and moved to Detroit, good mom, good dad, good brothers, good sisters-type family." I responded "Yeah," and

Steve continued: "Never got in no trouble as a juvenile. Never got in trouble 'til I was *thirty-six*." Steve proceeded with a narrative of a basically good man whose offenses have been few and nonserious. Marco's narrative began with the following prompt on my part:

> *Lo:* So—your life story.
> *Marco:* A lotta stuff. I mean—how should I say? I won't—I wa— I wa—
>   I was born in Honduras ah—
> *Lo:* Oh! You weren't born here.
> *Marco:* An' um, I grew up in a— in- in a ho-house [whorehouse].

Marco went on to tell a life story that stressed his heroic struggle to leave the criminogenic influences of his childhood behind.

In effect, the men's narratives had two beginnings: one announcing static, categorical identities, and a second foretelling the plot of detailed stories to come. This observation is consistent with classic studies of self-presentation in interaction. At the start of a formally arranged conversation, such as a research interview, participants emphasize role-relevant identities such as "ex-offender" and "researcher" (Schenkein 1978). These usually pertain to the reason that the conversation is taking place at all: the "institutional agenda" (Kuhn 1962, 194). These roles are only suggestive of "the general framework within which interplay will go on" (Strauss 1997, 57). As the conversation and hence the narrative unfolds, participants present more complex, informal identities and, correspondingly, more idiosyncratic plots.

I analyzed these linguistic channels to "getting to the story" in an effort to understand what the interview meant for my participants. All told, I believe that the implicit question that the men were addressing—if not the explicit question I was asking—was: "How did you come to be here?" This question was the *point* of the interview, what Agar and Hobbs (1982) have termed its "global coherence." Clearly I shaped "the point" in the direction of moral conduct—the interviewee's or criminal justice agent's—with my references to this (criminal justice institutional) place.

Making Sense of the Data: What Is Narrative?

Having transcribed the data, I was still at a loss for just *what* to analyze. Agar and Hobbs (1982) grasp the problem: "The more the informal interview is controlled by the informant, the less the ethnographer knows how to deal with it" (2). I needed a model for analyzing the narrative.

First, I had to determine what the narrative *was*. The operational definition of narrative eluded me. What makes talk a narrative? Is narrative simply the story of a single event? Or is it the whole interview? If several interviews were conducted with one individual, does narrative encompass what was said during all of the interviews combined? If the narrative is more than just the story of a single event, does it include greeting, introduction and conclusion, personal asides, and everything else of a present-oriented nature? Finally, does the narrative include my own questions and remarks?

In an effort to answer these questions, I reviewed some of the most frequently cited writings on narrative. An important understanding of narrative has been gained through Labov and Waletzky's (1967) deconstruction of narrative elements in talk. According to Labov and Waletzky, "The x-then-y relationship is the fundamental one in narrative" (31). Influenced by this work, I determined that a narrative must address a sequence of (at least two) events over time.

The so-called Labovian model of narrative structure has influenced many, who nonetheless conceptualize narrative as more of a running account—told either about one's life or about a single episode from it, during an interview or interviews (e.g., Agar and Hobbs 1982; J. Bruner 1990; Linde 1993; O'Connor 2000; Polkinghorne 1988; Spence 1982). This broad view permits analysis beyond that of internal organization to that of coherence as an ongoing project for people. It may consist in multiple stories, or accounts of single events. I chose to follow this latter group of scholars, permitting me the same broad view. As such, I collected twenty-seven narratives from my twenty-seven research participants, with the unit of analysis being the narrative.

On that view, the researcher clearly has a strong hand in producing the narrative, since the sum total of accounts told to her by each speaker is constrained (only) by her exposure to the speaker—that is, the number of interviews she conducted. This fact brings me back to the socially constructed character of "one's" narrative. Narrative must always be selective, and it helps to observe that even the narrative one records in a private journal is selective. The larger issue tied to the codification of "a narrative" is that of the validity of coding social life at all. Social life is always emergent and chaotic, while any sort of coding/classifying and theorizing (which requires the other processes), freezes and reifies. In systematically making sense of—that is, theorizing—the self-construction of violent men, I can only be candid about the freezing and reifying I do. These and other methodological decisions are among the "practical accomplishments" of selves that my research clarifies (Holstein and Gubrium 2000, 88).

So, I allowed that the narratives I collected were the running accounts bounded by my time with each research participant. As for which utterances from an interview are properly considered *part of* the accounts and thus "the narrative," Labov and Waletzky's (1967) model was again a valuable guide. They set out the following components of narrative: orientation, complication, evaluation, resolution, and coda. Evaluation "reveals the attitude of the narrator toward the narrative" (37). It establishes the *point* of the narrative. Evaluative statements have no standard location within narratives, but they nonetheless play a crucial role: "Unevaluated narratives are exceptional as representations of personal experience, and unevaluated narratives lack structural definition" (ibid., 39). Linde (1993) observes that "the evaluative component [of narrative] in particular establishes the kind of self that is presented" (81). Gergen and Gergen (1988) agree that self-narrative must make a point about who one is. Amending my earlier definition, for my research purposes I determined that a person's narrative consisted in what he said that reflected a sequence of events over time *and* offered an evaluation of self.

Many of the present-oriented comments of my research participants can be seen as evaluative. One such comment is Tim's introduction to his account of raping a girl: "An' uh, I—you kn— I—I— I—didn't- I ain't been lookin' forward to telling you this part of this thing because it bothers me a lot but uh." It clearly establishes Tim's attitude toward the rape story. In Labov and Waletzky's scheme, it is thus an essential part of the narrative as a whole.

What about remarks that are "administrative," pertaining to the interview and not to a particular story told within it? Consider, for example, this exchange with Ralph:

Ralph: You had them request me, right?
Lo: Yeah.

I contend that Ralph's remark is part of his narrative. A critic might protest that it is trivial. I would counter that its importance is revealed by the interactants within the research situation, and not by pre-empirical fiat. Events do not, in themselves, tell us the point of the story: rather, the narrator does (Gergen and Gergen 1988, 21). In this case, Ralph is establishing himself as having been specifically called to the interview and not chosen at random. This in turn is key to a point he makes later, proving his decency by virtue of his having been authorized to be alone with me.

Perhaps the critical reader will say that local remarks pertain to the immediate moment (that is to say, the moment just passed) and not the more remote past, which is the proper object of the narrative. I would counter that narratives often do include remarks pertaining to the immediate moment, even if just the "Yeah" that precedes an answer to the researcher's question (e.g., Labov and Waletzky 1967, 23). We should not preordain the *way* in which the point of a story is conveyed, whether by referencing an event that occurred in the moment just passed or an earlier event.[5]

By expanding my operationalization of narrative, the apparent coherence of the stories is improved. The narratives simply make more sense when present-oriented remarks are brought into view. Relatedly, the broader operationalization allows us to see a person's "life story" as an interactional accomplishment.

Analyzing Narratives

Having determined that I would analyze everything spoken by the research participant, it was still not obvious what I should attend to *within* it. Coherence is emphasized in much of the literature on narratives (e.g., Agar and Hobbs 1982; Linde 1993; Polanyi 1985; Polonoff 1987). The concept of coherence pertains to the basic function of self-narrative (see chap. 1)—to give unity to (i.e., to make cohere) one's life experiences and thus one's self. Agar and Hobbs (1982) delineate three interrelated levels of coherence:

1. *Global coherence,* where utterances operate in the service of accomplishing the overarching goal or goals of speaking.
2. *Themal coherence,* where utterances refer to "chunks of content" (Agar and Hobbs 1982, 7) that are part of a broader cultural world of the speaker (and listener). Themes include beliefs, goals, and values.
3. *Local coherence,* concerned with connecting one utterance to the next in a meaningful way (e.g., by elaborating on the previous utterance).

I chose to study global and themal coherence, as defined in Agar and Hobbs's model. The study of local coherence requires very close line-by-line reading, better suited to single case studies than to my large data set consisting of some very long narratives.

Earlier I commented that the point of each interview was evidently to address how the individual got "here"—here being the position (physical or symbolic) of offenders. I had not specifically asked the men to explain their long journey to a correctional facility, a halfway house, or—in every case—the status of criminal. Nonetheless, the answer was clearly given in all of the interviews. The question served a *global* function.

Besides the overarching goal of describing a life marked by deviance, there were many *themes* that ran through the narratives. Moral change/stability and heroic struggle were two of the most important themes. My analysis centers on them. I investigated the achievement of global coherence (the point) and themal coherence (particular meanings). I chose not to study stories of particular episodes as ends in themselves, but rather as means to telling a more or less unified *life* story.

I was particularly attentive to how the narrator used the interview. With so many different areas of focus, my analysis proceeded in several steps.

Step 1: Coded for a Variety of Themes

My transcribed narrative data were imported from Word into N5, a software package for qualitative research that is part of the NUD*IST series. I did all coding in N5.

The first step of the analysis involved coding all of the data according to any themes that seemed sociologically interesting. This was truly a "first pass" through the data, which helped to familiarize me with the men's stories. Early on, there seemed no limit to the number of remarkable things about the data. Themes at which one codes data in N5 are referred to as *nodes*. At one point I had 164 nodes. These included three basic branches of data:[6] personal and criminal justice data about the men (e.g., marital status, number of children, occupation, ethnicity); various themes in their talk (e.g., social control/support; misconduct in prison; types of crime; emotions; values; crime victims; self-criticism); and various themes in *my* talk (e.g., victims; values; myself; my emotions; rehabilitation). The themes were derived inductively; the criterion for making a node out of an observed theme was simply because it seemed interesting.

With so many nodes, I began to forget about some of them. Some perfectly interesting nodes had little data coded at them: I realized then that I had too many nodes. Were they all equally interesting? I began to review them for how relevant they were (1) across the narratives (the data set) and (2) within each individual narrative. This was a difficult task when one thinks all of one's data are fascinating. Still, I managed to reduce the number of nodes to ninety-five.

I also restructured the nodes to reflect progress in my thinking about the narratives. I began thinking about comparisons and contrasts—between people and between selves (e.g., over time)—as essential to the coherence of the narratives and thus to identity. The new structure consisted of eight branches, including social distinctions that the men drew; the men's talk about their genuine self; talk about the self over time; ways in which the men evidently used the interview; and ways in which I evidently shaped the interview. These branched into talk about their moral reform, talk about their moral stability over time, expressed resistance to my authority as interviewer, and critiques of the justice system. In time, this *second* generation of nodes emerged as the most important for determining what their stories were about.

First, I saw the men's stories as "about" either change or stability in the moral self. That is, the protagonist of the stories had been reformed since the most recent crime, or had stayed the same basic person over the life course. Whether one claimed moral reform or moral stability, as I came to call this schism, the protagonist was cast as a hero in his own life. What varied, in a manner divorced from the moral reform/stability distinction, was the particular foe (e.g., drugs, justice officials) one has consistently countered in the heroic struggle that is one's life.

A more general theme than these two concerned the reason for the narrator's social position as violent criminal. Earlier in the chapter I discussed this theme as conditioned by the setting for most interviews and references I made to that setting. But here I wish to emphasize its global nature, both sociologically and in my data. Scott and Lyman (1968) propose that accounts of deviance are fundamental to human social life, and I observed that for myself. Every other theme I identified (even the original 164) could be seen as a contribution to such an account. The interviews were essentially accounts. Here, then, was an elementary effect that I had on the narratives. If not for this audience, supposedly requiring an account, what other turn—I wondered—would the narratives have taken?

Step 2: Recoded Data According to Emergent Theory

I recoded all of the narratives to ensure that my brand-new framework was adequate for each of them. I found that it was. My theory had become "saturated" (Glaser and Strauss 1967, 111; but see Charmaz 2002, 689–90). More individually specific ways of talking about one's self—plots—fit into the reform/stability and heroism framework: they demanded no further categorization. For example, talk of one's personal agency—in the past and present—was a regular feature of all narratives. It served the new framework, however, rather than constituting its own branch.

The N5 software allowed me to probe for the relationships between themes. One text unit can be easily coded at multiple nodes and the software reports on the combinations/intersections and proximity of different nodes quickly and easily. Thus I was able to evaluate the general point of the narrative through various analyses of coding. The software helped me to roughly type the narratives as reform or stability, and in terms of one's heroic foe. For example, most of the narratives included talk of both reform and stability; it was the rare narrator who made reference to one alone. Yet, in some of the narratives that I eventually typed as stability narratives, references to reform were followed closely by talk in which the narrator rejects the notion of reform. The software's "proximity search" (identifying proximity of various coding within the text) systematically presented the narrator's undermining of his own reform talk. A simple example comes from Arnell, who said of the twelve-step program he is participating in as a condition of parole: "You know, take—the best part out for myself. You know. Whatever. You know wha'am sayin'? Try to get somethin' out of it. But—you know—I still don't like it here."

The number of references to stability versus reform was suggestive of the overall plot, as were those dramatic statements narrators used to signal the point of the story. This is not to say that the plot could, for any narrative, be reduced to quantitative calculation. Rather, the reflective task of identifying a general plot gives meaning to the story as a whole.

My coding to this point had failed to capture fully the interaction between researcher and each research participant, because one person's talk was coded at a time. I was missing a sense of the flow, including the texture of interaction, of each interview.

Step 3: Created Memos as a Running Report on Interaction

The next step in my analysis was to create memos on each research participant based on the original narrative. In each memo I documented the progression of all interviews with that participant. The memos read like a running summary of (1) how the man's story was unfolding, and (2) what was going on between us. The memo also contained rudimentary analyses of the interaction. An excerpt from a memo based on my interview with Hector follows. Abbreviated words and references have been spelled out; otherwise no changes have been made to the memo as recorded.

> Of record of violence, Hector says "I just defended myself—when I had to," giving a clear statement of victim identity. Interruption, someone enters to check on whether I'm "all right," I say yes "we're all right" but thank the visitor. Change pronoun to "we"—suggesting that I am aligned with Hector, also that I need no protection from him? I continue questioning: has he had felonies. He answers that he doesn't even know what felony is, thus presenting as an innocent in regard to the criminal justice system. I empathize, bridging social distance: neither am I clear (what a felony is), but I try to explain.

These memos helped me to study sequential communicative exchange in context. In this case, it led me to some mechanisms of co-production, whereby

I backed Hector's claim of being a benign sort of criminal. In this short frag-ment of the memo, one can see the achievement of local ("Change pronoun to 'we'"), and themal ("clear statement of victim identity") coherence.

Along with other notes-to-self, the memos contained reflections on com-munication that was "not there"—that is, comments unexplained by the narra-tor or left vague. Communication is not just a matter of what conversants say but also what they do not say (Iser 1978, 1989). Garfinkel (1967) notes: "The anticipation that persons *will* understand, the occasionality of expressions, the specific vagueness of references, the retrospective-prospective sense of a present occurrence, waiting for something later in order to see what was meant before, are sanctioned properties of common discourse" (41; empha-sis in original). What goes unsaid is precisely what one assumes all cultural members already know. The "not said" should therefore be suggestive of nar-ratives that rely on supposedly shared understandings. Accordingly, I searched for and noted departures from fully developed talk—for example, where all ambiguous speech is defined—as well as glitches in communicating.

Step 4: Recoded for Themes

I imported the memos into a new file, and created new nodes to code the memos. The two main branches (nodes) of this final analysis pertained to (1) narrative structure and (2) co-production of the narrative. I reclassified for themes, this time considering them as elements in the plots of each man's narrative. The themes/plot elements came to me as they had in the first step of my analysis: as phenomena of interest.

For the analysis of co-production, I attended to—among other things—the incentives the men might have perceived for narrating their lives in a particular way (see Dean and Whyte 1958, 35). For example, my apparent "insider" relationship with the agency's administrator no doubt might have motivated the participant to present a reformed self. I looked for references to the nature of that relationship, in the narratives or my talk. Along with Dean and Whyte (1958), I see no reason to believe the participant would present a *truer* self in another, nonresearch situation, only a different one.

Summary

To conduct research where research is an object of study, I coded both the substance of the narratives, which I conceptualized as the sum total of stories told to me by an informant, and I coded what happened during narration, including what happened that *permitted* narration. The latter sorts of data were interactional, including gestures such as requests for clarification by participant or interviewer. These gestures are usually left out of research reports, according to the view that they are inconsequential to the project of unearthing the true phenomenon that gets revealed through interviewing. But if the research encounter is seen as prompting narrative construction, then as many aspects of the encounter that are consequential to the point of the narrative, as one can recall, *must* be shared. Narrative is not revealed by research; it is made to order. If narratives are "tailored to the specific people who are the story recipients" (Polanyi 1985, 33) and more generally to their occasions for telling, then all that is entailed in obtaining narratives shape them, including those inputs conventionally known as research methods.

This chapter has elevated research methods to the level of contributors to the phenomenon of interest—to the level of variables. In the next four chapters, however, I will bracket my methods in reporting on the narrative themes I recorded.

REFORM NARRATIVES:
RETURN OF THE GOOD SELF

I used to go to Sunday schools and churches before I came to the
United States. But then after—ya know—after a while, the devil
overcome me and I got lost on the outer world.
　　—Nelson

Trajectories of the Moral Self: Introduction

Change or consistency in one's moral self over time was a major
theme of the men's stories. This theme is not surprising given the use of narrative in explaining oneself (Ricoeur 1984) and thus establishing a cohesive
self over time (Linde 1993; McAdams 1999), and cues to crime or sanctions
that I gave the men (e.g., "How did you get here?"), however neutral and
universal I believed them to be at the time. At two archetypical extremes,
I heard *reform narratives* and *stability narratives*.[1] These are broad ways of
discussing the trajectory or journey one's moral self has traveled over time.
I will sometimes call them narrative structures or forms.

The reform narrative posits the protagonist as having changed in regard
to criminal behavior. Reform is the *point* of this narrative. In contrast, the
stability narrative is not *about* moral reform. Rather, the stability narrative
posits the protagonist as steady in his propensity to act according to moral
principles, either because he has been mostly decent or because he follows
subcultural moral codes, or both. Most narrators used reform and stability

talk within the same narrative. Theirs were *elastic narratives,* the most common narrative structure.

Given the predominance of elastic narratives, ways of talking about the moral self may be seen as falling along a continuum. Moreover, ways of talking about the moral self are contingent upon situational as well as biographical and psychological particulars, as well as cultural templates. My data do not support the notion that narratives belong to the person. In fact, my findings concerning the situated construction of the narratives (see chap. 9) suggest that they are just as likely to be transitory.

In this chapter I will examine reform narratives told by five of the twenty-seven men in my sample. But first I will discuss the concept of narrative distance, an essential quality of narratives and the very basis for evaluating one's moral self.

Narrative Distance

For each one of my research participants, the *narrative itself* created distance between the speaker and the man who had deviated from conventional rules and was sanctioned for it. One "can never immediately speak the present in the present" (Linde 1993, 105). Even the "present" self is a past self by the time it is discussed or even contemplated privately. As Mead (1934) said, "The 'I' of the moment is present in the 'me' of the next moment. There again I cannot turn around quick enough to catch myself" (174). Regarding oneself as an Other is a sociological fact, made palpable by language.

John accentuated the distance between narrator and protagonist by referring to himself in the third person. In the uninterrupted talk that follows, he responded to my request to describe himself. He asked if he should describe himself "now or previously" and I encouraged him to do both. Thus he compared two different protagonists:

> John before was extremely selfish, self-righteous, well to a degree he's self-righteous somewhat now, but not like he used to be. Um, John before would just as soon whoop your ass as look at ya. John before would—well if John drank, John would go out and get totally wasted and probably do what Craig Nathan [unclear reference] did. And not care about it a bit. Um, John before was an extremely rude and disrespectful person. Uh, was out to get what he could for himself and basically screw everybody else and how they felt or thought about it. And John was very self-centered. Extremely self-centered. And John now is kinda—a lot more laid-back than what he used to be. Um.

John wa— now will think about things, instead of just act or react to the situation. Um, John goes out and tries to have fun now, where John before wouldn't do it. So. John will think more about others now than he will of himself. And John knows he needs to get his ass back in school [*laughs*], and is going to very shortly.

John-the-narrator criticizes both "John before" and "John now." Although he had far harsher things to say about "John before," even "John now" is fallible: for example, he is somewhat self-righteous, though less than "John before." It is by virtue of evaluating these "Johns" that John-the-narrator appears relatively good. Verbalizing and thus appearing to know that the present self is somewhat fallible amounts to a moral position.

Whereas John spoke of a past and a present self, Vaughan spoke of two past selves. He recalled telling a courtroom of listeners about the two Vaughans present at the murder of his wife, this in a book he published (with David Phillips assisting with writing): "And I no longer seemed to be like myself. It's as if I had become two people. . . . It's like I was watching the other Vaughan Booker stand up there and shoot those arrows, as if I wasn't doing it myself" (Booker and Phillips 1994, 65). The bad Vaughan shot five hunting arrows into his wife's body, killing her. A not-as-bad Vaughan simply looked on. The best Vaughan of all is Vaughan-the-narrator, speaking with shock and disapproval of the whole terrible scene. The depiction of multiple protagonists highlights that the present self is a moral evaluator. It also salvages a past self that was not as immoral as the actual violator was, as in Vaughan's case.

Narrative automatically creates the opportunity for pronouncing oneself a different person than one was before (J. Bruner 1990; Linde 1993). The concept of narrative distance explains the general ability of narrators to make moral assessments of self. In reform narratives, to which I turn next, the narrator emphasized the distance he had traveled from his past, deviant self.

Reform Narratives: Back to the Good Self

Five of the twenty-seven narrators told reform narratives, whose plot or point is moral transformation. That plot was well integrated across stories the individual told. The narrator spoke of essential goodness, however much one has strayed from it. Concrete plans for desisting from criminal conduct had already been implemented.

Reform narratives featured a critique of those variables that led, supposedly, to one's offending. Tré attributed his past violence, including the murder of another young man, to personal insecurity and a belief that conflict must be resolved through combat. The basic critique was launched in each storied event that made up the narrative. In other words, it appeared and reappeared across the stories that composed one's life story.

Essential Goodness

The critiques launched in reform narratives were thorough but they were not damning. The protagonist had changed for the better, but was nonetheless *essentially* good. Thus a change *to* a moral self was really a change *back to* a moral self. José captured this idea in a journal entry that he recited to me: "I see myself as the *problem*. But uh, it—but this is the place in which I get the help I need, to be the José Rivera twelve years ago." Prior to a decade ago, he was a good boy. At about age ten, influenced by criminal associates and their antisocial attitudes, he began to do wrong. He credited cognitive treatment with leading him back to the good person he was—to his true self.

Nelson's moral fall—culminating in a first-time robbery—was depicted in religious terms, as the effect of evil thoughts and alcohol in his life. For a time he followed this decadent path, but he was, at the time of the interview, back to his essential self thanks to religious faith and abstinence from alcohol consumption.

> *Nelson:* Yeah. I was like—I was like— it was like one o'clock in the morning. I was drunk. I went in the gas station actually to buy cigarettes. But the alcohol and the—the evil thoughts just pop up in the—head, ya know. Uh— decided to rob the guy. I didn't have no weapon. I coulda got killed.
>
> *Lo:* Did you pretend to have a weapon?
>
> *Nelson:* I— yeah. Pretend that— actually I didn't really pretend. I had just had my hand in my— in my coat pocket. And, I coulda get killed. Because it's very serious. But now that—uh—I came to prison an'— worked through a lot of these programs—uh—AA programs an'—NA programs an'—like here, teach you a lot about life skills an' stuff like that. Behavior modification I was takin'—when I was in South Woods. Uh, I was also takin'—uh—auto mechanic—course. So I learned—a lot—that would protect [unclear] me from comin' back to prison.
>
> *Lo:* So, uh—how did—you said "evil thoughts"? What was that?
>
> *Nelson:* Um, I guess—ya know—like the devil was tempting me.
>
> *Lo:* Are you a religious person?

Nelson: Yeah, I'm a Christian.

Lo: A Christian.

Nelson: Yeah. I was born—actually I was born in a Hindu home. But I never follow up Hinduism. My mom and my dad is Hindu. My— I have one sister who is a Hindu. I have—uh—an [unclear: "ex"?] brother who's Hindu. Two other brothers is Hindu and—um—I have two sisters who's Christian.

Lo: Did you become Christian in prison?

Nelson: No.

Lo: No. On your own—before?

Nelson: Before. I used to go to Sunday schools and churches before I came to the United States. But then after—ya know—after a while, I—the devil overcome me and I got lost on the outer world. So.

Lo: I'm sorry: lost what?

Nelson: On the outer world.

Lo: Other world?

Nelson: Well, actually it's like—you have the narrow path in life which leads to eternity, and you have the broad way that leads to death and hell. So I got strayed away on that. But after comin' to prison, going to church again, I realize my mistakes—that I made and I learn a lot from that too.

Nelson and the others who told reform narratives are not claiming that the *criminal protagonist* was good, which, we will see, is a moral stability claim. Rather, the claim is that a certain pre-criminal protagonist was good, but strayed or fell from that position of moral decency. Hence, Clarence depicts his drug dealing, drug use, and related violence as an overlay on his true self: "So, when I don't do anything—that no more, I just be me." He also said: "There always been good in me, you know?"

In reform narratives, lack of agency characterized the criminal past. That is, given drug or alcohol addiction, antisocial peers and environments, negative attitudes, and so forth, the protagonist's actions were more or less uncontrolled. However, today's narrator is mastering these criminogenic factors, and thus his offending patterns. The course of one's agency, in reform narratives, is comparable to that in "desistance narratives" identified by Maruna (2001). Desisters in Maruna's sample narrated themselves as basically good people whose circumstances led them to criminal behavior. "The offending came from out there, not inside" (Maruna 2001, 93). Against great odds, these men and women reportedly liberated the decent person that had always existed inside. They arrived at self mastery. Likewise, the reform narrators in my sample talked of recovering the capacity to live a law-abiding life.

Ongoing Strategies for Desistance

Maruna (2001) states: "If such an enormous life transformation is to be believed, the person needs a coherent narrative to explain and justify this turnaround" (85). A plan for desistance was a central component of the reform narratives, just as it was of Maruna's so-called desistance narratives. Reform narrators were rather concrete about how they had changed *and* about how they would sustain the change. The strategy consisted in reversing those processes that purportedly caused offending. The causal factors cited in reform narratives were not markedly different, more or less numerous, or more or less plausible than those cited in stability and elastic narratives. They included poverty, alienation from school, substance abuse, antisocial peers, antisocial environments, and antisocial thinking patterns. Compared with the other narrative forms, in reform narratives these factors were mentioned more often and across event stories.

Reform narrators discussed specific ways in which they accomplished reform, in the present as in the past. For example, Tré told me how he avoids confrontations in the correctional facility: "I just stray away from 'em. I just stray away from a lot of people." For example, he would rise especially early in the morning so that he could be alone to think. He craved time alone. He shared a room with five other men and rejected their "childish ways" and tendency to ignore others' feelings—precisely those qualities he criticized in his past self.

The task of changing the factors that led to crime was seen as formidable. José was preoccupied with how to implement his plan for desistance once released from a correctional facility. He had doubts about staying in a relationship with a girlfriend who had not changed along with him: "Like I was tellin' you about my girl, now I really don't know *what* to do." Desistance was pictured as a process that would likely never end.

José loved his "girl" but disapproved of the wild habits and partying of her family and friends. He objected to one friend who, while staying with his girlfriend, had sex with a boyfriend in the presence of José's girlfriend's twelve-year-old sister, whom she was raising and whom José considered like a daughter. His censure is framed as a lesson to his girlfriend:

> So that made me feel better that she threw her friend out the house. So like, the month— a matter of fact, I got the letter *here.* That she accepted her friend

back in the house 'cause their relationship as friends has been too long. An' they forgave each other, this and that. An' I told her like this: I said "Any little incident happen with that girl? In the house? . . . Just don't even bother writing. Or asking for me or nothin'.' 'Cause I'm giving you too many [*sic*] advice and I'm giving you too many warnings. I'm learnin' the hard way and I don't want *you* to learn the hard way. I'm tryin' to tell you things before it happens."

For José and many of the men I interviewed, desistance involved doing good deeds (here, trying to help a girlfriend and her sister) and sharing one's life story, with the idea that others might avoid making the same mistakes. In my data, stated plans to do good deeds were fairly common in both reform and elastic narratives, but virtually absent from stability narratives. Yet plans for desistance broadly and redemption specifically tended to be more concrete and more realistic in reform narratives than in elastic narratives. Hence, whereas Ralph, who told an elastic narrative, presented himself as *currently* serving in the role of counselor in the facility—a claim that was not credible—José talked about *becoming* a counselor like those ex-convict counselors who were his role models. José said: "You know, maybe come back here in like—in a year or two an' be a counselor. You know and there's a lot of things I want to change in my life. Meanin'—you know—ah—be a better man."

The view of change as a process is consistent with the "one-day-at-a-time" rhetoric of twelve-step programs. Informed as it is by belief in a higher spiritual power, the twelve-step philosophy teaches that change is partly contingent on mutual help and sharing of one's personal experience (Swora 2002). José considered sharing his story to be critical, not only because it would help others. He conceived it as "the only way I'll get my respect back in society."

Reform versus Elastic Narratives: An Illustration

The reform narratives of two men, contrasted with an elastic narrative, will help clarify its features. William told a reform narrative in which he attributed his drug use and robbery to a contrary attitude and antisocial peers. He detailed what that attitude consists of, and he introduced it as problematic in different event stories. He said that he once engaged mainly in prosocial activities (e.g., sports)—that is, he was originally good—but had grown restless and came under the influence of the street. William draws a distinction between his essential prosocial self and the deviant he became. "Just start doin' the wrong thing. Just start lettin' my attitude take over my *self*."

Just as William distanced his present self from the one taken over by his "attitude," he planned to distance his future self from influences that would only encourage the bad attitude. He strategized about avoiding those friends he used to spend time with, saying "I don't want to deal with no—associate with nobody that I did wrong things *with*. You know? 'Cause—only thing you can try to tell me or try to convince me is to come out here and do the same thing." William anticipated an extended struggle to leave crime behind him, but was nonetheless optimistic.

In passing, William shared that he had an attention-deficit disorder. William might have used the disorder as an excuse for his antisocial behavior (see Scott and Lyman 1968, 49). Yet it does not figure into his particular reform plot at all. A clinical disorder might have "naturalized" his past bad attitude, whereas William is inclined to depict it as a temporary phenomenon over which he has gained control. The fact that William did not include the disorder in his narrative suggests that the "facts" of a person's life, rather than dictating one's life story, are resources (see Gubrium and Holstein 2000; Maruna 2001, chap. 3).

José also told a reform narrative. In fact, he and William shared a similar profile as young minority men whose criminal histories consisted mainly of illicit drug use and robbery. José spoke at length about turning away from a life of crime: "But it's my choice whether to go out there to do the same things I was doin' or not. You know. And—I wanna—I'm changin' and I wanta change to—to the best I can." He told me: "I wasn't such a bad kid 'cause—I could always say that for myself—until I started hangin' around with the wrong people." In order to continue on a prosocial path once out "in the street," José intended to reverse the pattern whereby he became involved in street crime, by distancing himself from "the wrong people." He revealed: "But my greatest fear is—my biggest biggest fear? It's going out there completely. 'Cause I haven't been out there—in— by the time I go out there it'll be five years. But it's like goin' out there and really knowing—ya know, lookin' at new faces. The same people that was out there before, some of them are—still alive, some of them are dead. Ya know. It's that—I don't want to go back to the same environment." José's plan of isolating himself from noxious influences would be difficult to implement, because many of his family members, including his father, were offenders and drug users. He went so far as to consider a "move away from the family." Thus he presented himself as committed to change, whatever the price.

Tim's elastic narrative provides a contrast. He told me: "I'd like to go do something where I can help people—give someth— kind of give somethin' back, you know? Just like I said, I got a sensitive side to me, you know? An' I—I'd kinda like to do that. It'd be a way of expressing some compassion, understanding." As much as Tim wished to do good deeds at this point in his life, he was easily thwarted. He had the idea of becoming an emergency medical technician but lamented: "I— but I—I found out that I can go to the school, but because of my prison record, I probably wouldn't get hired at a hospital . . . that kind of put me on hold." As a result, he said: "I don't know *what* I'm goin' to do. I don't know *what* I'm goin' to do. I'm just gonna play it by ear, where I'm at right now." Obstacles had thrown him off the course of reform. Specifically, the justice system interfered with his efforts to redeem himself. Tim speculated on other courses of action but these were not well thought out. For example, he said that he has thought about moving to Florida or Nevada. When I asked him if these or any other states do not restrict licensing for emergency medical technicians, he replied that he does not know; he vaguely stated that there must be some place without such restrictions. In short, Tim had no alternative reform strategies in tow.

Summary

All of the men I interviewed claimed moral decency in the present, but how they arrived at such decency varied greatly in their narratives. In this chapter I introduced my distinction between three sorts of narratives—reform, stability, and elastic narratives—which reflect different trajectories of the moral self. Current "life course" studies in criminology focus on the actual events and disruptions that conduce to change in offending patterns. I did not set out to research the phenomenology of the life course, as some criminologists have recommended (e.g., Sampson and Laub 1993; Ulmer and Spencer 1999). But something on the order of a phenomenology of the life course did emerge, centered on oneself as a good person. That is, my informants stressed their *experience* of change or stability in *moral* selves over time as a key theme of the life story. To know these men is to know that they have changed or remained basically the same ethical actor.

Also in this chapter I closely examined reform narratives, which featured a trajectory from essential goodness to moral decline and back to goodness. The distance between narrator and protagonist that characterizes *any* narrative was emphasized. Though desistance was presented as an ongoing process, entailing practical activities, the narrator had already made a marked break from the deviant self.

STABILITY NARRATIVES: NEVER A BAD SELF

'Cause I was the type in the biz like I used to feed all the kids
in the neighborhood.
　　—Dwight

Seven of the twenty-seven narrators told stability narratives. Whereas
reform narratives are about desistance, stability narratives are about steady
moral character. The protagonist was presented as a moral or good person,
if not in the exact moment of offending then in one's life generally. The
protagonist had consistently abided by subcultural values—standards of
behavior—and/or was dependably good in the conventional sense—or at
least as good as other people.[1]

In reform narratives, the difference between the protagonist or past self
and the narrator was emphasized. Not so in stability narratives, where that
difference was presented as more or less insignificant. The protagonist was
the narrator and vice versa. Nor were desistance strategies a necessary part
of stability narratives, because one's criminal self was described as moral or
as very short lived.

Accounts—both justifications (one takes responsibility but the action was
not so bad) and excuses (one minimizes responsibility) (Scott and Lyman
1968)—were vital resources for those telling stability narratives. That is, embedded in life stories of being a consistently decent sort were explanations of
violence that framed the actor's (role in) harmful conduct in ways that cast
him in a decent light.

Larry's Stability Narrative: An Illustration

Larry had killed a man while driving under the influence of alcohol (DUI). For this offense he was convicted of aggravated manslaughter and sentenced to twenty years in prison. (He served less than five years in prison when he was paroled.) He called the DUI "just somethin' that happened." Initially citing alcohol abuse as causal, later in our interview he contradicted that statement: "I—in *my* heart, I believe that it wouldn't have mattered if I was drinkin' or not: that woulda still happened." In Larry's narrative, he had always been a responsible person. His substance abuse was extraneous to—and extricable from—his essential self: "I mean, I'm not comfortable with—my drinkin' and my drug behavior. But when I put the drugs and the alcohol—down, I pretty much like who I am, what I'm about, and what I'm capable of doing." Larry's essential self thus lies in the potential goodness of his character. He attributed his current residence in a correctional facility to a "carefree lifestyle" and to "emotional immaturity" but did not attest to any change in his lifestyle or his personality. In fact, he stated his hopes for a future free of cares and responsibilities: "What I want is like a permanent vacation."

Larry's "good" identity was established by excising criminogenic agents (e.g., drugs, alcohol) from the narrative, not because he had given them up but rather because they were not deemed part of his true self. Larry's criminological perspective on his offending was tentative: "I think what it is is that I've just made bad decisions. At times." He was also dubious about his need for reform. Of the treatment he had been exposed to, he said: "Well, the only thing I can say about that is that the uh—information that they give you can help you." Larry claimed a fundamentally good identity by defining his deviant conduct as irrelevant to who he really is. This is comparable to Tim's insistence that he has "a sensitive side," behavioral indications to the contrary aside.

The majority of narratives that I heard, including Tim's, incorporated reform *and* stability talk. I call them elastic narratives. Elastic narratives emphasized moral stability but included some reform talk as well. In this chapter I will first describe stability *talk* as it appeared in both elastic and stability narratives, after which I will outline some features unique to stability narratives. Chapter 7 offers a closer look at elastic narratives.

In order to present themselves as consistently decent regardless of past offending, narrators used four general tactics, which were closely related and often used interchangeably. These framed one's offending (1) as good or (2) as fleeting and atypical of one's true self; (3) shifted the focus of stories and the overall narrative away from one's criminality; or (4) secured the moral role as one's harshest critic.

Crime as Good

Framing one's crime as good is comparable to "justifying" crime in the sense that Scott and Lyman (1968) defined that term, though my data concern justification of one's self and thus actions generally, and not just a single action. I found three sorts of justification that crime was good: constructing oneself as an honorable offender, extolling masculine aggression, and presenting deviance as sport.

Honorable Offenders

In some stability talk, images of honorable deviants were presented. The narrator affiliated himself with mythic male nonconformists who followed their own set of ethics, if not always the ethics of conventional society. Less principled offenders were denounced.

Kevin prided himself on his ability to stay true to his values during more than eighteen years behind bars. When I asked Kevin if he had changed much in prison, he answered: "I've pretty much managed to keep the same personality and character I had." In a letter from death row, he attributed the steadfastness of his character to "codes of honor": "Because of my codes of honor my hands have always been tied. Not too long ago a precious woman I know got on my case about my principles and said things along these lines, what have my codes gotten me, have they kept me warm at night? My principles have gotten me nothing. . . . But logic doesn't apply to principles." Kevin has lived according to higher principles than others do. His liberty and physical well-being have been compromised as a result of his moral integrity.

Hector and Joe-Ray likewise distinguished the protagonists in their narratives as honorable offenders. Hector regretted the passing of a culture of "mens of honor." A lifelong boxing enthusiast, Hector frowned upon today's boxing culture, which he characterized with the lament: "Very little honesty. Very little justice." He continued: "Guys—ya know wha'a mean—ask you to fight—today. Ya know. Before you put your hands up, you be wise to look behind you."

I have categorized Hector's boxing as honorable deviance, which begs the question of whether *he* thought of it as deviant. My interview with him suggests that he understood boxing as occupying a middle ground between mainstream and street cultures. He first learned to box in juvenile detention facilities. At age seventeen, when Hector entered a new high school in the community, he was challenged to box by other youths. In describing that challenge, he conveyed a reluctance to box because he was not violent: "I was a peaceful type of person—ya know, I wasn't—violent. Ya know. But if I was offered out [dared to fight], ya know, I would come out." There Hector depicted boxing as violence. Hector's evident talent caused him to be labeled as a boxer. In time, Hector came to love the sport and depicted himself to be a virtuous sort of boxer. He described his current fighting as an art: "I'm on a hi— much higher scale now. It's more like a— the martial arts expert, ya know." The early protagonist in Hector's narrative was forced to fight. The later protagonist is a principled member of the fighting community. Fighting is not altogether legitimate, but he does it honorably.

Joe-Ray presented a comparison of two kinds of drug dealers. One kind is ruthless in the pursuit of money and the lifestyle and respect that money affords. He aligned himself with a different sort: "guys that do it peaceful. You got guys out there that actually don't want no type of trouble." "Is that you?" I asked. He replied: "No! That *was* me." In his (elastic) narrative, Joe-Ray criticized a past self that, though criminal, was nonetheless decent compared to his peers.

Steve minimized his criminal history, in part by focusing only on those actions he had been sanctioned for. (I examine such focusing on sanctions rather than behavior, as a technique for establishing moral stability, later in the chapter.) At the same time, he recounted his loyalty to accomplices. He complained that he had received an excessive prison sentence for burglary, his only felony: "Cause I don't run my mouth, I don't snitch." Had he snitched, he would have received a much shorter sentence, as his accomplice did, but he is "from the old school." For Steve, being "from the old school" is consistent with being essentially decent.

Arnell did not glamorize the violence he had committed but simply called it a neutral fact of life where he comes from. Thus he referred to having engaged in violence that was not violence: "You know, see uh— before—like I said, I was just sellin' drugs. But once I've got really into—well see, I will think—fightin' ain't violence. Heh [*chuckling*]. When it's street, anyway. You know. If you fight somebody, that's—uh—like *normal*. Ya know—an' uh—you know—from where—the streets that I come from."

By redefining violence, Arnell redefines himself as a normal neighborhood resident. He is nondeviant in his community, though he displays a consciousness of a different, mainstream way of viewing violence. He is not dishonorable.

Masculine Violence as Good

Violence *against* women, in contests *over* women, and *on behalf of* women is endorsed by a patriarchal culture arguably gone underground.[2] Such forcible gender displays were also endorsed in stability talk. Chivalry in one's account highlighted the good done *through* violence.

Whereas the three forms of masculine violence coincided in stability talk, they received somewhat different treatment. Specifically, violence against women was *not* presented as decent in itself, evidenced by the universal tendency to neutralize such incidents (see also Mullins, Wright, and Jacobs 2004). In contrast, the other two forms of masculine aggression were presented as righteous per se.

The contrast is vivid in Reuben's stability narrative. In the following exchange he refers to an extended episode involving both certain violence against a man with whom his girlfriend had had an affair, as well as probable violence against his girlfriend:

> *Reuben:* Well, I had an assault charge like last year.
> *Lo:* What was that about?
> *Reuben:* Uh. Well, my girlfriend and—some other guy. I caught them two.
> *Lo:* So—
> *Reuben:* [unclear] fight.
> *Lo:* You and the— you and the girlfriend or you and the guy?
> *Reuben:* Me and the guy.
> *Lo:* And—then he filed—charges against you?
> *Reuben:* U— *no.* Um, after I beat him up, I got—mmm—very upset with my girlfriend. And started yellin' at her an' me and her started fightin.' So that's what I got locked up for.
> *Lo:* Oh, so *she* filed charges.
> *Reuben:* Yeah, they took me. She didn't press charges though.

Reuben minimized his domestic violence by referring to it as a fight. He also stressed the fact that he was not ultimately charged. But Reuben described his beating of his male rival in bold terms ("I beat him up"). Similarly, Tim was intrepid in stating his purpose in shooting his girlfriend's ex-lover: "I figured I'd kill him, he can't talk: a dead man can't talk." His rape of a teenage girl is handled far more delicately, even shamefully, with a caveat that recounting the episode "bothers me a lot." Indeed, tactics for framing oneself as good in the conventional sense, like remorse, were applied to battering much more than to the other two kinds of masculine aggression—violence in contests over women and violence on behalf of women. The latter two kinds of aggression were usually presented as *themselves* good.

As Reuben and Tim's stories make plain, masculinity might require the protagonist to do violence to a *male rival*. Tim said of the aforementioned shooting: "The fact that he was—that he was with Amanda wasn't settin' so easy with me." Explaining his manslaughter charge, Max was able to sum up the incident—the killing of his girlfriend's husband—in one sentence:

Lo: What was the incident?
Max: It had to do with an individual who would not give up his wife at the time.

Max subsequently admitted that killing the man was a mistake, saying, "I didn't handle it the way I should've handled it." Still, he implied, when a rival will not "give up" a woman, aggression may be required.

Masculinity also warranted violence against other men for the *protection* of women. Marco reported that, while in his teens, he was expected to protect his sister: "I had to go to um—my sister was not doin' too good in school an' some people were botherin' her so I had to go around there." Dwight shot a neighbor who had raped his girlfriend's teenage daughter. He explained that he did what he had to given his role as "man of the house." Dwight's safeguarding of women is a constant thread in his storyline. Whereas Dwight talked of his moral reform in regard to his conduct *toward* women—he admitted to having raped many in the past—he did not attempt to relegate his thinking about masculine aggression against *men* to the past.

I asked Wayne, whose criminal history included several serious assaults, if he felt any regret about having hurt people. He replied that he did, and stated that "there isn't any excuse" for violence, then revised that blanket statement: "But, if there's someone who would hit or hurt a woman, or whatever, I'd hit him! I would!" Tim said that he resented the disparaging talk about women he had to listen to in prison: "It used to offend me, havin' to sit and listen to that crap. I don't feel that way about women." These protectionist claims are rooted in conventional chivalry, which is no less celebrated in popular culture. It should also be noted that most crime, even violent crime, is conventionally condoned and even lauded under certain circumstances. In stability talk, virtuous aspects of offending were emphasized wherever possible. Describing crime as honorable, chivalrous, or as mastery of some game extracted a bit of virtue from a criminal life.

Deviance as Sport

The gaming aspect of crime was often discussed appreciatively in stability talk. Deviance was a sport—it offered "sneaky" and other thrills (Katz 1988a)—and the narrator took pleasure in it in the moment of narration. The audience was invited to appreciate the fun aspect of the crime.

John seemed to relish telling the story of his friend's recent violent confrontation with a reckless school bus driver. John revealed that he too was eager to beat the bus driver. When I asked what he thought a beating would have accomplished, he answered: "It woulda made us both feel a lot better [*laughing*]!" Thus he demonstrated his willingness to resolve conflict through physical fighting for the sake of immediate gratification in giving what he called "a good old-fashioned ass-whipping."

James became animated when he described his skill and bravado in shoplifting to his classroom audience. He seemed to delight in sharing precise details about his thefts and the street value of stolen items:

> *James:* I was taking Yamaha boom boxes, 1,500 dollars. Out of Bennett's. I was killin' Bennett's. I was je—
> *Student:* [*giggles*]
> [Other students break out in laughter, along with James.]
> *James:* [*laughing*] Why you looking and start laughing?

James reveled in the observation that he was "killin'" the largest department store in town. When this comment met with laughter from James's interlocutors, the fun of the offending was extended to the present speaking moment.

Ralph valued his cleverness in manipulating others, as well as the cool, comfortable life he had been living prior to his incarceration. He denied that he had committed robbery, rape, and burglary, as his record indicated, yet he was fond of the image of himself as shrewd. Without specifically naming any crimes, he presented the hypothetical smart and "sneaky" criminal he *would* be if he *were* a criminal:

> *Ralph:* I mean if you had to look at me and say "Well, what kind of criminal is he?" Uh. I ain't the type that like to go hittin' nobody over the head. [*laugh*]. You know wha'a mean? I damn straight ain't no rapist. Um. I ain't no purse snatcher. Uh. I'm too cool to be a drug dealer. Ya know. So, if you had to classify me—yeah—from the type of lifestyle that I was livin'—from the way I was brought up—you

could say—I'm more the sneaky type. I'm more of the white-collar crime. That way if I'm goin' out, I'm goin' out. You know, I want some loot. You know [*chuckle*]: some *real* money. You know wha'am sayin'? So. That's the type of person *I* would be. Um. You got to set up some type of bank job for *this* thing 'cause—if I'm goin' to jail for years, I got to have *money*. It's got to be *planned out*. I don't want no *mistakes*.

Lo: So it involves a challenge.

Ralph: Exactly, so. That's the type of person I would be. Um. 'Cause I always thought. I always think. You know. I always use my head. Um. Nah, I ain't into that violent thing.

In Ralph's fantasy, he is a clever rogue engaged in highly lucrative, well-planned crimes. Such crimes are incompatible with violence because he is simply not so pedestrian as to be "into" violence.

In addition to presenting one's crime(s) as good, some men placed the crime(s) on the margins of their life story. The crime did not define them. Either it was extraneous to who they *actually* were or a persona manifested at or suggested by the crime scene defined them instead. This pattern of defining the self *contra* criminal behavior underscores a basic observation of much of the literature on identities and narratives (see chap. 2), that self-construction processes are creative and active.

Crime as Momentary: "Taken Out of Character"

Some men relegated admittedly immoral conduct to a brief and meaningless episode of their lives. The conduct is not indicative of who the narrator truly is; rather, his true, good self momentarily disappeared. Joe-Ray summed up this position: "You can—you can actually do somethin' that—can take another individual out of— out of they character." He even applied this argument to me, so commonplace was the phenomenon: "If—somebody probably could do somethin' to you that will— can really take you out of your character. I mean, it happens all the time." Joe-Ray attributed being taken out of character to another person's provocation.

Peter was taken out of his good character literally by accident. While attempting suicide by auto collision he killed a man—another driver. Peter said of his essentially nonviolent self, "In all of my thirty-eight years, I could—uh—tell you how many times I've gotten into a—a confrontation which—resulted in any—uh—physical—altercation—and s— on my one hand, and still have plenty of fingers left over." He expressed his lasting sense of shock.

Even after four years, "it just doesn't seem real." The self he knew was not the self that had taken a life.

The momentary, criminal protagonist baffled the narrator. Emotions and cognitions were frequently summoned to explain being taken out of character. These were depicted as external to one's true self, hence the narrator's incapacity to understand them. Harry was surprised by his rage upon learning that his wife had betrayed him, leading to his attempt to kill her: "I went ballistic. I couldn't believe how mad I was myself." Lyle considered why he had committed armed robbery although he did not need the money: "I oh—oh [don't know]: I was just beat. I don' even know." Joe-Ray's recent aggravated assault and robbery took place at a casino and began with a bold grab for the victim's bucket of chips: "It had to be at least like forty thousand dollars worth of chips. Somethin' like that. But um. I just grabbed it: I took it. On my way walkin.' I was—I was just buggin' man." Being beat (bored), bugging (being crazy), feeling anger and lust are all instigators to uncharacteristic action.[3]

In some stability talk, emotional states were foundational. That is, their origin was beyond explanation. More often, though, the narrator described situational prompts to strong emotion. This was the case for Joe-Ray, in his account of the aforementioned aggravated assault and robbery at the casino:

> Yeah, I was stressin.' I had a female at the time and—I had two females. I had one female that was gettin' on my nerves, I had another female that was pregnant an' was *really* gettin' on my nerves, so. No excuse but I was just drinkin'—um—you know, I was broke at the time. I ain't had no more money after havin' a *lot* of money and—I was—I don't know what I was thinkin.'

Vaughan also established situational strains that caused an unagentive state of mind, which then led to his killing his wife with a bow and arrows. In his memoirs he wrote the following:

> I was coming home in the early hours of the morning, pretty intoxicated. On approaching my home I saw a man coming down the steps, apparently leaving our house. I went upstairs and found Gail awake, sitting on the edge of the bed, smoking a cigarette. I asked her about the man.
> "Who was the dude I saw leaving?"
> "What are you talking about?"
> "You know what I mean. Who was he?"
> "Your son's father."
> It was as if I had been hit over the head with a baseball bat. You've heard the saying "see red." Well I saw red. Every possible hidden or dark emotion

that I had came to the surface. I remember the flash, the anger. (Booker and
Phillips 1994, 69)

Vaughan "saw red" after his wife implied that she had cheated on him. His
book details the consequence of that implication, and thus Vaughan Booker's
position as victim.

Similar is Tim's account of aggravated assault, in which he sustained a fair
amount of beating from an exploitative employer before fighting back under
the spell of rage. Before describing the physical altercation, Tim explained at
length that the employer owed Tim back pay for his work as an apartment
manager. When the man demanded a lesser amount that Tim had borrowed
from him, he replied, "I guess you'll just have to take it out of my check. So I
said, better yet, just take it out of what you owe me and give me the balance.
Ya know, you owe me twenty-eight hundred dollars—jes' deduct it from that
and give me twenty-four hundred dollars." The employer became enraged
and attacked Tim.

> An' then uh, he came— brought me over this table, chokin' me, bent me over
> this table an' was chokin' me an' finally I just got— I just came up off the table.
> I pushed him away from me, went to the door, opened the door, stepped out
> into the hallway. Well he came out into the hallway with me. Punched me in
> the stomach, slapped me in the face, punched me in the stomach *agin,* slapped
> me agin, knocked my glasses off, an' then, he—ya kn— he was runnin' his
> mouth a lot, talking all, I don' kno— remember all what he said, but he was
> talkin' all kinds a crazy. And I was mad *then.* I mean, I—I—when my glasses
> went off my face, I could feel the anger comin'—you know? an'—an' uh—there
> was a brief pause then an' he punched in the stomach agin, an' when he did,
> I—before I even knew it, I hit him with that cup. I—I jes' hit him with the cup
> an' he went down immediately an' when he went down, I just started hittin'
> on him. Hit him a couple times. He tried to crawl away from me an'—his
> head was split. He tried to crawl away from me an' I—I jes'—I was mad, you
> know. An' I don' know—I jes' got *mad.*

Tim is first a victim of his employer's financial exploitation, then of his
employer's prolonged assault, and finally of his own rage.

Even when a particular type of crime was ongoing by nature, the protagonist could still be described as acting out of character in each individual crime
episode. A good example of such ongoing crime is battering, which nine of
the men told me they had perpetrated. Larry said of his domestic abuse: "I
jes'—my first wife, I hit her a few times. I was in such rage." Alternatively,
emotion built up over many years could, in some accounts, provoke a single

atypical action. This is akin to the frustration-aggression hypothesis, an influential psychological proposition stating that frustrated satisfaction of goals or needs may provoke violence (Berkowitz 1989; Dollard et al. 1939). Oren allegedly killed his father in a psychotic, delusional state, the cumulative result of years of abuse:

> Lo: Were there—fingerprints leading to you or is this just an impression?
>
> Oren: There was no weapon—nothin' really. I just said I did it. I—I had a dream—I had a violent dream. . . . I had—I was like—this cross of—I was dreaming like—I was this knight? But one of those futuristic types of knights, ya know. And I've always hated waterbugs: I can't stand waterbugs [chuckle]. Always hated waterbugs! And anyway, I was—this knight. I was in this field. This nice, sunny day. Ya know, set down my—armor, and this sword and this [unclear] pistol. I turned around and there was this waterbug. And um, I was about to jet, but—I didn't 'cause—I was tired of running from things anyway, so. I—I picked up [unclear], and instead of running, I grabbed a sword and—charged.
>
> Lo: You charged the waterbug?
>
> Oren: [chuckle] And I started hacking at it and hacking at it and hacking at it. And then after a while, I just—booked [chuckle]. It wouldn't stop moving! So I left! I was gone! You know. And, when I was running—I remember I was running through the field, and I [unclear] felt there was snow—behind me. And I was running—something sharp hit me? An' I woke up, and I was in the middle of the street. And it was some ice cold wind hit me [laugh]! Anyway—I said—ya know—I was like, I thought about it. I said I did it! Ya know. 'Cause I know I wanted to. Honestly. . . . Ya know. I mean—I don't even like huntin.' I haven't been in the country for years: I can't stand huntin' [chuckling]! . . . If my life was in danger? That's somethin' different, but. Just—take somethin' out? I could never do it.

Oren took responsibility for his father's murder but did not, in fact, know himself as a person even capable of violence. He reasoned that years of being dominated by his father, which led him to feel like he "was in a cage," made the use of force possible for him in one trancelike moment.

The frustration-aggression hypothesis also has a place in Vaughan's account of murdering his wife: "Every possible hidden or dark emotion that I had came to the surface." Tim likewise described the assault on his employer in terms of accumulated frustration: "I hit that guy before I even thought about it. I just did it. I guess it was just all built up inside of me an' I just let it go."

These "moral stability claims" of having been taken out of character are in some ways similar to the *reform* narrator's view of his moral fall. In both cases, one's essential self was suspended at the time of offending. The key difference between them is that "being taken out of character" occurs within a very short period of time. The self is *not* himself for only as long as the harmful action lasts. The absence is so fleeting that extensive analysis is uncalled for and therefore is not typically provided.

Nelson referred to the moment before robbing a gas station when "evil thoughts" "popped" into his head. A few exchanges later, though, Nelson described the influence of evil as lasting for some time. He had been a righteous sort until "after a while, I— the devil overcome me." On the basis of this more thoroughgoing critique, I typed Nelson's as a reform narrative. In Nelson's narrative, he would continue to abstain from drinking and would attend church in order to keep the devil at bay. But in "out of character" stability talk, desistance is a pointless goal since the narrator is a noncriminal. Only during those short-lived episodes did a different, unfathomable character appear.

Shift in Focus

Another tendency of stability talkers was to shift the focus of the story away from deviance. In other words, the stories were emplotted along nondeviant lines. The protagonist's goodness in the crime scene and/or more morally neutral traits were emphasized as characterizing him.

Good, Even at the Crime Scene

Some narrators highlighted qualities commonly associated with goodness, such as kindness and concern about others' welfare. Many stressed that they were caring fathers. The men also called attention to traits that, on their surface, do not seem to be about goodness. James and Ralph, for example, made much of their verbal shrewdness and adventurous spirit. Above and beyond the fact that contemporary Western culture indeed does take cleverness and innovation to be "good" (see, e.g., Dudley 1994), the men posited these personal qualities as being used *for* good, time and again. Most ingeniously, these qualities were used for good even in *deviant* episodes of one's life.

Shawn quit the army because he missed his family. Larry quit the Marines because he had been assigned to an infantry post, where he was, he believed, unlikely to learn skills needed for a legitimate livelihood. He explained: "So when I went in the Marines, I went in the Marines with the intentions of turning that into a career. Learning a trade. *Becoming* somebody. Bein' a man. Well, I get in there, and uh, somehow or another I felt as though they kind of like uh—pardon the expression—screwed me over? I signed up for aircraft mechanics? Something I thought that I would be interested in doing, make some money at. And they wind up puttin' me in the infantry.... And uh, I didn't see any future in that? Except for maybe become a professional hitman?" Thus Larry was deviant *because* he did not want to become a criminal ("professional hitman"). He wanted, rather, to become a law-abiding breadwinner.

Tim and a friend took turns raping a teenage girl. Afterward, Tim asked the victim if she was all right. He also made some verbal attempt to get his friend—who was allegedly more brutal—to leave the girl alone. He also reported being upset that his rape victim was humiliated at trial. Once arrested for the rape, Tim escaped from detention—remarkably, on two consecutive occasions—because he was worried about his pregnant wife. He turned himself in after the first escape.

Dwight stressed moral reform when it came to sexual violence. Yet his talk about certain other crimes, including other crimes of violence, emphasized moral stability: he was never very much in the wrong when it came to these. He used several tactics to buttress his presentation as decent, including talk of his own victimization and his good, caring qualities. Previously I referred to Dwight's shooting of the man who raped his girlfriend's teenage daughter. At the time, Dwight himself was awaiting trial for a rape. His account of the shooting incident was saturated with references to his own conflicted quest to do good, given his sense of manly duty to his girlfriend and his responsibilities to people generally. For example, he referred in this scene to his kindness to the neighborhood children.

A brief account of Dwight's involvement in prison riots also suggests that he is a man burdened by moral obligation. His violence—here only alluded to—is warranted by his integrity as well as victimization by others. He replied to my question about his involvement in past riots as follows:

> *Dwight:* Yeah, I was involved in a couple of—uh—quite a few of 'em.
> *Lo:* Why? What was going on then? What got you involved?
> *Dwight:* Well uh [pause]. Uh. The right going to work. Uh. Didn't like bein' mistreated by—the—officials—authority—in authority, I'm sayin'?

Lo: So what was—what were your actions in it?

Dwight: Uh. Just wanted to stand up and do the right thing. 'Cause I got tired of doin' what people tellin' me to do, an' there was so many things they asked me to do. Uh—prison rights—that's why we went through with it. Or, they'd come in an' uh—hit you upside the head an' throw you out in like in a yard—throw you out in the yard an' there's people all over you—jest throw your stuff all out in the yard. It was a mess.

In these examples of Dwight's stability talk, he is a good man put upon by others.

Victimhood

Dwight was one of many narrators who emphasized a victim identity. Self-identification as a chronic victim served as a hedge against an alternative identification as a villain. History offers numerous examples of "victimhood" supplanting offender identities; narrators may be individuals, groups, and whole societies.

Usually the narrative simply emphasized one's protracted victimization: the connection to one's own offending was not drawn. Shawn discussed his experience of abuse throughout childhood. From age five through the age of fourteen, he was sexually molested by his father and uncle. Shawn's presentation of this story is introduced in talk about what he had done wrong in his life. I had prompted Shawn to evaluate his actions in regard to his most recent conviction for breaking into the home of a fellow drug dealer and attempting to rape a woman who was the man's girlfriend:

Lo: Um—do you think your mistake was like what happened—ya know—with the guy? With the woman? Or do you think you—do you wish you never [had] gotten involved in drugs in the first place? Like where do you think the—your mistake started?

Shawn: When I was young. Bein' abused as a child. Physically, emotionally, and sexually.

Shawn blurred the boundary between crimes he perpetrated and crimes done to him, thus dissolving his agency in the former. It is possible that he misunderstood the meaning of my question, or perhaps he acted as if he misunderstood. An alternative possibility is that victim and offender identities are difficult for him to distinguish, so conjoined are they in his lived experience. Clarence also answered a question about his offending with an answer about victimhood:

Lo: What uh—what kinds of drugs were you involved in?

Clarence: You basically name it, I tried it. An' uh—that was a totally shut-down for me because of—I didn't have no self-esteem. If I had some, it was very very low. I didn't like myself. And life didn't matter. I been shot, cut, stabbed. You know. Just on account of trying to sell drugs.

Unlike Shawn, Clarence is able to take advantage of the notion that there are no victims of drug trafficking per se. Thus does he emphasize the various harms done to him "just" because he engaged in that activity.

Other narrators claimed that victimization directly instigated a criminal action. Larry attributed drunken fights he had gotten into over the years to other people's harassment:

Larry: But if I'm *drinkin'*, I wouldn't advise you to—to mess with me.

Lo: Right.

Larry: But see tha— I think that's the key there: mess with me. Not because I'm drinkin.' Because I've had some *good* times when I was drinkin.'

Accounts of self-defense fall into this category, such as Tim's stories about finally matching his employer's physical blows with some of his own. Much prison violence and street violence was talked about as responses to actual or potential victimization.

In some remarkable cases, the protagonist was a victim while he was perpetrating crime. Hector depicted himself as a victim even in his account of child neglect and abuse. On one occasion, high on speed and marijuana, he was moments away from beating his seven-year-old daughter, who had been crying out for food. He stressed his own hurt during and after the incident: "And, I was about to tear her little butt up and took a second look at her. And I looked at her. The baby was small. She was small. Ya know. And I— add up the—I noticed that she was small. And it hurted me real bad. . . . And I fed her, but that incident—scarred me deeply." Tim likewise framed his abuse of other people as hurtful to him:

Tim: You know, I—you know—I've had a lotta—I've been involved in a lot of abusive relationships—with—not only other men but with *girls-*

Lo: Mm-hmm.

Tim:—you know—because of alcohol, gettin' drunk, stuff like that myself.

Lo: Your being abusive.

Tim: Yeah. I—I became the abuser.

Lo: Mm-hmm, mm-hmm.

Tim: An' uh, you know—it broke my heart.

Tim cast himself as a victim throughout his life. Even in the context of rape, he felt manipulated by his victim, who terminated consensual sexual relations before he had achieved orgasm: "I dunno, I just felt uh—I felt victimized, I guess. You know, uh. I dunno, it just wasn't fair. I didn't think it was fair." In narrating the story of rape, Tim alternates between acknowledging that he did rape the girl and that his action was "cold-hearted," and depicting it as a far lesser offense than other sexual violence because the girl appeared to be sexually responding to him, hence not altogether coerced: "That's why—that's what I was *sayin*.' Was that she was—it was a willing, consensual situation. An' then she said '*No*.' An' I was *wrong*—to intimidate the girl like that—you know, I was wrong. An' it'll never happen again. But I—I was wrong, I did it, an' it was wrong but—even then—even at that point—she was a willing partner. You know. I—because I never—I never laid a hand on her—to hurt 'er. I mean, I never punched her, I never slapped her, I didn't even grab her hard. I didn't do anything to her like that. I—I was jest on an intimidation game. Like I said, if she would have resisted, if she jest—if she woulda got up and got bold with me, I woulda ran out of that place, man. I never done anything like that in my life man. My—she would've scared me to death, if she woulda done that to me." Tim offers the counterfactual idea that the girl held unrealized power over him. She might have fought back, which he calls an action taken against him ("done that to me"). In that case he would have been "scared . . . to death." His point is that he was not altogether an offender and in fact was a would-be victim in the rape scene. His use of the hypothetical scenario, where the victim turns on him, is crucial to his making that point.

The hypothetical scenario is an important part of the story, as Labov (1982) explains: "The contrast between what did occur and what did not but might have occurred serves to evaluate the narrative. Negatives, futures, modals, and comparatives thus enter into narrative structure" (226; see also J. Bruner 1987, McKendy 2006). Accordingly, Ralph's deliberation on the kind of criminal (white-collar) he would be if he were a criminal, discussed earlier, helps him make the point that he is like a criminal in the best sense, but still *not* a criminal.

Wayne was another chronic victim. His deafness shaped his narrative; most of his oppressors were hearing people who failed to understand him, beginning with parents who refused to learn sign language. In Wayne's narrative, some attack—usually verbal but occasionally physical—prompted each of his many acts of violence. During one of many of his experiences in jail, he assaulted a police officer:

> So, they released me—and later, I had a problem again, and then I had *another* problem again. And the last time, I was drunk. The police arrested me. I went in the hall . . . and—when I had felt better, they're like Okay. The police came and the sheriff came. And they wrote something and gave it to me. And I told the police, "I don't want to write: I need an interpreter." And the police said, "You're an interpreter crybaby." And I told the police, "Please bring a TTY [communication device for the hearing impaired] so I can contact my lawyer." And the police said, "You're a deaf crybaby." There are two things that I needed to have provided: the interpreter and the TTY, and the police said I was a crybaby. So I got really mad and I hit the policeman. He fell down, and he got hurt.

In Wayne's description of events, he has had a series of "problems" that have led to his repeated arrests. His assault on a police officer was prompted by the man's disrespect, mediated by Wayne's anger.

Harry provided one of the most victim-oriented narratives I heard, in which the protagonist is a victim even as he offends against others. Within the first few exchanges of the interview, Harry revealed that his foster mother had sexually molested him when he was only four years old. Displaying no small amount of consciousness about his "life story" as heard by others, he said: "As a matter of fact, whenever I'm talking to someone about my life, I include that simply because [*clears throat*] most of the people who give me interviews and stuff like that, they need that in their—uh—their little journals or whatever. They have to have—well, they don't have to have that, but it's a bigger part of what has happened to me." Contrary to that broad statement of the significance of early sexual victimization, Harry did not subsequently draw any particular connections between the effects of having been abused sexually and his various crimes.

Harry was a righteous victim in a relationship where *he* was the abuser. He prefaced talk about his second marriage with: "And um I have to be honest [*clears throat*]: because I was on the drugs, I was a very abusive and abrasive individual." Thus the account begins with an allusion to his frankness. He interrupted the account at various points to tell short stories oriented around his goodness. These included (1) caring for his ailing father while he was hospitalized for terminal cancer; and (2) spending an inheritance to furnish the apartment he shared with his wife, buying "everything she wanted, and everything I could provide, that's how our relationship went." Before actually getting to the account of battering then, Harry managed to frame himself as well as his battered wife as particular characters—selfless and selfish, respectively.

The emplotment of Harry's life as a tale of his own victimization continued over the course of two long interviews. His account of attempting to kill his wife by pushing her out of a speeding car, is as much about her shooting him in self-defense as it is about his original deed:

Harry: Uh [*laugh*], somebody had told me—called me from work—and told me that they had seen my wife transporting people around in my car. And uh I just kind of went ballistic. And when she showed up, I went down this long, dead-end, hollow type of place, and at the time I was going, I was going about seventy-five or eighty miles an hour? I reached over and opened the door and tried to push her out the car. That's how fuckin' mad I was [*chuckle*]. But, y— you know, sh— in the end, when she held on, when the car stopped, that's when she shot me.

Lo: She had a gun?

Harry: Yeah. She had my gun.

Lo: And did you go to the hospital?

Harry: Yeah. Yeah I did.

Lo: In that situation, so you were trying to push her out the car door . . .

Harry: Mm-hmm, I was really pissed about what had . . .

Lo: —trying to kill her or trying to . . . ?

Harry: Trying to kill her would probably be a more accurate statement.

Lo: And then, she's trying to kill you back?

Harry: Ooh. She—she knew where she shot. She wasn't trying to kill me. She was just—just trying to get me to leave her alone. That's probably the best way I could tell you.

Lo: Do you see her action as self-defense—then?

Harry: [*sigh*] Yeah, according to the situation. Yeah. It had to be construed as—as—as—uh—

Lo: Is that how you saw it?

Larry: Yeah, that's—that's how I saw it. That's how I forgave her. You know? Um, cause the night she shot me, she came to the hospital to see me. Cause I—I—I didn't press charges. And when she—

Lo: And did she—did she press—charges?

Harry: No, she couldn't press charges cause she—she was the one who shot—shot me.

Lo: Right. But she didn't say, you know I—

Harry: [*smiling*] —because I had been kicking her out the car or something? No, she didn't say anything about that. She didn't say anything
about that.

Lo: Uh-huh. Uh-huh.

Harry: So, um, and—and we tried to make it work from there but it
just—you know—sometimes you just—the magic's gone.

Harry's evaluative remarks about the incident, culminating in his assessment that the "magic" of the marriage was "gone" after the incident, serve
Harry in his self-portrayal as a morally decent person. His concerns are conventional and humane—not those of someone who has perpetrated extreme
violence.

Foolishness

Like victimhood, foolishness is a characteristic that seems to be antithetical
to intentional misconduct.[4] The men's stereotype of the fool as essentially
noncriminal is borne out in Hector's discussion of his earliest delinquency.
He told me: "Some little guys that—knew pretty much about stealin' and
knew Main Street downtown like they knew the palm of their hands, I started
hangin' out with them. Not really bein'— a good s— yeah, not really bein' a
good thief or anything."

The good, victim, and foolish personas, in fact, often coincided in the same
account. Hector explained that it was his naïve trust of a devious friend that
led to his adult conviction for auto theft. He joined his friend for a ride in
what he later learned was a stolen car: "I didn't st— I couldn't drive. Ya know.
I didn't really steal a car. It was a friend of mine. [He] promised to teach me
how to drive. But he came around one day showin' off a car. . . . So he said
'Well, slide over here in the seat.' And see I was too stupid to just simply get
out of the car, go around the other side, and get in the driver's seat." A police
officer pulled the car over. Because Hector was behind the wheel, he was arrested for auto theft, while his friend was not. Hector the narrator accessed
the officer's own recognition of the ruse to verify his victimization: "He [the
police officer] said 'Let me tell you somethin.' Somebody in this car is not
your friend.' He said um 'Whoever—was drivin' the first time is a professional driver.' You know. He said 'I noticed the change in drivin.' Ya know.
You weren't driving. You didn't—you didn't drive it here.' He say 'But I have
to arrest you because—you were caught behind the wheel.' Ya know? He said
'But I'm gonna— I'm gonna tell you again. Somebody in this car is not your
friend.' And he looked at Nat." Again, Hector's lack of sophistication about
deviant matters is contrasted with the scheming of his peers.

Joe-Ray highlighted his ineptness in perpetrating his recent casino thefts:

> *Joe-Ray:* So I'm tryin' to make it out of the casino, he chases me, and the chips falling all over the place; I guess he got his chips back. And on my way out the door, I bumped—[*sigh*]—on my way out the door, it was um—there was this lady—walkin' down the street. An' um, I think her name was Linda. An' um, I snatched her pocketbook. An' um—
>
> *Lo:* The chips—you already—didn't have the chips or anything?
>
> *Joe-Ray:* Yeah, they was fallin' an' everything. Uh, I had—the amazing thing is I'm still bein' chased! Heh! Yeah, still being chased.
>
> *Lo:* What were you thinking when you grabbed her pocketbook?
>
> *Joe-Ray:* "What the hell am I doin'?"
>
> *Lo:* You just needed—you knew her—was she a friend of yours?
>
> *Joe-Ray:* No, I didn't know her. And, when I did that, I guess—from the van and everything, she fell. And um, I don' know, I ran back into the casino. I don't know what I was thinkin' about. And then I ran back out of the casino, and I just threw that down.
>
> *Lo:* Threw what down?
>
> *Joe-Ray:* The pocketbook. I threw that down.

In a different story, in which the police conducted a drug raid at his apartment, Joe-Ray is also the foolish offender. He had been partying with his friends in the apartment, but just prior to the arrival of the police he happened to leave to make a brief phone call at a booth on the street. His foolishness in not trying to evade capture is plainly stated: "They had all my friends up against the wall with their hands behind they back. And it was my room, so like a idiot—well, not like a idiot—I consider that this is a good—yeah, like a idiot. I went back into the room. And I said 'Look, this is my room.'"

The protagonist of the story is not so much bad as he is dumb. Joe-Ray moralizes about this dumb protagonist by reflecting aloud that being the kind of idiot he was (an inept criminal) was actually a good thing.

Ralph elaborated on his foolishness in accumulating so many driving violations that he was eventually jailed for them. In fact, this foolishness served some moral good. It was a source of entertainment for his aging father:

> *Lo:* Why wouldn't you have a license?
>
> *Ralph:* I don't know. I guess it was like I didn't want to pay the money. 'Cause I owed like two thousand dollars in fines.

Lo: Oh.

Ralph: You know. And, um the tickets. And I was like "Shit. Now I could do somethin' else with this money!" You know how you just get selfish sometimes [*laughing tone*]?

Lo: Ohh! I see.

Ralph: And be like "I'll pay 'em this year." You know, "I'll— I'll pay 'em—income tax time." Uh and never wind up doin' it. Ya know, and. Or, my car would get taken. I'd be like "Shit! I'm gonna get me another one!" [*laughing*] As soon as they take my car! I'd be like "Well I got to go get insurance, I got to go do this, I got to do that" and I'd go buy me another car. I'd go out and spend like a thousand dollars and get another car. Come back. My father—I used to come over my father house and he'd just be like. You know, my father— some of the things I do, I think I cracked my father up. You know? 'Cause it's like I've always been the mischievous one. You know. So. I don't really get into trouble but I get into trouble.

Lo: Right.

Ralph: You know. So, to him it breaks the monotony and the boredom between the rest of the kids. You know, so. That's [*chuckle*]—that's pretty much—I'm like his livelihood. You know? I'm the excitement.

The self-declaration of being foolish may trivialize or normalize the illegal action, as it does in Ralph's case, but it also conveys acceptance of responsibility for that action now. Neither the protagonist nor the narrator, then, is an essentially criminal type.

Sanctions

It was common in stability talk to focus on what one had been *sanctioned for* rather than what one had *done*. For example, Ralph made the following claim to being like "normal" people based on what he had been incarcerated for in his lifetime: "I did—I think I got in about just as much trouble I think as any normal, normal person. Ya know? Maybe—you could say—I ain't gonna say this really to the extreme—'cause most of the time I got locked up, was just getting locked up for driving without a license. Driving with no insurance. Those were the most times I got locked up."

James recalled having been pulled over by a police officer, at which time he learned that he had a number of outstanding warrants. In narrating this discovery, he left his actual innocence questionable, referring to those charges as "things like I had never been caught" and saying "I never—let's say I never been to prison that many times." Prison time also served as a reference point for Lyle.

> *Lo:* Um, did you have a lot of juvenile arrests?
> *Lyle:* Only like five. But I ain't never did no time or nothin.'

At the start of my interview with Steve (age forty-five at the time of our interview), he presented himself as a newcomer to crime, stating: "Never got in no trouble as a juvenile. Never got in trouble 'til I was *thirty-six*." Later in the interview he framed his rap sheet (criminal history) as minimal based on a more complex appraisal:

> *Lo:* So that's the only thing—like you said, that's the only thing on your rap sheet?
> *Steve:* That's the only felony I got.
> *Lo:* Oh. And—are there [unclear] misdemeanors?
> *Steve:* Yes, misdemeanors, uh DWIs, things like that—but they been so long that they're not even on your record now.

Steve's report that he had a number of very old misdemeanors on his record contradicts his earlier remark that he got "in trouble" for the first time at age thirty-six. If we judge Steve to have meant "prison time" when he said "trouble," like many of his fellow narrators, then his narrative gains coherence.

Looking at the narratives generally, I clearly played a role in orienting the interviews toward sanctions. I asked the men about arrests and rap sheets, felonies and misdemeanors. Frequently, I relied on such questions to stimulate discussion. I spoke in justice system terms and used the system's own classification of crime seriousness. It might be said—though it would be difficult to establish precisely—that I *cued* the men to consider their offending experiences in *terms* of the justice system. I would like to make a related but more cautious claim: the discourse of the justice system and its cultural products pertaining to who offenders are (e.g., heroes or rogues), and the narratives of individual offenders are mutually constitutive. The co-constitution of such discourses about crime and criminals occurs at least in part through person-to-person interaction. A focus on sanctions, and various other ways of talking about crime, is reproduced in this way.

To return to the narrower point of this section, the focus on sanctions is a device that makes the narrator's history seem less deviant than it would seem based on "actual" crimes. This device is not necessarily used consciously. It appears that persons long involved with the criminal justice system come to think and speak of their offenses in terms of system responses. According to O'Connor (2000), the focus on charges and sentences in the speech of many offenders indicates a deflecting of personal agency (53–58). I maintain that such speech also serves their self-presentations as morally consistent.

Negative Referents

A shift in narrative focus to someone worse than us can make us out to be relatively good. James had such a negative referent in his brother, who had killed a girlfriend. He said: "I'm a shoplifter. And my family comes down harder on me than him. I say 'Isaac's a killer!'" James's brother Isaac provides a point of contrast against which James's deviance appears not so bad. Negative referents can be drawn from one's direct interactions as well as from popular lore and history, as was evident in my interviews. Arnell protested his failure to be granted parole by claiming: "I'm not Charles Manson or nothin.'" Tim expressed concern that people would mistake him for a "truly" violent rapist:

> *Lo:* What are you afraid that they're gonna think?
> *Tim:* I dunno. There's jest—there's just so many sex crimes anymore. Uh, and rape. Rape just creates so many images in people's minds. I mean some people—say rape—one person might relate—they start seein' somebody with a hatchet or somebody with a gun, somebody with a knife or a rope or—I mean different images! An' uh—I jest—I'm afrai— I jest don't want to get—have people thinkin' that I'm one— a person like that. You know, I don' know, there were jest different circumstances in my situation. I got the charge, but the circumstances were totally different. It wasn't *like* that.

We frame ourselves in terms of other people (Jenkins 2004; J. Turner 1999). Stability talkers in particular benefited from distinguishing themselves from more serious offenders. Situationally, I encouraged this means of forging identity. A question I asked many of the research participants was "Have you ever met anyone you would call evil?" With that question, I effectively implied that the narrator is not himself "evil" but may have encountered evil *others*. Besides what I had to say, the discipline of criminology and the criminal justice system contribute the idea that criminals may—indeed *must*—be contrasted and classified (Henry and Milovanovic 1996). To compare oneself with a negative referent makes perfect sense in the context of the interview and the macro context in which "violent criminals" are made (Fox 1999; Jenkins 2004, 161).

Bad Seed Critiques

Three erstwhile stability talkers launched blanket critiques of themselves, to the effect that they are essentially "bad seeds." Tim said that he grew up thinking of himself as the "black sheep of the family." James reported: "I'm just the bad one out of the bunch" among his siblings. Steve said: "My dad never had a ticket in his life. I don' know *what* happened to me." Because these narrators otherwise stressed their moral decency, I was initially at a loss as to how to interpret these "bad seed critiques."

Then I noticed that these critiques were refuted just as soon as they were articulated. An analysis of talk in the proximity of the critiques, and their narrative contexts generally, suggests that bad seed critiques accomplish two things. First, a pronouncement indicating "I may be bad" offers a new platform for pronouncing, "Actually, I *am* good." Second, it allows the narrator to take up the righteous position of self-critic.

James condemned a contemporary protagonist by detailing his moral shortcomings: "And it—ya know—to this day, my mother still an' my father still is like 'I don't know what's wrong with you.' I said 'Well maybe I'm just a bad seed.' Ya know. Every time I start somethin', I don't complete it. But if I can start some trouble, I can start that and finish that. But what comes with it is always jail time. Ya know. So now I'm in transitional living and, I did upon— I did it to my*self*. I wasn't sent there by no parole officer. By nobody—I been—you know, I called and signed up myself. And I've been there a couple of weeks and I feel it's gonna work for me. Because I'm—you know—you live up to people's expectations, and it's not like bein' in jail. I'm gay, right? And, it was rough for me in there. But I stood up my own ground." James's bad seed critique, prompted by his parents' indictment, is certainly comprehensive. Yet it is just the beginning of a longer and more favorable claim about the self. Following the critique, he moves to a statement of his apparent reform. Reluctant to spend any more time behind bars, he reports that he volunteered for a treatment-oriented residence that, he believes, is "gonna work" for him. Lastly, he alludes to homophobic victimization in prison and his triumph over it. He thus refutes the notion that he might be bad beyond repair and he refocuses the discussion on his victimhood.

I classified Tim and James as elastic narrators because of their sporadic reform talk. By contrast, Steve was a stability narrator in my analysis. His bad seed critique preceded an appeal to his good qualities. It also enabled him, like James, to inhabit the role of self-critic. Steve uses narrative distance—the narrator's moral superiority—without claiming reform.

Lo: Right. But so you've never assaulted your wife or you—?

Steve: No, I'm not going to beat no woman, you know?

Lo: That's not you.

Steve: No. I wasn't raised that way. See, I don't have—my mom and dad—I never seen my mom and dad fight *or* argue. I never seen my mom drink in her life. I seen my dad drink two beers in his whole life. My dad never had a ticket in his life. I don' know *what* happened to me.

Lo: What do *you* think?

Steve: I don't know! [*laughing*] I guess I'm different. I [unclear] know I'm a good person. I—you know—I'd do anything for anybody I can. I'd give you my last dollar or whatever. I don't know. I have uncles that's alcoholics, and—aunts that's alcoholics, I don't know: I must have picked it up from one of them guys—I don't know.

Lo: I see. And your burglary and stuff like that—property crimes— uh—is it about money, or what—wha—how do you—?

Steve: No. It was nonsense! It was stupid: I was working, making good money.

Just as quickly as Steve distinguished himself as different from his extremely decent parents, he maintained his self-evaluation as "a good person." Steve called attention to his generosity, then offered some tentative explanations for his deviance, which he had earlier established as trivial. Failing to explain his property offending, he critiqued the protagonist for engaging in it simply because he did not need the money. Steve thus managed to critique his protagonist without damning him. The "bad seed critic" plays with the idea of a basically deviant self, only to finally dismiss this idea from the narrative.

Summary

Stability narratives featured consistent decency over the life span. Several tactics were used to claim consistent moral decency despite having committed violent crime. These tactics amounted to claims about the self—for example, that one was taken out of character in the crime scene—and ways of refocusing the narrative, such as by presenting oneself as a perpetual victim, sometimes even in the act of offending. Any one narrator tended to use multiple tactics.

Similar tactics are discussed in other studies of offenders' accounts, where one can find both sympathetic and unsympathetic readings. An example of a sympathetic reading comes from Halsey (2006), who shares young men's reports of why they violated probation conditions. Some actually violated in order to maintain desistance from crime. Halsey concludes that some violations "had more to do with systemic factors than, it would seem, any foul play or wanton intention to buck the system or 'stick it' to authority figures" (Halsey 2006, 160). An example of an unsympathetic reading is from Gilgun and McLeod (1999), who report on intensive interviews with adult male perpetrators of sexual violence. They describe Tim, who said that he "trained" victims of pedophilia but also convinced himself that the relations were "mutual"—that the boys "wanted to be doing it" (180). Gilgun and McLeod are "horrified" (185) by Tim's claim of having believed he was engaging in morally acceptable sex. In these studies, accounts reveal circumstances or pathologies of offenders. For my research purposes, these aspects and hence the truthfulness of the men's reports (including reports on the way they saw or see things) are only relevant as anchors for self-identification.

ELASTIC NARRATIVES: CREATIVE INTEGRATION

Every time I start somethin', I don't complete it. But if I can start
some trouble, I can start that and finish that. But what comes with it
is always jail time.

—James

Elastic narratives emphasized moral stability but *also* included reform talk. The reform talk in elastic narratives was sparse or else shallow, so that the narrative was evidently not "about" reform.

In characterizing the reform talk in elastic narratives as shallow, I mean two particular things. First, accounts of one's crimes were contradictory, vague, or both. Quite often, one's life, including but not limited to one's reform, was broadly described (for example, one previously enjoyed a "fast" lifestyle that was condemned) but specific crimes were neutralized. Second, desistance, like offending, was attributed to vaguely stated factors. In addition, desistance was conceptualized as an already completed process, so that strategies for desistance in the future were insubstantial.

Based on those criteria, fifteen of the twenty-seven men I interviewed told elastic narratives. Their life stories were marked by a poorly integrated plot and "weak evaluation" (Taylor 1985) of their past harmful actions, with little commitment to desistance as a consequence. The fact that a majority of the research participants told elastic narratives is considered at the end of this chapter, after the narratives themselves are deconstructed.

Poorly Integrated Plot

In many elastic narratives, accounts of one's crimes tended to be vague or inconsistent. As a result, the plot of reform was not well integrated throughout the narrative—across specific event stories—as it was in reform narratives.

Reform in the Abstract

Some narrators tended to state that they had changed overall, but then neutralized specific crimes. John's critique of his deviance, including an attempted escape from jail culminating in an assault on a deputy sheriff, was stated abstractly. He said: "John before was extremely selfish, self-righteous, well to a degree he's self-righteous somewhat now, but not like he used to be. Um, John before would just as soon whoop your ass as look at ya." Given the question that prompted this response, "How would you describe yourself?" it is not particularly surprising that the statement is abstract. Perhaps it is in the nature of "description" to summarize: a more concrete question probably would have generated a more concrete response.

What *is* noteworthy is that John's criticism of his earlier self was restricted to this abstract summation. When it came to stories about specific episodes in his life, John was far less disapproving. In fact, he seemed delighted by his victories in a variety of conflicts with other people. In his critique, John condemned his tendency to "act or react" without thinking. He nonetheless enjoyed sharing the story of the assault he might have perpetrated against a reckless school bus driver:

> *John:* A friend of mine was having problems with her grandson's bus
> driver. And the woman—with kids on the bus tried to run her off the
> road.
> *Lo:* It was a woman with kids on—who?
> *John:* The woman—the driver—
> *Lo:* Oh the driver.
> *John:* —of the bus, tried to run—
> *Lo:* Oh with kids on the—
> *John:* —my friend off the road.
> *Lo:* Oh.
> *John:* And there were kids on the bus.
> *Lo:* Hmm.
> *John:* And she got all pissed off about it.
> *Lo:* Hmm.

John: Zipped around the corner an'—parked her car on the middle of the street an' the bus came around the corner, stopped, and she went up to the bus and basically told the driver that—she needed to step out of the bus so she could get her ass whooped for endangering the lives of the children like that, and for endangering her life. . . .

Lo: Was your friend arrested?

John: Uh, she was—she was formally charged—and—

Lo: With what?

John: —uh, it's still in the court. Aggravated nothin'.

Lo: Mm-hmm.

John: But, um, I'm gonna have to—be going to court with her sometime because—I was with her when it happened. So. I mean [*laughing*], if it wasn't her it was gonna be me [*laughing*]!

Lo: What do you mean?

John: I dunno. If she hadn't pulled over and—

Lo: But what—?

John: —gotten out and told the bus driver to get out of the bus to get her ass whooped, I was going to.

Lo: Uh-huh. You think—

John: You ju— you don't do that with school kids on a bus!

John seemed to enjoy recalling this conflict. He volunteered that he would have used violence just as his friend threatened to do. Reform would appear to be inconsistent with this story. And John's remark that "John before would just as soon whoop your ass as look at ya" seemed not really to be relegated to the past.

John also excused his shooting at a sheriff—the charge for which he was recently incarcerated—as a necessary defense of his family, who might have been killed if John had not assisted a former cellmate in an escape. He added that he ultimately did no harm to the sheriff, shooting at his car rather than at his head. While criticizing an abstract protagonist in his narrative, John distanced himself little from the protagonists depicted in actual episodes of his life.

Tim, like John, condemned very broadly the fast lifestyle and thinking habits of his past self, which prompted his wrongdoing. That was a diatribe spoken very generally. When Tim accounted for particular crimes, lifestyle and thinking habits were not cited as reasons for his actions. He had more self-exonerating explanations in these accounts. For example, Tim criticized his youthful self as violence prone: "I mean I used to—I would fight at the drop of a hat. When I was younger." He immediately qualified that he is still apt to fight if justified: "I mean, I—even today, if somebody tries to hurt me, I'm fightin' back. I would defend myself. But I won't go pick on somebody." In fact, Tim characterized himself as provoked by his victims in his most serious crimes, including a rape and an attempted murder.

Unspecified Causal Mechanisms

At points, Tim attributed past offending to alcohol abuse: "There—there is a *pattern*. You know, I just recognized the pattern. Uh, it's either—there's either—when I'm drinkin', it's either a broken relationship or it's a crime." In a subsequent interview, Tim proposed that his abusive behavior was the result of his drinking: "I got caught up with some people I cared about an' became kind of abusive myself. You know? When—you know—if that hadn't been the alcohol, it never would've happened." Tim's statements of alcohol causing his crimes are, linguistically, passive constructions: when he drinks, "it's a crime" and abusive behavior "happened" (see O'Connor 2000). Later in the very same interview, Tim denied that alcohol itself is ever an impetus to wrongdoing: "An' I certainly know—I know that alcohol itself ain't bad—I think it's jest the drinker, how the drinker approaches it." Previously, Tim failed to specify *how* alcohol caused offending in *specific instances*. He relied instead on the observation that alcohol was simply *present* at the scene of most of his offenses. In doing so, Tim can waver, across the interview, between blaming the protagonist (which he does in pointing to "how the drinker approaches it") and citing external causes, as suits a desired self-presentation. This was a general pattern in elastic narratives. Criminogenic agents were identified, but the mechanisms by which these led to crime were not made clear. It was especially common for narrators to point to substance abuse as the ultimate cause of their violent crimes, but to avoid specifying the causal link between substance abuse and crime.

Exceptional is Cyrus, who suggested that drugs caused crimes because he needed money to buy drugs. He insisted: "If it wasn't for the drugs—ya know—it wouldn't a—none of this never woulda—*none* of this never woulda unraveled. None of it." Yet a robbery that resulted in murder is not explained by economic need, since he had money at the time. Cyrus's theory of drug-induced crime was inadequate to the task of explaining all of his offending.

Cyrus spoke of cognitive causal factors—his past thinking being "selfish" and "messed-up" in the context of an early juvenile offense in which he robbed a woman of her pocketbook. He did not theorize in this way in accounting for his three murders. His passive and awkward construction of one murder is illustrative: "The one in '70, that was just a straight-up robbery, and the guy pulled a gun and we got him to shoot me and—ya know—he got shot." Cyrus here offers no explanation at all for his crime. Indeed, linguistically, he hardly establishes himself as the agent in the shooting.

Weak Evaluation/Commitment to Desistance

Elastic narrators typically spoke of reform based on weak evaluation. Philosopher Charles Taylor (1985) makes a useful distinction between weak and strong evaluation in order to conceptualize human choice and action. The weak evaluator is a "simple weigher" of alternatives who determines whether he or she desires one alternative more than the other (ibid., 23). The weak evaluator judges only the "inarticulate 'feel' of the alternatives" he or she is faced with (24).

In contrast, the strong evaluator judges *desires themselves* as more or less desirable. For example, a desire to do good deeds may be judged as honorable: the desire itself is favored. The strong evaluator takes into account what kind of person he or she wants to be. "Motivations or desires do not only count in virtue of the attraction of the consummations but also in virtue of the kind of life and kind of subject that these desires properly belong to" (Taylor 1985, 25). Taylor argues that strong evaluation is necessary for true agency.

Generally speaking, I found strong evaluation concerning one's desistance in reform narratives. I found far weaker evaluation concerning one's desistance in elastic narratives. In a reform narrative, the narrator does not want to engage in criminal actions because he is disinclined to be a person who does so. In contrast, the reform described in elastic narratives was very often a rejection, not of doing crime, but of the criminal experience, including the taste of alcohol (Tim), the exertion of the criminal lifestyle (Max), and the strains of incarceration (Cyrus, Tim).

Whereas Cyrus offered his "messed-up thinking" as well as drug use as causal factors in his long offending career, he framed projected desistance in terms of *neither* factor. Rather, he had simply grown weary of life in prison, having spent nearly half of his life behind bars:

> *Lo:* So you'll definitely try to abide by all the stuff [parole conditions]?
> *Cyrus:* Yeah, pretty much. I don't see—ya know—this here anymore, ya know. And even though this here—I mean—you got to hold yourself accountable for this here: for being in this position. . . . And um— not that it would be ea— it—not that it would be easy to come back if the sit— circumstances was different. You just get tired of this, ya know. Get tired of this.

Cyrus was tentative about whether he would desist for certain ("pretty much"). In the narratives, weak evaluation and tentativeness about desistance went hand in hand.

Tim, like Cyrus, had spent many of his years incarcerated, and similarly spoke of the toll it had taken on him. Despite that toll, both men lacked confidence about avoiding prison in the future. Tim reveals a fatalistic attitude about the prospect.

> I just don't want—I don't plan to go back to prison, but anything could happen—you know? Emergency could come up. So I just don't know—I don't know—I just kind [of] play it by ear right now. I been to prison four times. I can't remember all my juvenile stuff. I been to Juvenile Diagnostic Center in [city]: I been up there twice. I been to Red River School for Boys [unclear]. I been to the Jarvin House twice. I don't remember how many times I was in juvenile detention. But I'm just sick of it. I'm sick of it, man. I'm jes' burnt out on the whole thing. I just—forty-eight years old or I'll be forty-eight in September an' I just—man, I just don't want to be in prison. When I'm—when I'm [chuckle] fifty-five or sixty: that's just not where I want to be. You know, I'd like to find me a little girl I'm compatible with or somethin', you know, to share things with and stuff like that. Jes' mellow out, you know?

During one interview Tim pronounced that his values have completely changed since his younger years: "I've had time to think about things, analyze things an' uh, just sorta reevaluate my priorities. You know, a lot of things. An' my value system's totally different than it had been." However, Tim did not associate that change with a vision of a crime-free future, nor did he speak specifically of what had changed. The following statement from Shawn sounds remarkably similar to Tim's. It further illustrates the correlation between weak evaluation and uncertainty about the future:

> *Shawn:* I can't say I'll never commit another crime. God forbid. But— if—anything could happen. 'Cause—I think if you push a guy farther enough, he's gonna do whatever— what they have to, ya know: he's gonna do whatever he has to, to survive. Just like a female. She's gonna do whatever *she* has to, to survive. So. Like uh— ya know. But uh, God forbid, I hope I never have to turn back to what I did—was. Ya know.
> *Lo:* Yeah.
> *Shawn:* I didn't like that life.

Shawn, who most recently had been convicted of rape, was fatalistic[1] about the possibility of committing future violence. He only expressed a desire to desist from crime, because he disliked the criminal life.

Lyle, my youngest research participant, was neither fatalistic nor pessimistic about the future. However, he shared with other elastic narrators a fuzzy plan for desistance. Lyle wished to write a book in order to tell his life story.

> *Lo:* What's the book gonna be about?
> *Lyle:* About my *life!* Autobiography. Ya know, I mean I'm gonna put in details. How I came out the hood. Ya know. And just *made* it.
> *Lo:* Mmm.
> *Lyle:* Got locked up. Still having the chance. And just *made* it.

Lyle also hoped to become a major basketball player. He had not yet "made it" nor was he assured of "still having the chance." But his book/plan for desistance assumed that he had: "'Cause I know—a person who'd want to *read* that. Ya know wha' I mean: keepin' it real. Especially if I make it to the NBA. So they can look at me as like—ya know wha' I mean—he just ain't no guy that just had all this money, and just went and played basketball. Ya know, I came from—the 'hood. Ya know wha' I mean?" The book—a rags-to-riches story of a boy from "the 'hood" who becomes a celebrated athlete—would obviously be based on Lyle's desired vision of the future. The narrow chance of Lyle's achieving his vision is less noteworthy, for present purposes, than the fact that Lyle had little to say about *how* he would avoid offending in future. He called his instant (current) robbery offense "a mistake"—a response to boredom. Yet he disclosed several other robberies for which he had not been caught. He spoke precious little of those crimes and of what caused them.

Lyle offered some general ideas about why people commit crimes, such as their not knowing any better or choosing to offend—interestingly, two explanations that criminologists position as contradictory.

> *Lyle:* A lot of people sometimes do it on *purpose*. But, they don't know no better.
> *Lo:* Is that w—would you describe yourself—that you didn't know any better?
> *Lyle:* No, I knew better! I'm sayin', I—
> *Lo:* But you still did it on purpose.
> *Lyle:* I still— what I did, ya kn' wha' mean, I *did*. I mean, they can't say—oh uh, I was sick or I didn't know or I can't regret that—it was just—you know. I just *did* it. I mean it happened almost three years ago. I *been* moved on.

Lyle resisted my challenge, claiming in essence that his reform is complete. No further efforts to maintain his right ways are needed ("I *been* moved on").

He rejects exculpatory explanations ("they can't say . . . I was sick") but offers no alternatives. Evidently, Lyle's book/story will feature the fall that came with being incarcerated ("Got locked up") but not any moral fall.

Contextualizing Weak Evaluation

The predominance of elastic narratives in my sample (fifteen of twenty-seven) warrants close consideration. There are two social contexts I take into view to understand elastic narratives. One is the culture of free-market individualism. The other is contemporary governance through self-responsibilization.

The contemporary culture of free-market individualism, which characterizes advanced capitalism, underwrites the method of policy-making known as cost-benefit analysis—a method with which agents select that social action which grants the greatest benefit, quantitatively calculated. Cost-benefit analysis precludes consideration of the values of agents, which of course encompasses who the agent (e.g., nation, individual) wishes to be. At least nominally, then, it stands at odds with moral evaluation of action, including evaluation of the moral self.

Cost-benefit analysis is an exemplar of Western rationality and Western ends-orientation (Kay 2005). It is Taylor's (1985) weak evaluation writ large. Garland (2001) considers the ascendancy, since the 1970s, of such economic reasoning to decide policy as a historical phenomenon that is running parallel, in the United States as well as England, with that of a general concern to control dangerous others. The state is newly oriented toward both efficiency and governance. In the correctional arena, governance occurs, as Foucault (1980) observed, by managing offenders' subjectivities.

One dominant contemporary discourse concerning offenders has it that their "criminal minds" are the cause of their offending. Crime begins and therefore ends with the individual. To the extent that efforts to *reform* offenders are made (as opposed to merely incapacitating or managing them), a popular policy and program target is the way offenders think. Since cognitions can only be accessed through speech, treatment programs (Fox 1999) and criminal justice decision makers alike look to speech for evidence of change or, conversely, intransigence. Offenders' talk is regulated. Consequently, McKendy (2006) observes that the offender is in an "impossible situation." He or she is "required to speak as a self-possessed responsible agent—as a victimizer—even as his subjective experience is that of a relatively powerless victim" (479). One strategy for dealing with this situation, McKendy observes, is to "pay lip service" to the responsible self by "pasting in" talk of an agentive self in an account of powerlessness. I consider the elastic narrative as a result *and* an indicator of broader cultural tendencies. These pay lip service to the public good through careful weighing of what yields the greatest net benefit, but actually proceed as if sovereignty will be overcome at any cost.

Summary

Elastic narratives included both reform and stability talk but emphasized the latter. These narratives consisted of relatively shallow reform arguments and tentative and insubstantial plans for desistance from crime. The plot of reform was inconsistent across event stories. When speaking of future desistance, elastic narrators rejected the criminal experience rather than criminal identity. I considered these contradictory discursive positions as exemplary of the orientation of contemporary decision makers to net gain. Cost-benefit analysis is a paramount method of policy making today, but the policy options are now constricted, geared toward control. The offender-narrator's privileging of future choices that will feel better than crime and punishment reflects that method, while it also accommodates to the new discursive strategies of control. Elastic narratives allow the narrator to hedge his bets on what the audience truly wants to hear.

Polletta and Lee (2006) remind us that stories whose "normative conclusions are ambiguous" (718) may be most effective for stimulating acceptance of one's claims, since what these stories are saying is open to interpretation. The indeterminacy of the elastic narrative invites listeners to relate to something in it and thus to agree, whatever listeners' prior viewpoints. But note that the discursive contexts I presented as contributing to the elastic narrative may also be seen as shaping the other two narrative forms—reform and stability narratives—which were inherently less ambiguous. Such effects are simply subtler and thus less amenable to observation. All persons characterized as "violent offenders" in our culture are vilified for lacking empathy and for devaluing human life, as we project our own tendencies onto the few. The workings of the metanarrative are mostly obscured from view, and so "violent offenders" resist by contesting either the characterization or the ascribed deficits, as pertaining now or ever. Elastic narrators use multiple strategies of resistance.

8

TALES OF HEROIC STRUGGLE

And so it happens that if anyone—in whatever society—undertakes
for himself the perilous journey into the darkness by descending,
either intentionally or unintentionally, into the crooked lanes of his
own spiritual labyrinth, he soon finds himself in a landscape of
symbolical figures (any one of which may swallow him) which is no
less marvelous than the wild Siberian world of the *pudak* and sacred
mountains. . . . In our dreams the ageless perils, gargoyles, trials,
secret helpers, and instructive figures are nightly still encountered;
and in their forms we may see reflected not only the whole picture of
our present case, but also the clue to what we must do to be saved.

—Joseph Campbell, *The Hero with a Thousand Faces,* 1949

But when I was incarcerated I read the Koran, which said everyone
goes through some ordeal, everyone's persecuted and overcomes it.

—O. J. Simpson in Jordan, "The Outcast," 2001

Besides moral decency, a second major theme in the narratives was
heroic struggle. Whether a stability, reform, or elastic narrative was told,
some struggle or struggles figured into it. Struggle was part of the men's
storied identities.

Framing one's life in terms of struggle gives it meaning—indeed, a highly
celebrated sort of meaning. Gergen and Gergen (1988) observe that struggle
is a universal theme of life stories. I heard of protagonists nobly struggling,
alone, against particular, and particularly formidable forces, to achieve their
goals.

Popular culture routinely depicts the good, usually male protagonist bat-
tling hostile forces, which all but overpower him until a momentous gesture
of agency by the protagonist prevents such a fate. Accessing that cultural
model is therefore another way of identifying oneself as a moral agent. The

narrator as hero redeems his past to himself and to others. In this light, a tale of heroic struggle is a way of co-opting the label of outsider and subsequently reintegrating oneself into the societal mainstream (Braithwaite 1989).

In this chapter I focus on the men's storied struggles. I describe what they were seemingly struggling to achieve and what or whom they were struggling against—that is, their foe or foes. Toward the end of the chapter I consider the link between the two themes identified in the stories—moral decency and heroic struggle. The heroic struggle was at least partly framed as a defense of one's moral rectitude: that is, to either maintain the constant moral self or to safeguard the moral reform one has worked hard to achieve. The struggle against some external foe also translated into the ability to separate self from that foe (a reform claim) or it deflected attention from one's responsibility at the crime scene (a stability claim). Finally, the struggle against the justice system was in many ways a struggle to let one's own story of moral decency be heard.

Nature of the Heroic Struggle

The men's struggles reflected, at bottom, a tension between the self and society. The men were lay sociologists of a sort: they thematized influences from other people on both identities and behavior. Their observations were combative, not neutral. There was a general wish to liberate oneself from the strictures of other people. *Society* was in some cases internalized: for example, as pro-criminal attitudes learned from peers. In other cases, society was a completely external entity, such as an agent of authority. I refer to these internal or external social forces as *foes,* because all of the narrators approached the tension between self and society in adversarial fashion. The narratives were told in the idiom of combat, with its protagonist usually a lone hero.

Joseph Campbell (1949) suggests that the heroic tale is a universal story form through the ages. Others argue that the individualistic moral worldview in which heroic tales are grounded is particularly male (C. Gilligan 1982) and particularly Western (Markus and Kitayama 1991). Thus, only Western male scholars see heroic tales as universal. My research participants were all men and the majority of them were Westerners. Those who were originally from non-Western societies (e.g., Nelson)[1] differed little in their characterization of an autonomous self under siege. However, across narratives there were differences in the level of aggressiveness used to describe one's heroic tale, and the role of other people in assisting the hero. That is, the interpersonal nature of the struggle was a variable.

John spoke antagonistically about reintegrating himself into society. Others might continue to label him as criminal but, he declared: "Don't come around me with that bullshit, because basically you're gonna find out I'm a lot different now than I was." His talk of redemption involves an aggressive warning to potential critics. Also concerned with social reintegration, José depicted a journey that demands his diligence and patience: "An'—I took this like a man. I'm doin' it like a man. An' I'm a get out of it like a man. And, no matter how—what time, or—what distance it takes, or years, for me to sp—uh—'spunge [expunge] that [from] my jacket [criminal record]? I'm a do it. But I'm—prove—not only to myself, not only to my family but to the state, that I wasn't the person they thought." José's tale of struggle is plainly masculine, but he speaks less aggressively than John and brings other people into the struggle with him—for example, as witnesses to his reform. He is concerned about what these others think. Both John and José strived to gain respect and understanding of who they really are. In addition, they loathed their degraded offender status and sought to free themselves of it.

Respect, understanding, and freedom were fundamental goals that narrators were struggling or had struggled to achieve. Typically these were related, so that one sought to be understood as someone worthy of both respect and freedom. There were other, less common goals, including a relationship with God and mental serenity. Even when narrators shared the same basic goal (e.g., respect), they often conceptualized their foes—those forces blocking the way to achieving the goal—quite differently. I organize the discussion in terms of internal and external foes.

Internal Foes

The internal foes identified by my research participants were the "usual suspects" from contemporary lay discourses about what causes crime—certain attitudes, mental illness, and addiction. Here, the obstructed goal was typically one's own reform.

Attitudes

In many narratives, antisocial attitudes were keeping the protagonist from achieving his goal or goals. Reform-oriented narrators criticized previously held attitudes that directly supported criminal action. The narrator had largely defeated such attitudes, including denigrating attitudes toward women and ideas about what "the good life was."

In his quest to gain respect as a conventional member of society, José contended with his antisocial attitudes, learned through association with delinquent peers. The correctional treatment José was participating in was cognitive in orientation, and he discussed at length having changed his thinking patterns about decision making, conflict resolution, and functional relationships.

Having made inroads into antisocial attitudes, José—at the time of the interview—was wrestling with anti-*self* attitudes. He expressed a great deal of self-doubt about achieving his vocational goals and reacceptance generally post-release. Concerning the realization of his dream of counseling youth, he said: "But it's somethin' in me that's stoppin' me. I don't know what it is. Probably it's fear or—fear of disapproval from the people? But I guess the only way I could do that is by doin' it anyway." In view of that statement, José seemed to be winning his battle over self-doubt. Other narrators shared this struggle. Like José, Vaughan referred to the need to change attitudes promoting antisocial behavior as well as attitudes preventing him from achieving greater, prosocial aspirations. In Vaughan's words, even after defeating antisocial patterns, one might be paralyzed by failure to recognize personal accomplishments, strengths, and potential. His need for both kinds of cognitive change occurred to him after reading the Bible. In his memoirs he shared: "You have to become consciously aware of attitudes before you can start to change. You have to become aware of the fact that you don't see things that way anymore, that you don't harbor anger the way you used to or whatever it may be" (Booker and Phillips 1994, 93). Vaughan's turning point in a struggle for spiritual redemption comes with a realization that he can change *and* that he has already changed.

The struggle to improve self-worth was discussed as an end in itself and as a means to keep from reoffending. Hector spoke of his battle to realize that he is good: "And um, always had positiveness in me but—I'm more knowledgeable of it." Tim expanded on a similar idea: "I probably got the best self-image now that I've ever had in my life. But I don't see myself as a criminal. I see myself as a victim. But I also see myself—I mean, I saw myself as a criminal. In some of my things. I don't see myself as a criminal *now*. But I—you know—a few years ago, that's the way I saw myself. You know, I changed myself about seein' myself that way because it was creatin' negative images about myself to myself. To just say 'Well I'm a criminal,' that's not a very positive, assertive thing to say about yourself. You know, you start believin' that stuff, and then the next thing you know you're doin' what *criminals* do." In Tim's vocabulary, a positive self-image is vital to his mental well-being. He felt oppressed by a negative, criminal identity. Adding heft to the seriousness of the problem, he proposed that a criminal identity (somehow) promotes offending: a labeling theoretic prediction (H. Becker 1963; Kitsuse 1962; Schur 1971; Tannenbaum 1938).

Among those men who were struggling with self-doubts, only José sought to conquer self-doubt by engaging with other people. The other narrators described that conquest as one accomplished alone, such as by looking within. For them, interpersonal relations would not facilitate renewed self-confidence.

Mental Illness

Oren and Peter were two men with much in common. Both had sustained long-term abuse from their fathers. They suffered from mental illness, reportedly as a result of such abuse. They talked openly about the etiology of their illness and its past and present symptoms. Oren and Peter had both committed murder and attributed the crimes to their mental illness. Both men struggled with persistent anxiety and psychosis. Peter also suffered with depression and suicidal thoughts.

Whereas they had long struggled to find peace of mind, they were succeeding in that struggle at this point in their narratives. Oren, who had murdered his abusive father in a psychotic rage, described how he had been managing his illness:

> *Oren:* I was seeing a psych once a month. An', I had a lot of self-help programs . . . "Anger Management" and all that. And I was learning how to speak to people. And I was facing things. My need for it was diminishing, ya know. I didn't—need it so much 'cause I found myself—if I just *talked,* I didn't have that anger or that hopelessness and I wasn't feeling paranoid anymore . . . so that helped a lot. And I found I wasn't zoning out anymore.
> *Lo:* So you didn't need medication to control the zoning out?
> *Oren:* Nah. I found I didn't need it. You see I didn't have a need to zone out. So. Start goin' and I was tryin' some things out. Ya know like well, "Let me try talking to him this way." And, that's how I was doin' it. Until we— I finally got off the med. And, so far, I haven't had problems, ya know. Um. But like I said, this is in prison. I haven't done it on the streets yet.

The future was uncertain to Oren, but he had come very far. He spoke of his triumph in ironic terms: having been confined to a treatment-oriented correctional facility, where he is "physically locked up . . . on the way I got spiritually free."

Peter too described a battle won thus far against mental illness. He was learning new techniques of self-talk for managing anxiety and depression. He also benefited from being able to share his experiences and feelings with empathic others; Peter was one of the few men reluctant to leave the correctional facility for the outside world.

> *Lo:* So you're saying that—now you find that this is a very good place
> for you.
> *Peter:* Very—very comfortable. You know, I'm not so anxious. Uh, I c—
> still can get anxiety attacks. Uh—I'm seeing a psychiatrist one to two
> times a week—ya know—our sessions. Um, an' *that's* been going very
> well. My therapist said that, "Pete, just pretend—you have a cold.
> And it's gonna go away." So that helped a lot.

A few other men told me that they suffered with periodic depression. Yet they did not conceptualize it as a particularly potent force in their lives, nor did they speak about conquering depression in interpersonal terms. Cyrus, for example, admitted to feeling sad that he has only weak ties to family. "Sometimes I be sayin' . . . 'What the hell would be the difference if it just ended right now?' There ain't a lot of people that would *care*. Ya know. And like that's kinda—ya know—feel kind of bad about that." Cyrus avoided these feelings of sadness by saying that it was his own fault that those ties had atrophied, and there was nothing to be done about this sorry situation now.

Addiction

Addiction to drugs or alcohol or both was a battle fought by most of the narrators. They generally concurred that this battle had been or was being won. Note that, for twenty of the twenty-seven men I interviewed, participation in a twelve-step program (e.g., Narcotics Anonymous, Alcoholics Anonymous) was required. The twelve-step philosophy offers its own distinctive metanarrative, depicting a battle fought one day at a time with the aid of a higher power. This metanarrative framed many of the stories I heard. I heard no narratives in which addiction was said to have lasting power over the narrators.

James discussed a cocaine addiction that he had beaten. Sounding a common theme among narrators, James reported that it was fairly easy for him to give up cocaine. He boasted that in prison he abstained: "I coulda did anything I cared about in doin' down here, but I chose not to do it." Although James attributed his initiation into theft to a need to finance his cocaine habit, he explained *persistent* shoplifting as due to a different sort of addiction. His enduring foe was "an addictive personality."

External Foes

External foes were more often summoned than internal ones. If one takes an interactionist approach, the distinction is of interest not because it indicates exactly *what* aggravates the speaker. Rather, the pervasiveness of external foes indicates how the speakers tended to depict existential trouble—in "I" versus "them" terms. Identity was, for most, fundamentally riddled with conflict with other persons or entities.

Environment

Environment was a leading obstacle in the narrators' lives. The prison environment and the community outside of prison had challenged them in two related ways. First, the narrators had to struggle to avoid victimization in both settings. Second, these settings thwarted their ability to live right. Violence, for example, was demanded in prison and in one's criminogenic neighborhood.

Most narrators depicted themselves as having triumphed in the struggle to avoid victimization in prison or in the street. A simple change in behavior patterns allowed them to be in a menacing place without becoming its victim. Thus Steve depicted the Detroit he hails from as an inevitably bad place, which he nonetheless negotiates successfully:

> *Steve:* Even sitting in Detroit, at the street I used to live on—my
> brother's house, you don't sit beside a window like this [*gesturing*]: it's
> bad business.
> *Lo:* Huh.
> *Steve:* You can find somebody to blow your window off.
> *Lo:* Huh.
> *Steve:* [*softly*] You get used to it.

Victimization is akin to a choice in Steve's construction: "You can find somebody to blow your window off." Being victimized in prison is likewise avoidable:

Cyrus: That rape thing, if you just leave that type of situation alone, and especially if a—young guys don't get drawn into that, they're better off.

Arnell: But—you know—my second time—out in—when I went to prison, I knew how to jail. You know, that's knowing how to *move*. So once you know how to move, won't nobody bother you. An' like I said, it's how you carry yourself.

José: People got their theory messed up about prison. You know and the only way you could put yourself in a predicament that you might get beat up or somethin' is your disrespect.

None of my research participants posited the prison environment as an enduring foe. They had all succeeded in "holding their own" and "preserving their manhood" there. Even those men who were still behind bars said that prison did not pose a lasting threat to physical well-being.

Emotional injuries due to prison, such as a lasting bitterness, were less readily dismissed. Talk of such injuries was typically embedded in an indictment of a more despised foe than prison per se: the criminal justice system. Even when a narrator condoned prison for some people and some crimes—including their own—he had a store of criticism for "the system." Shawn, whose criminal history included multiple rapes and assaults, had been released from prison approximately five weeks before our interview. He had this to say about it: "I mean, thank God there is prisons 'cause there's some people should go. I mean, I committed a crime and I shoulda went to prison for it. But . . . they give you too much time. I mean, some of the time they give you, it makes you bitter." Shawn's appraisal was policy- and not place-oriented. This was true of the many other criminal justice policy critiques I heard. The antagonism seemed to be directed toward the system that meted out prison and other incapacitative sentences. Supporting this finding, just as much resentment was expressed about a lack of self-determination while under *community* supervision—probation or parole. I return to the justice system as foe later in the chapter.

Many narrators were still fighting or at least expected to have to fight to avoid the power of criminogenic places to *make* them criminal. Some narrators anticipated that the strong and the gifted could win the fight against a "rough" neighborhood. For Lyle, the influence of neighborhood was only as bad as residents allowed it to be. Lyle's planned autobiography, which culminates in basketball stardom, suggests that he resisted the ghetto influence in the past: "Ya know, I came from the 'hood. Ya know wha' I mean?

Everybody's shooting people, hustling. An' I just—I ain't *go* that way." Lyle positions himself as one who managed to remain unaffected by the ghetto. There is a contradiction, however, since he also used "the 'hood" to explain his robbery. Lyle shared that his immediate family lived in New Jersey, but he chose to stay in the Bronx with his uncle and cousins. He regrets the decision, saying: "If I ain't never come down, I wouldn't have got in no trouble, ya know." In accounting for his one reported crime, Lyle attributes influence to the Bronx.

If Lyle *did* "go that way"—if he did get taken in by his surroundings—he nonetheless did not *stay* that way. He credits his character as well as his athletic talent for helping him win the battle over the 'hood. Others have not managed to do so:

> *Lo:* You think women's basketball's gonna be good?
> *Lyle:* Yeah, I would say so 'cause they got a lotta female talents. Ya know? As far as—I be watching a lot of college games. I know a lot of girls that when I was home, go to the park, and they got a lot of talent with them but they in the 'hood, ya know wha'a mean? They can't get that out of 'em.
> *Lo:* What's—what do you mean when you say in the 'hood? Like what— what is—?
> *Lyle:* Like—ya know—the ghetto. Ya know. Projects . . .
> *Lo:* But what does it do to you?
> *Lyle:* It doesn't do *anything* to you unless you let it do somethings to you, see wha'am sayin'?

In his narrative Lyle was extraordinary in managing to get the 'hood "out of" him.

Dwight was allegedly winning the struggle against his neighborhood. He talked about challenges he confronted each morning on his way to work. When drug dealers and prostitutes approached him to make an offer, he told them "Nah, I ain't got time." He explained: "See I use my mind." His new cognitive skills trumped his setting.

Other narrators did grapple with living in a criminogenic place while still holding onto decent values—precisely the struggle Elijah Anderson (1999) discusses on a community-wide level. Clarence stated that his low wages gave him no choice but to live in the same ghetto area he had lived in prior to his incarceration on drug-related charges. Despite the drugs readily available in his community, he maintained—against the concerns of his parole officer— that he was ever vigilant against relapsing: "I'm [in] jeopardy every time I walk out the front door, you know wha'am sayin'? I don't put my *recovery* in jeopardy."

The justice system failed to recognize, as Clarence did, that his own self-discipline permitted this détente in the struggle against the criminogenic neighborhood. In fact, the justice system undermined his self-identification as a responsible agent by making lifestyle choices for him. He devoted more of his narrative to his struggle against the justice system than to his struggle against place.

Other People

Even apart from certain environments, other people were said to challenge the self. The narrator was exploited, abused, and/or disrespected by others through different phases of his life. Tim and Shawn viewed the world as a hostile place from their earliest days. Both had been subject to abuse by caretakers. As youths they were bullied. As adults they were cheated. In prison they had to assault to avoid being assaulted. The variety and number of foes cited in their narratives was indeed remarkable. Relatives, acquaintances, spouses, and victims were named, along with lawyers, judges, parole officers, and other persons with power over them. All people were potential opponents.

John's narrative did not depict a struggle against abusive others, but he was nonetheless hostile to the potential slights of people generally. He described his adoptive parents as very caring—his strongest allies during ten years spent in prison. Yet for a while he considered suing them for a settlement received when John's natural brother, adopted with him, was killed by a drunk driver: "I could take everything that they'd gotten. Heh, I don't see any point in it." The battle against others was also seen in tirades against those who would deprive him of opportunities due to his ex-convict status. It was seen in contrived disputes with me, addressed in the next chapter.

Aligning himself with other deaf people, Wayne struggled against mistreatment by hearing people and biases against the deaf. He portrayed himself as an effective activist on behalf of the rights of deaf inmates. He protested the message that the deaf are stupid and detected it everywhere. Wayne identified hearing people's chronic failure to understand and respect him, and eagerness to take advantage of him, as central problems in his life. These had also supposedly instigated his various violent crimes.

Some who struggled against other people emphasized, rather than respect or understanding, the simple desire to be left alone. Steve was one such narrator. He characterized the women in his life as trying to hold him back: "Ya know, I just—I might be drinking—get off work on a Friday and I want to take off and go to Detroit, hanging out up there with guys and girls up there, you know? And I ain't tagging the old lady along, you know?"

Oren also longed to be left alone. For this reason he hated the rural area where he had been sent to live as a child and, later, where he was stationed by the army: "You can't hide in the country [*chuckle*]. Ya know, everybody knows everybody." He also claimed to despise authority figures, which he attributed to his father's abuse. He felt that he was winning the battle against authority and for autonomy. Not only had he freed himself of his father by killing him, but he expected his intellectual abilities to land him a job in science, enabling him to work with minimal direct supervision. Of family and friends, he told me that once back at home, "I want them to get the idea that I'm like just off-limits from them."

It was mainly young narrators who described a struggle against peers who would sway them back to antisocial behavior. José (age twenty-two), Tré (twenty-three), and William (twenty-one) stand out among those who saw a need to be vigilant against the influence of antisocial peers. José told me:

> *José:* 'Cause it's—they still doin'—the friends that I so-called had then, they're still doin' the same thing.
> *Lo:* Right.
> *José:* I'm sayin.' And now that I'm—these four years that I've been locked up, I've changed in different ways, that I don't want to go back to that.

Beyond feeling alienated from such irresponsible friends today, José appears to have rewritten the past, questioning whether they were ever his friends at all ("that I so-called had").

Nelson depicted his one-time robbery as the result of temptations nurtured by "the devil"—evil personified. He explained: "You have the narrow path in life which leads to eternity, and you have the broad way that leads to death and hell. So I got strayed away on that." Though Nelson was in recovery from alcoholism, he pictured "the devil" and "evil thoughts" as ever on the horizon, not just for him but for all people. The devil is an external foe who provokes internal addiction.

Criminal Justice Authority

The criminal justice system was a foe in the majority of the narratives.[2] Its authority inhibited achievement of a host of goals but primarily liberty, respect in the community, recognition of who one "really" is, and economic success.

Most of the research participants were under correctional supervision—probation, parole, or that of a correctional facility—and most expressed feelings of resentment about being supervised. Many spoke of specific conflicts they were engaged in with agents of the criminal justice system. They described heated disputes concerning potential or actual violations of the conditions of their supervision. The system was personified in stories of abuse. Police and correctional officers were vicious, judges were unfair, prosecutors were ruthless and apt to humiliate defendants, public defenders were indifferent, and probation and parole officers were either negligent or overly strict.

The battle against the criminal justice system was unlike any other in a variety of noteworthy ways. This foe was especially *powerful*. Indeed, the criminal justice system was said to abuse its power. Kevin believed that business interests drove criminal justice decision making in his case, leading to his sentence of death: "[Large company] has a lot of political power down in Somers County. So there has been backdoor politics." Without money, the men had been inadequately represented by public defenders. Larry contended that the affluent thus get away with committing crimes: "But because I was poor, I had to take a public defender. And my opinion is, the public defender didn't know what was goin' on an' he didn't care, whatever. And uh, ya know, so I get twenty years. Ya know? You— there's so many cases that people with money that do these type of things, they get off."

The power of the justice system is extensive. It includes the power to define who the narrator is. Claims of innocence to a crime could be ignored. In court, Marco said, "I could be say that I'm innocent, the next thing that I know—you know—that don't count." Agents of the system routinely rejected one's claims to moral decency—both claims that one had changed or had always been decent. Harry described such rejection by a judge after Harry had abused his four-month-old son: "And uh, my second wife, she was even in the courtroom, she was trying to explain to the judge that he's not like that. You know? It's just one incident, you know. But that didn't work either." In that example, Harry's wife assisted him—unsuccessfully—in his struggle against the power of the criminal justice system to define who he is.

Shawn was also unsuccessful in his battle against criminal justice authority. He was classified as a "sexual predator" as part of the state's community notification policy. This was the most serious classification a sex offender could receive, and he believed himself to have been misclassified: "See, there's guys in the prison that have worse offenses than mine, and got labeled less than me. And then there's guys in prison that got lesser offenses than me, and got labeled the same as me. And, I don't know how they go about labelin' 'em or what." Because of his designation as a sexual predator, communities in which Shawn resided would be notified of his address and criminal history for the rest of his life. Though he said he had no intention of challenging the classification, it imposed a serious hardship: "I'm thinkin': 'How you expect a guy to live and stay in society, if you're not gonna let them live nowhere?'"

Ralph struggled against a justice system that had wrongfully defined him as a rapist in the courtroom and continued to define him based on that charge by denying him parole. He concluded with resignation: "This ain't the first time I been knocked or kicked flat out, so it probably won't be my last." Ralph did not feel that he had yet vanquished his foes, but persisted in crafting ways to establish his innocence, so that he might at least defeat their ability to classify him as a criminal. He would not be outsmarted.

Nor does the system's power to define end with formal supervision. Tim struggled with the reification of the offender label. He would ever be identified with his crimes given his criminal record: "I'm the bad guy even if I'm right or wrong." He offers a concrete illustration:

> You and me, for example: you know, you don't have a prison record. You make a mistake and you're gonna get some play. You know, they're not gonna be as tough on you. But, with me, I make the same mistake an' jest bein' human, I'm not sayin'—I'm not talkin' about criminal behavior. I'm jest sayin' somethin' that—you know. Uh, speedin' ticket or somethin' like that, you know? Say you get a speedin' ticket, I get a speedin' ticket, you know an' first time for you, first time for me. But I got a record. Ya know, it's things are a whole lot more *intense* for me. An' it jest—it puts me under a hell of a lot of pressure.

The struggle against the justice system was very often formal. In comparison, other struggles were less likely to involve institutional action. Larry had a lawsuit pending against the Department of Corrections in his state for an assault he sustained from correctional officers. Kevin had filed various appeals as well as a request for clemency from the governor, prior to his execution.

After John shot at a sheriff's car and then fled, he feared abuse from justice agents if he turned himself in, so he demanded a written promise that he would not be abused. He recalled, "We took off. And, of course I kept in contact with Mom throughout the time—we were gone. And she finally told me, 'Give yourself up; it'll be a lot easier.' And I said, 'No, I'll never make it back to [State] alive if I do that.' And she said, 'Well, I can get the guarantee from the Sheriff's department and the police department that you won't be harassed when you get back.' And I said, 'Well, I want that guarantee in writing.'"

The justice system was depicted as a particularly sly adversary. Many of the narrators criticized the rhetoric of treatment, which they said contrasted with a reality of actually facilitating recidivism. Arnell made this point: " . . . called themselves tryin' to rehabilitate me but all that did was made it worse because the places that they was sending me to, like the youth house, you know, you go there, all your friends is there." Larry likewise implied that the system is duplicitous, its stated goals false: "It's crazy, ya know? And then when you get in to the prison system, and see how it operates and the parole and things: it just—I just shake my head because I think I'm intelligent enough to know what's goin' on. That I don't know how sincere they are about rehabilitation, tryin' to help anybody, you know."

The battle against the criminal justice system was unique in the way it seemed to consume the narrators and to dwarf other battles. Ralph's griev-ances against the victim who had wrongly accused him were forgotten. His main opponent was the justice system. Reuben talked about the inevitable pull of the rough neighborhood to violence. Yet he did not narrate a struggle against the influence of the neighborhood. He shared an intention to relo-cate—to Africa, in fact—but he explained the plan in terms of avoiding the American criminal justice system. Whatever else preoccupied the narrator, it seemed to pale in comparison with criminal justice processing. In particular, struggles to free oneself of criminogenic influences hardly seemed to matter as much as the struggle to free oneself of formal restraints.

Clarence experienced the justice system as exerting excessive influence in areas of his life that he considered private. A choice given to him by his parole officer was experienced as overly intrusive: "You know, makin' me live with my mother when I don't want to live with my mother." He also protested having to participate in yet another treatment program in the community. He expressed his frustration in terms of abuse of power: "They feel they have so much control, you know, everybody—you know wha'am sayin'—gets mad, you know." Clarence's rage at this foe tended to be muted: here it is projected onto "everybody." He may have been reluctant to risk too much resistance against so powerful a foe, with whom I might be aligned.

The crimes of the men in my sample were tethered to formal consequences. This allowed many of them to focus their life stories on sanctions rather than on their own conduct, and more specifically to employ the stories in terms of struggle against unfair sanctions. James violated a parole condition, but he pointed to a bureaucratic error in protesting the sanction: "And I get sanctions one time, you gonna give me six months because of your negligence?" Tim assaulted his boss, and had his parole violated because of it. He resented the resulting prison term: "Ya know, when I got arrested an' everythin' an' I went to court, I didn't get any credit at all—for the seven years, that I was clean." The wrongdoing the men had done was dwarfed by the greater wrongs done to them by the justice system.

Finally, the battle against criminal justice authority was unusual in that it seemed almost inevitable for narrators with lengthy criminal justice involvement. Men with short criminal records seemed less likely to position the criminal justice system as a foe. Reuben, William, Nelson, Vaughan, Tré, Peter, and Oren had relatively short records. With the exception of Reuben, none of these men said they considered the justice system in an adversarial light. In fact, Tré, Nelson, Peter, and Oren identified with the system during the interviews. Oren claimed to hate authority but curiously not criminal justice authority, which had played a helping role in his salvation. Of the treatment-oriented but nonetheless secure facility he was in, Peter said: "I like the structure." Tré told me: "I get into arguments with other residents all the time because I'm more for DOC [Department of Corrections] than I am for the inmates." No doubt Tré's position enraged many of his peers, for he was advocating for what was likely their fiercest opponent.

The Moral Self as Hero

The trajectory of one's moral self—mostly reform or mostly stability—and heroic struggle are not discrete features of the narratives. Rather, the two themes are interrelated.

First, the men made moral reform and moral stability claims in *heroic terms.* The moral self had fought valiantly to arrive at or to maintain his decency. Hence José's commitment to achieving a public status as a non-offender no matter what: the effort will be hard but he is "doin' it like a man." Likewise, Dwight fends off drug dealers in his neighborhood as one going into battle, but armed with the weapons of decent people: "You got to use your coping skills. You know wha'am sayin'? Ain't nothin' about being weak." Kevin's heroic struggle against the justice system *was* a struggle to be recognized as a morally righteous person. "I'm not this monster that they make me out to be," he insisted more than once.

Second, a heroic struggle with a foe that had been defeated was a way for narrators to claim that they had changed—that theirs was a story of reform.

Both José and William denounced antisocial peers and antisocial attitudes that their peers had passed on to them, which allegedly led to their wrongdoing. Their reform narratives partly hinged on the prospect of maintaining distance from antisocial peers even after returning to the community. Many men argued that the criminal justice system tries to keep the protagonist from changing through labeling processes. They struggled against that process.

Third, a heroic struggle served to *deflect personal agency,* especially when the struggle was against an external foe. This enhanced the coherence of stability claims. If the justice system, other people, or a criminogenic neighborhood were responsible for one's offending, then the self, even during one's offending, could be presented as decent. For example, Larry's stability narrative is supported by his conflict with the criminal justice system. He contended that the justice system is unfair, and that he and others in prison have been targeted arbitrarily: "I think the difference between the person outside in society, and the guy who's incarcerated is that we just got caught." On the basis of that argument, Larry is able to claim that he is as good as anyone else and always has been.

Fourth, struggle with the criminal justice system was very often a struggle to claim moral decency and thus to defy stigma. After nearly killing his baby, Harry was unable to get a judge to honor his claims of being a consistently moral person. Harry reported: "He said that—what he said was I don't seem to possess the characteristics of a person who is really remorseful." During sentencing for aggravated assault, Tim beseeched the judge not to let the prosecuting attorney characterize him as an indecent man: "Fact that I'd been to prison before, that I been arrested for—you know—other things an'—all that stuff, he [the prosecutor] just kept focusin' on all that. An' um, then I got so scared, I just—I got outa order in court. And pleaded with the judge. I said, 'Your Honor, don't let this guy do this to me!' You know, I said, 'He's just tryin' to hook me up! Because of my record: things that I can't change, things that I've already served time for that are dead issues, they have nothin' to do with what's goin' on here today.'" The criminal record was used by others, and especially agents of the justice system, as a snapshot of who the "criminal" is. Tim contended that his story, a dynamic one, and not his official record captures his true moral identity. The courtroom was one venue for struggling to make his story heard.

Summary

Each one of my research participants cast himself as a hero in his life story. The theme of heroism was evidently informed by a Western masculine paradigm in which an autonomous self is in conflict—often quite violent conflict—with society. Nonetheless, there was variation in the role of other people in one's struggle and the extent of aggressiveness in talk of struggle.

Whether one's foes were conceptualized as internal or external to the self, they originally stemmed from social sources. Internal foes included one's attitudes, one's mental illness, and one's addiction. External foes included one's environment, other people, and criminal justice authority. Most of these foes were central to explaining one's criminal behavior. The narrators spoke of prosocial beliefs and behavior patterns diverted as a result of corrupting influences. Social learning and control theorists consider social influences—external ones and those that have been internalized—as criminogenic or protective, but folk theorizing about such influences has received far less attention.

The heroic struggle was the basis for an identity as a valiant fighter with a victorious future. In the epic struggles celebrated in our culture, the hero—usually male—does not stay down for long. So it was that many of my research participants tended to script victory for themselves at the close of their tale of struggle. It was problematic for these narrators to encounter an indomitable foe. In that event, they anticipated alternative plans for defeat. Members of José's family were criminal influences, so he talked of moving away. Lyle could not change the ghetto he came from, but spoke of leaving it via an illustrious basketball career. Reuben shared a plan to move abroad in order to get away from the justice system. These were fantastic visions of the future, but they spoke a truth about the subjugated position in which the narrators found themselves.

Indeed, the heroic struggles of one's life endowed subjugating experiences with moral purpose. The men did not identify themselves as oppressed, alienated, and labeled, but rather as those whom others—and particularly "the system"—tried to oppress, alienate, and label. An extreme case is Kevin, who was ultimately unable to overcome the criminal justice system in a battle for his life and who was reviled in much of the mainstream local news. He was able to write his own heroic tale as a righteous man who fought to the end. Narrative—more precisely, narration—was itself a battlefront. In the next chapter I examine how the research (and I) were drawn into battle, and thus into the construction of the speakers' identities.

THE SITUATED CONSTRUCTION
OF NARRATIVES

The same way you see me? . . . That's how I am. I mean—that's just me. I hurt you more quickly—I ain't got to touch you.
— Ralph

Rather than *criminal,* as he has been labeled, Ralph narrated himself as simply shrewd. Likewise, he was shrewd in talking with me and called attention to that situated shrewdness. The interview was a vehicle for narrating himself as a certain person. So it was with all of my research participants. Their narratives were constructed in important ways in the interview (Presser 2004). In this chapter I will clarify and offer examples of these mechanisms for the *co-production of data.* I will demonstrate how moral decency was established, stigma defied, and heroic struggle carried out through these mechanisms.

First, the fact and the nature of the interview were used to signify something about the self, such as having changed in a morally significant way. Second, many of the research participants solicited and/or inferred my evaluation of them. The evaluation provided a second opinion in support of their self-claims. Third, features of the moral self and struggle were enacted during the interview.

The main point of this chapter is that the narratives were *not* "inside" of the narrators waiting to be expressed. They did not *come from* the men. To say this is not to deny that unconscious psychological states and desires, embodied characteristics, and biographical particulars shaped the narratives (see Gadd 2003; Hollway and Jefferson 2000; Messerschmidt 2000). Rather, it is to emphasize that the narratives, however much narrators molded them from antecedent conditions and personal resources, ultimately emerged *in* the research interviews. More broadly, it is to take an ethnomethodological stance on my research (Lynch 1991b) and in this way to think critically and reflexively about the storied identities of offenders.

Pervasive Social Influence: What This Analysis Is Not

In chapter 3 I concluded that sociologists have generally shied away from or have explicitly denied the open-ended and creative nature of social interaction between researcher and those the researcher studies. In particular, empirical studies codify research effects, as though these are containable. I am sympathetic to the tendency: research on a particular phenomenon proceeds only if other phenomena can be ignored, held constant. Fortunately, my research question, concerning the production of narrative, allows me—more, encourages me—to leave the research interaction in the frame.

My analysis ignores some basic kinds of social influence, because they are either well established as influences or because they are not isolable. I will not focus attention on certain pervasive ways in which self-reports are clearly context bound, including that they respond to the reason for self-revelation or include more or less, and different, sorts of information depending on the context. I have already suggested that the interviews generally provided a forum for giving accounts, or explanations, for deviant behavior and status. Each narrative was therefore fashioned to satisfy the requirements of a proper account: for example, using the currently acceptable "vocabularies of motive" (Mills 1940). I have also indicated that the moral ambiguity of elastic narratives allows the narrator to hedge his bets on what the researcher-as-evaluator wants to hear and will, perhaps, sanction or reward. The possibility that the researcher will affect the informant's future shapes the narrative.

Defendants say things in an attempt to reduce sanctions (Goffman 1971). Mitigation is not the only reason for or influence on what they say: it is simply one. Thus, again, my contention that multiple factors shape our stories. It is clear that if I had interviewed the men at an earlier stage of criminal justice processing, I might have heard more denials of responsibility for the instant offense, which would have made for different life stories. In my sample, Kevin was the only participant whose sentence stood to be changed (i.e., commuted) at the time of our interviews. Likewise, the narratives would probably have been different if I had had more evident power to affect criminal justice processing.

The narratives were tailored to me as an audience: they were means of making a certain impression (Goffman 1959). I view impression management as a particular social force that drives the other dynamics that I will study in this chapter. In addition, the narratives were tailored to the interview in that they are more complete (Labov 1982, 244, n. 3) and pertain more to one's social self (Chanfrault-Duchet 2000, 62–63) than they might be if told in a nonresearch setting. The narratives were thus cast as public artifacts in ways that I appreciate but will not probe.

Nor will I specifically consider the influence of what I communicated and what I did *not* communicate on the narratives. Such influences were clearly evident in my data, however. An example pertains to the commonplace lack of coherence of elastic narratives: in many such narratives reform talk was used for abstract monologues but stability talk was used for stories about particular events. In effect, I permitted this lack of coherence by not calling attention to it. I have found many other instances where I ignored leaps and ellipses in the telling of a story. For example, I abstained completely from challenging Kevin on all that was missing from his narrative, including an adequate account of the robbery-turned-murder that led to his execution.

Sometimes I did challenge a narrator on lack of coherence or on some stated inconsistency in his narrative. The consequences (e.g., resistance to the challenge) were always fascinating. The narrator expected me to accept the narrative "as is" and my violation of that social convention was not often appreciated. Recall, for example, that Lyle responded to my pointing out inconsistency in his criminological logic with: "It happened almost three years ago. I *been* moved on." An exploration of the possible effects of what I communicated (through words and gestures) and what I did not, on the narratives, is obviously a study in itself. Some such effects will be alluded to in regard to the three mechanisms I delineate for the co-production of data.

What I will show in this chapter are not the insidious effects of other people on what we say—effects that are difficult if not impossible for the analyst to extricate from *what* we say. Rather, my intent is to illuminate certain tangible ways in which the narratives are shaped by the research interview in particular.

The Interview Indicates

The interview was an event in the men's lives and thus in their life stories. Moreover, the interview was an "identity-rich" event. The interview *event* signified two other events that ramified in the narrative: first, being asked to participate in the study, and second, participating. These events carried both positive and negative meanings about the self. Signification was active and subjective. The interview was a flexible resource (Holstein and Gubrium 1995). It meant what the participant interpreted it to mean based on personal, "imported" associations, my own cues, and emergent features.

The interview with me indicated the participant's status as an offender. Note that the informed consent form, which I gave to each informant at the start of our first interview, indicated that the purpose of the research was to "learn more about people who had been involved in violent crime." Thus, the *research* positioned the participant as an offender, if somewhat vaguely. (I opted for the vague "involved in violent crime" over nouns such as "violent criminal.") Arnell protested offender status on the grounds that his past violence, including the shooting of a fellow drug dealer, were demanded by life in a dangerous ghetto: "You know, *he* [the victim] coulda been sittin' where I'm at right now, talkin' to you, or me, an'—I would rather it be me anyway but my intentions wasn't on actually killin' the guy. But you know things like that happen."

Like Arnell, Steve narrated himself as decent and contested the very fact of the interview for suggesting otherwise. My interview with Steve was not scheduled in advance. When another participant—a fellow halfway house resident—did not show up to be interviewed, I asked Steve if he would not mind talking to me on a moment's notice. He was hesitant at first, explaining that he had a minimal criminal record. Steve used the fact of the interview to suggest that he is not a criminal. He commented at the beginning and at the end of the impromptu interview that he was actually a poor candidate for my research. In closing, he apologized: "I'm probably not much help to you but you know." Thus Steve rejected my "criminalization" of him, implied by my asking him to participate in the study.

In direct contrast is Dwight, who confided early on that my interview with him might be one of the longest I would have. Dwight also differed from Steve in telling an elastic narrative, as opposed to a "pure" stability narrative. Dwight's theory of his offending incorporated multiple causal factors going back to childhood deprivation. Thus was the promised length of the interview an indicator of the *kind* of narrative he would tell. His long tale reflected a winding journey through life, back to the proposed causes of his offending.

In Cyrus's narrative, he is suffering greatly from having spent so many years behind bars. Our two meetings, spaced approximately six months apart, came to represent his sorry situation. Cyrus had regularly been denied parole release. Each time he was called to the interview room—the library, which served as a meeting place generally—he thought he was being called to a parole hearing. He said: "That's why when they called me up for this time here, I thought this is what it was." The interview was a symbol of his failure to gain freedom. In addition, the fact of a *second* interview—six months after the first—marked Cyrus's failure: his parole eligibility date was more than a year past by the time of the second interview. "Nothing too much changed," he said despondently, except that he was "way over" the parole eligibility date.

I also interviewed Ralph twice, with an interval of six months between the interviews. Like Cyrus, Ralph conveyed more despair over his confinement during the second interview than he had during the first. Ralph, however, was one of those narrators who posited himself as triumphing over the corrupt forces of the justice system. Accordingly, he stood tall against those forces when he said to me: "Told you I'd probably be here." With that statement, he defied the power of his foe to catch him off-guard. I was a witness to his resistance to the state's psychic control.

The interview was written into many of the men's plans for redemption (see Maruna 2001). I suggest that men's agendas for giving back started in the moment—in the research setting. They were not merely intended for future use; the interview was not just a forum for talking about a plan to be implemented elsewhere. Many of the participants appraised the storytelling itself as contributing to society, and specifically to reducing crime.

Concluding our first interview, Ralph said: "I do want to say I— I hope you got a lot out of this—this afternoon. Um. Is there anything you—want to ask me yourself?" For José, the interview was expected to improve the criminological knowledge base. He said: "As far as you doin' studies on different—ya know—uh, criminals or whatever? That's somethin' that's gonna better you 'cause you understand us more." Remarkably, José's reform was in part occasioned by the interview—or at least that is how the story would be told in future. Having thoroughly established his intentions to change, José spoke of telling future audiences about the interview. Participation in the interview was being "written into" his tale of reform: "So when I hit the street, I could talk about or, maybe say like one year, two years from now, I could be talking to kids and explaining to them that I was sitting in front of you—a lady like you—and she was—ya know—studying on criminals. An' I was telling her my story or whatever like that."

Although José's interpretation of the interview as a moral turning point was unusual, the interview as an act of redemption was not. Dwight, like José, talked much about his plans for the future. These plans included precisely what he was doing in the moment:

> *Lo:* What is [it that] you want to do?
> *Dwight:* What we doin.'
> *Lo:* You want to—uh—what?
> *Dwight:* Share the—the—the experience—and reach out an' help—an' help others—uh.

The belief that redemption, especially for reformed deviants, comes through sharing one's story with others is well documented (e.g., Maruna 2001; Modell 1992).

To summarize, far from being a "time-out" from life lived elsewhere, the interview was an event *in* one's life. For some it was an invalid indicator of their offender status, which was protested. For others it was indicative of the direction one's scripted life was taking, either toward triumph or temporarily defeated. Either way, the men narrated themselves using the interview as a reference point.

A Second Opinion

In the previous section the interview was shown as indicating something about the narrator, even apart from its specific content. Other mechanisms engage the content of the interviews. In this section I consider how my evaluation of the narrator figured into the narratives.[1] To some of the men, my moral or mental assessment of them was important as confirmation of self-claims. I did not necessarily verbalize an assessment, even when one was solicited. Typically, the men simply inferred my opinion of them. Why did my opinion matter? Where did my authority come from?

Whence the Researcher's Authority?

Peter, who suffered from extreme anxiety and depression, told me about his plans to include family members in some counseling sessions. He asked me: "What do you think about that?" I was initially surprised that Peter would seek out my clinical impression of him. I wondered about the source of my supposed expert authority.

The researcher's position in relation to the research participant is, first, as the *instigator* of the interview and thus an authority figure. Mishler (1986a) writes: "Typically, the aim of an interview is defined by the interviewer who also controls its shape and flow as well as the form and intent of specific questions" (245). I *caused* the interview. I called the participant to the room. Facility administrators allowed me to interrupt the day's routine. I had power in making the interview happen (Presser 2005).

I was also obviously acquainted with some of the administrators, thanks largely to a career background in criminal justice. Usually the fact of knowing an administrator was made plain when those administrators introduced me to the research participant. Sometimes I explained the relationship to a research participant, upon questioning. My apparent "insider" relationship with the agency's administrator probably motivated participants to present more positive selves than they would in a different situation (see Dean and Whyte 1958, 35). Several participants made reference to what I might report to organizational administrators, usually at the close of interviews.

What, though, explains the idea that I had insight of a clinical sort? First, at the New Jersey facility where I met thirteen of my research participants, the clinical director—herself a Ph.D. identified as "Doctor [Surname]"—was my intermediary. Second, I informed the men that I was doing my doctoral research and that I taught college courses. Most of the educated people whom they met were counseling staff, and so the supposition that I had the same kind of expertise is understandable. In any case, the fact that I was taken to have expert authority suggests that such authority gets constituted at micro levels (see Molotch and Boden 1985) by interactants, and is not always based on "structural" positions.

I Am Not Deviant, Am I?

My opinion primarily served to vouch for the men's nondeviance. At the end of my first of nine interviews with Kevin, he closed with the remark: "I hope you don't think I'm a nut." Thus he sought my assurance that he was not a mental deviant. Kevin was concerned that he be seen as a normal person, if an especially intelligent one. Two days before he was executed, I asked Kevin how he wanted to be remembered. He replied: "I think you've known me long enough and spoken with me long enough to know that I'm not some kind of uneducated monster like they make me out to be." My relationship with Kevin—spanning eight months—was a resource for conjecturing my appraisal of him.

Ralph's narrative relied very heavily on denial of having raped a woman— the crime for which he was convicted. His was a moral stability narrative. He solicited my opinion for the purpose of confirming that he was not, in fact, a rapist. My assumed clinical expertise and my female gender were equally important aspects of my assignment as evaluator. In the exchange presented below, Ralph asked me to verify how I felt being in the interview room with him. Contending first that if he really "is" a rapist he should be confined to a mental hospital, Ralph bid me to continue the appraisal of his real self:

> *Ralph:* Now, I don't know—based on me having this interview, or—
> How do you feel? Do you feel comfortable? Do you feel like you in
> here with some nut [*chuckle*]?
> *Lo:* [*shakes head*]
> *Ralph:* Huh, okay [*laughing*]. You know wha' I mean. I'm—people have
> a sense of understandin' and feelin' comfortable with people. You
> know wha'am sayin'? They know when a person is—sincere or they
> know when a person is real or they know when they around some-
> body that just ain't got all they scruples.

Ralph involved me as a partner in his clinical assessment of self, by reason-ing that I would have felt uncomfortable with a truly immoral man. In the following exchange, Ralph urged me to attest to this syllogism: a rapist would not be brought to a facility with female staff; he was brought to a facility with female staff; therefore he is not a rapist.

> *Ralph:* Would you bring him to this facility, knowin' you got women
> work here? Would you? On a *personal* basis, would you do it?
> *Lo:* Well, it's uh—it's the treatment services or whatever over—maybe—
> I'm just—like—well I'm not really sure.
> *Ralph:* No. Honestly.
> *Lo:* Yeah, I don't really know.
> *Ralph:* As a doctor's point of view.
> *Lo:* I don't—well I'm not a doctor *yet*. I don't really know—
> *Ralph:* I know, but you studying to be a—okay, as a—
> *Lo:* Yeah, I mean—[pause] I don't really know, because I don't know—
> maybe there's nothing like— I don't know New Jersey that well.
> Maybe there's nothing like it in New Jersey.
> *Ralph:* Okay. Where you from?
> *Lo:* New York City.
> *Ralph:* New York? Same thing. New York and New Jersey the same
> thing. We right over the bridge, girl! You— you— you right there!

I was rather uncooperative in Ralph's project of proving innocence of rape. The exchange can be analyzed in terms of the following conversational "moves":

1. Ralph asks my basic opinion of him.
2. I decline to give an opinion.
3. Ralph refers to my expert authority.
4. I deny authority.
5. He rejects my denial.
6. I claim lack of knowledge because of geographic difference. I thus take myself out of the assigned structural position, instead speaking as a layperson.
7. He rejects that claim by bridging the distance between us as laypersons.

My effort to remain neutral—to avoid evaluating him in moves 2, 4, and 6—led Ralph to a succession of alternative ways for narrating his "decent" identity. In move 7 he used autobiographical "information" ("I don't know New Jersey that well") that I happened to provide in move 6, to appeal to our spatial/social proximity. Ralph's claim that we are from proximate places ("We right over the bridge, girl!") is punctuated by the familiar and gendered "girl" he then used for the very first time in our encounter.

Thus did Ralph make me a resource for identifying himself as nondeviant. More than once did I fail to assist in Ralph's project. With the following spontaneous question on my part—I was seeking clarification about the sentence Ralph was serving—I managed to imply that Ralph is someone who is appropriately incarcerated:

Lo: So you were—so you're looking at—w— I don't follow. How much longer should you be here?
Ralph: I *shouldn't* be here.

My question, which admitted to a double meaning, provided Ralph an opportunity to make a repair that was laden with meaning for his identity as a "regular" person—someone who should not be in a correctional facility.

This second exchange with Ralph underscores the fact that social interactions, including interviews, are always open to chance occurrence. Meanings "emerge, develop, are shaped by and in turn shape the discourse" (Mishler 1986b, 138). Strauss (1997) refers to face-to-face interaction as "a fluid, moving, 'running' process" (57), the course of which "is due in considerable part to unwitting responses made by each participant" (60). The researcher's statements and questions cannot be fully accounted for in advance; even less so can their assumed meaning. Like Gadd (2004), who interviewed batterers, it was only upon analysis that I detected my failure to give sought-after affirmation. I cannot say that I regret such failure, both because I view the exchanges as yielding "the data" and because I had no sense in the moment that I was affecting his self-story.[2]

Inferring Agreement

More often than outright solicitation of my evaluation of them, narrators simply inferred my agreement with their self-evaluations. Harry, who emphasized a victim identity, told a story of separating from his wife, after which she took all of their furniture while he was out of the house. "Well, you can understand my anger when I got there and there was nothing there." Steve sought my empathy after I asked him to elaborate on a domestic assault against his wife. He framed the incident, for which he was charged and convicted, in terms of an argument. "Well, we was cussing, screaming—you know how it goes." Concerning assault generally, Larry argued: "If I make you mad enough—ya know, or if somebody else makes you mad enough—ya know, you're gonna strike back." All of these men used stability talk in which their actions were presented as no worse than those of other people, including me. Accordingly, I should identify with them and their actions.

One might protest that these references to my empathy were more like verbal tics than thoughtful inferences. Such a judgment suggests indifference to linguistic data and the relationship between linguistic expression and culture. Agar and Hobbs (1982) provide a useful model for that relationship, with the concepts global, themal, and local coherence:

1. *Global coherence,* where utterances operate in the service of accomplishing an overarching goal or goals of speaking.
2. *Themal coherence,* where utterances refer to "chunks of content" (Agar and Hobbs 1982, 7) that are part of a broader cultural world of the speaker (and listener). Themes include beliefs, goals, and values.
3. *Local coherence,* concerned with connecting one utterance to the next in a meaningful way (e.g., by elaborating on the previous utterance).

The different kinds of coherence are mutually constitutive. As such, local coherence serves themal and global coherence. And all verbal expressions—even ones that are stated more or less mechanically like "you can understand"—have social meaning within a particular speech context. Here, they are consistent with an assertion that I do understand because I am morally *like* the speaker.

Enacting the Moral Self and Struggle

With use of the preceding mechanisms, narrators took the interview or the interviewer as indicating a certain identity that they claimed for themselves. In this section I introduce a somewhat more dynamic mechanism positing the interview as an enactment of one's "true" identity. This mechanism resonates with Messerschmidt's (1993, 1997) structured action theory, except that the behavior that accomplishes the desired identity—keeping the appointment with me, for instance—is not (necessarily) criminal. As in Messerschmidt's theory, the behavior is constrained by local and extralocal circumstances. Again, I focus on the local. The research site is a forum for the action-cum-identity work.

Kuhn (1962) demonstrated that the interview between a social worker and his or her client may be seen as "a constructed situation in which an individual can act out, at least in conversation" who she or he is (203). Although Kuhn was not referring to research interviews, his point is applicable to my data. My participants used the research interview to embody a particular version of themselves. Note that Kuhn's expression "act out" (and my own "dramatization") seem to distinguish real life from the interview, the latter serving as a warm-up for the former. I prefer the term "enact"—as in enacting the self—to indicate that action that occurred during the interview was real and important: not merely rehearsed for more important conduct elsewhere, no more and no less "constructed" than action occurring elsewhere. In enacting a particular self, the men were being a particular self and/or engaging in a particular struggle in the present speaking moment. I was at all times a participant in these enactments—usually an unwitting one. The men positioned me as they did themselves along gender, race, class, and other so-called structural lines.

Moral Qualities on Display

It was quite common for the men to act, during the interview, in ways that conventional society values, and to present that they were doing so. For instance, Dwight, in discussing his newly responsible self who keeps appointments no matter what, referred to having kept *our* interview appointment that day.

Honesty was the moral quality alluded to most often, perhaps due to my explicit request that the men share with me candidly. José stated: "It's like— I'm honest for any staff member or with you. There's anything you could ask me, I'll tell you the truth. There's nothin' I can— I have to— I gotta hide. 'Cause I did the mistakes on my own." Likewise, when I asked Joe-Ray whether his old friends would try to lure him back into offending patterns after his return home, he conceded that this is likely, prefacing his reply with: "And to be completely— 'cause I know honesty comes first?" His honesty— moral integrity—underscored the commitment to desistance that followed: "But nah," he says, "I can't do it. I refuse to do it." Steve favorably compared himself with *less* honest men. He advised me: "Be careful what you ask me now 'cause men don't like to answer, but I'm going to tell you the truth, so be careful what you ask." The research itself provided Steve with the opportunity for framing himself in terms of those other, less moral counterparts.

Doing Moral Conformity

In addition to piecemeal enactment of moral qualities, there were more dramatic stagings: presentations of "doing" moral conformity. Beyond the conformity reflected in the interview as a whole—simply going along with it constitutes deference—I was struck by the men's resourcefulness in creating opportunities to more palpably *be* a noncriminal.

Some of the men went out of their way to advise me about something, where the advice was specifically related to their criminal past and redemption. Dwight, a convicted rapist, advised me about maintaining personal power and satisfaction in relationships with men. He had just finished discussing his reform from the misogynist rapist he had been:

> *Dwight:* I say this because uh—I'm hopin' yourself—you know wha'am sayin'- you know, you is a good person.
> *Lo:* Hmm. Thank you.
> *Dwight:* And, I just met ya. Ya know, you a good person. So, I'm hopin' that—that you don't get—you're stuck with some [unclear] guy—you know wha'am sayin'—
> *Lo:* [*chuckle*]
> *Dwight:* —don't want you for—don't want you for you.

José used a more dialogic technique to challenge my unagentive thinking just as, in treatment, he was encouraged to challenge his own. My status as a nondriver came up in conversation with José when I commented on a municipal transit strike that complicated my trip home.

> *Lo:* I don't drive.
> *José:* Nuh-huh?

Lo: No.

José: Why not?

Lo: 'Cause I n— it just never—I just don't know how.

José: You don't know how or you never took the time to learn?

As discussed previously, redemption was achieved through such gestures in moral reform narratives. José did not just tell me about his plans to be a counselor: he counseled *me*.

A remarkable case of moral performance in the interview involved Clarence. As I prepared to mark the microcassette for recording the interview, I asked Clarence if he would like to provide a pseudonym. He told me the alias he had used for past criminal activities but then very quickly bristled at the idea that I must assign a pseudonym at all. When he asked me why it was necessary, I tried to explain. Unable to make myself clear, I finally said that it was "Just like that." This remark greatly irritated Clarence. He snapped: "Well, *this* is how it is." I gained an understanding of Clarence's position during the discussion that followed:

Clarence: That was fake about me, so I use a fake name, but now that— you know, I'm in recovery for a lot of things, I'd rather use my real name.

Lo: So it sounds like you're—you're thinking—you're feeling like that's a false thing, that you don't want to be part of that anymore.

Clarence: I don't want to be part of that anymore, and I don't be part of that anymore. Everythin' I do [unclear], I use my real name. I had— all of my identification's in my real name.

Lo: Yeah.

Clarence: My birth certificate in my real name. This is me, you know. That right there is from— [referring to my initial recording of his alias]

Lo: Yeah. Yeah, that—I just put that—

Clarence: That's part of my past, using different names and stuff like that—you know wha'am sayin'?

Lo: I see.

Clarence: I'm not doing that— [unclear: with?] the real me. Like, if I can get past a lot of things, but, what they do in the criminal system, if you give 'em a fake name, they—they lock you up under that fake name. Even though they know who you is, but they process all your paper work under that fake name. But they will add your real name to it so, you know, just for birth records and all that. So.

Lo: I see. So it's rea— it sounds to me like you really kind of feel like you made a break from this other identity that you had. Is that true? Or am I getting the wrong—?

Clarence: Yeah. Right. I mean, I worked from that other identity. See, that identity was into a lot of—other things, such as goin' to jail, gettin' out, using drugs, selling drugs, and all that. So, when I don't do anything—that no more, I just be me. Clarence. Ya know, that's who I am. That's who I was born. Clarence.

Soliciting my opinion or expressing concern about my opinion showed the narrator who did so to be a conventional sort. For what is more conventional than caring about what "straight" people with formal authority think? Many of the men were quite concerned about what I thought of them and showed it. Ralph was vocal about this concern. "You know like—ev— even here with you. It's like, Okay. Now that I expressed myself, like Damn! What will she think?" In stark contrast were those who made a show of not caring by rejecting my opinion, as discussed in the next section.

Defying Conventional Authority

The interview also served as a forum for opposing conventional culture. It was well suited to the task. The interview is a mainstream cultural artifact (Atkinson and Silverman 1997; Cicourel 1964; Fontana and Frey 2000). To manipulate it at all is to be subversive. The interview was also permitted and regulated by the justice system. Hence the interview was a convenient battleground for defying *criminal justice* authority. There were particular and often fortuitous ways in which my research participants were able to challenge those in authority, including me, through the interview.

Getting Over

The criminal subculture involves, among other things, "getting over on" or "hustling" conventional persons and institutions, and in particular the justice system (Anderson 1999). Reuben hustled in and through our interview. He made no effort to hide his current marijuana use but instead explained it as medicinal. In fact, he planned to give the same explanation to the probation officer following our interview.

Reuben: You know wha'am sayin', just to keep a little bit of vision as well as my—drops and things.

Lo: Right.

Reuben: That's what I was gonna tell the supervisor, so she won't be on no funny stuff. You know wha'a mean, when she check my drugs an' say whatever. . . . . It's good that it's on there [the tape recorder] too.

Reuben was confident that the fact that the account was taped ensured its acceptance by the probation officer. He accessed power through the interview to avoid being sanctioned. The interview figured in his hustle *and* the hustle exemplified Reuben's self-portrayal as a rebel.

John depicted his present self as mischievous but ultimately decent. He framed his offenses as sport. He enacted his mischievous side during our on-campus interview by calling attention to having parked his car illegally:

John: Now where's the security office again from here? [*laughs*]
Lo: Why do you need the security office?
John: Um, campus police.
Lo: I think it's by Percy [building]. You know where that is?
John: Well, all I know is I took—I parked over in the "A" Decal parking lot [*chuckles*]. Which I probably shouldn't have done.
. . . .
John: Well, if I get ticketed, I'll just pay the fine an' tell my PO [proba- tion officer]—
Lo: Call it [unclear].
John: Yeah, call my PO. "I got ticketed. I parked in the spot. I didn't re- alize that it had to have a decal" [*laughs*] Bullshit—bullshitter [*hearty laughter*].

In jest, Kevin vowed to come back from the dead, after his execution, to "stalk" me. He personalized the remark: "I like you college girls." James made a similar comment to one of my students who had been especially confrontational with him. "I'm comin' back for you, Missy," he said. It is not clear, and perhaps not crucial to determine, whether these situated acts of deviance were used to signify subcultural allegiance or merely to play with the labels others had assigned to them.

Defying Roles, Rules, and Labels

At the start of our interview, I asked Arnell to tell me anything he would like to about his life, and he replied with more than a little contempt: "You got to ask me some questions." This remark can be understood as both a defiance of my power to dictate the terms of the interview, and a call *to* a "standard" interview protocol and the power of interviewers. Both interpretations reflect his sensitivity to power imbalances. Likewise, Arnell was a harsh critic of the justice system's abuse of power.

Reuben's narrative featured disdain for and struggle against authority. He breached not only the conventional expectation that he would answer my questions, but also conventional use of language. During one exchange, I asked Reuben to clarify for me his past and present charges. As the story became more complex (e.g., an arrest for marijuana possession uncovered an outstanding warrant), Reuben began to signal indifference to the meaning that I took from him. He used "Mm-hmm" and "Yeah" whether I understood his meaning correctly or not.

> *Lo:* So what were you—what were some of your other arrests for?
> *Reuben:* Drugs. Weed. Beer.
> *Lo:* Oh, so like—uh—the beer one was just—'cause you were a juvenile?
> *Reuben:* Right. And um, the weed I got caught with—and I had a warrant—for this—charge that I'm on now.
> *Lo:* What's the charge now?
> *Reuben:* It's—um—possession. It's a possession charge. It wasn't really—
> *Lo:* It was for marijuana?
> *Reuben:* Mm-mmm. Cocaine.
> *Lo:* Uh-huh.
> *Reuben:* It wasn't marijuana.
> *Lo:* What— you mean—was it stuff you were using or stuff selling?
> *Reuben:* Mm-hmm.
> *Lo:* Which— which?
> *Reuben:* Selling.
> *Lo:* Uh-huh.
> *Reuben:* Yeah.
> *Lo:* Crack or powder?
> *Reuben:* Yeah.
> *Lo:* Both?
> *Reuben:* [*irritated tone*] Yeah.

Reuben abdicated a speaker's conventional responsibility to affirm meanings when they are correct and, moreover, violated the common expectation that affirmative words signify that meanings *are* correct. But he did not consistently abdicate that responsibility. He repaired my derived understandings in his own time. In this way Reuben gained power in the interaction (see de Certeau 1980).

Kevin refused to sign the informed consent form in its standard form.

He returned the form to me by mail: he signed it only after writing in some additional disclaimers. In a letter he referred to this action: "Come now Lo, you know I'm not the average bone-head in prison." Kevin staged himself as an extraordinary inmate—he inferred that I recognized this—who holds his moral ground. He wrote: "This way I can still assist you with your study, and protect myself. Don't be to [too] bent with me. I'm under constant attack."

Under constant attack indeed. Kevin's federal appeals had repeatedly proven unsuccessful in overturning his murder conviction. Whereas Kevin was unable to save himself from being executed, he was able to enact a desired self as both defiant and good ("I can still assist you") with me. That moral identity was obviously important to Kevin. As he said during one conversation, "Anyone who knows me knows I'm not a punk, a coward, or stupid." Kevin's self-described essential attributes were given substance through his firm stance concerning the consent form.

It is noteworthy that Kevin had nothing substantive to gain from me by portraying a certain self. His impending execution was all but certain, and he fully recognized that I had no power to stop it. Kevin's example suggests that offenders are involved in more than just "conning" when they present moral selves.

Rejecting My Opinion

Just as earlier I described narrators who sought my opinion, real or conjured, there were those who made much of *rejecting* my opinion. Their rejection dramatized their struggle against authority and, in most cases, against a contemporary justice system that professed to know their psyches.

John had a plan to start a business that would be staffed by ex-convicts only. With this plan John generalized his personal claim to decency, to *all* ex-convicts. After describing the plan to me, he added: "You might disagree with me an' . . . you're entitled to your opinion [*laughing*]." John narrated himself as going against the grain all his life. Notwithstanding that identity born in struggle, he had changed into someone who now fights prosocial fights. I thus interpret his statement of resistance ("you're entitled to your opinion") as part of his struggle.

James, like John, told an elastic narrative that pitted him against criminal justice agents. Introducing himself to my class of university students, James dismissed our formal education in criminal justice: "Whatever you all are goin' to school for, what you're majoring in—as far as criminal justice—is totally different when you lookin' at it from my perspective." He thereby established himself as one who has privileged knowledge of the justice system, laying the groundwork for his subsequent position that the justice system is partly to blame for his criminal history.

A similar rejection of what I presumed to know about his situation came from Clarence. He railed against the message of his treatment program, that he must avoid criminogenic environments lest his reform (and thus his reform narrative) be undermined. He aimed his critique at me: "I'm [in] jeopardy every time I walk out the front door, you know wha'am sayin'? I don't put my *recovery* in jeopardy. You know wha'am sayin'—but, it just—you know, there's drugs all around in these corners. You know, come on, face it, I don't [live] like you all live. I wasn't raised like y'all was raised." For Clarence, I represented a justice system (run by mostly white middle-class people like myself) that was hopelessly ignorant of the real-world conditions of a poor black ex-convict. Clarence critiqued my supposed middle-class bias, thereby critiquing the system. His hostility seems to be directed at a justice system/society that fails to distinguish between criminal and street-identified residents of the inner city—which he used to be—and decent people who merely live there (see Anderson 1999). Had Clarence seen me as an ex- or current offender, or as more culturally similar to him, the interview may not have occasioned such an angry reaction, or even a critique.

Oren too inferred an assessment on my part. Regarding a certain emotionally intense phase of his life, he reflected: "That's weird, I know, but—that's how it was." He tended to speak to a supposed failure on my part to understand him correctly. Describing the extent of his psychosis as a result of his father's abuse, he was a particularly harsh critic: "I tell you, I used to be afraid he had the house bugged. I'm serious [*chuckle*]. You know my—I used to be afraid he had the house bugged. Never went in the fridge. Never went in the fridge! Afraid to turn the TV on [*chuckle*]. Ya know. I'm tellin' you: you just don't get it! [*sigh*]." Oren's repeated message to the effect that I did not "get it"—did not appreciate his narrative—reflected his heroic tale in which others (including an abusive father) consistently failed to recognize his humanity.

Enlisting Me as a Participant in Struggle

I was enlisted as a participant in the men's struggles. In his story of struggle, Kevin was fighting for his life on many fronts. The justice system was his main foe. He cast me as a partner in that struggle. In fact, Kevin knew me to be an anti-death penalty activist and thus something of an advocate. Not surprisingly, then, he spoke of the battle against his execution as one I waged with him.

Our roles were very gendered. Kevin protected me in battle. At the close of most of our phone conversations and in his letters to me, he urged me to "stay strong." During our last few calls, Kevin commented that I sounded sad on the phone. Immediately he comforted me, for example by saying: "It's part of life, baby girl." During the next phone call he raised the topic of my ordeal: "Lo, now the last time I spoke with you it was kind of hard on you." Kevin positioned me as traditionally feminine (e.g., sensitive) and assigned himself the complementary role as my manly hero. I played a tangible part in his story of struggle, which also enabled Kevin to enact a good, masculine self.

Wayne, a deaf man, had long struggled against the interference of hearing people in his affairs. His was a very unagentive life story in which hearing people caused his deviance or simply got him into trouble, time and again. His romantic advances toward me implied the same thing.

> *Wayne:* It's better to leave the message with Anthony [halfway house director]. The hearing people? I wouldn't do that. Because I'd really rath— rather have more privacy—
>
> *Lo:* I see.
>
> *Wayne:* With you. And with the hearing people: you know, I don't want them to have to get in touch with you for me or—
>
> *Lo:* Yeah. Mm-hmm.
>
> *Wayne:* —whatever. Because—they'll say "Okay" and they won't say what I want them to say.
>
> *Lo:* Right. Right.
>
> *Wayne:* And they might just call and bother you on the phone or something.
>
> *Lo:* Okay [*chuckle*] Um. That's good, so I will—tell Anthony.
>
> *Wayne:* And—I'll give him the message if there's something for me to tell you and keep it private.
>
> *Lo:* Good. Okay!
>
> *Wayne:* And I need—for you to get a TTY [communication device for the hearing impaired] would be nice, but-! Maybe—you could rent a TTY. Because—when I'm here—ya know—I could call you or you can call me: it would be fun to talk to each other back and forth. But it's better if you have a private number. Because I don't want the other residents to call it and have access to it. I don't want the other people to have it. 'Cause they might bother you and get me in trouble.

The notion that hearing people cause Wayne's troubles is conveyed through his attempt to create greater intimacy with me. Thus did the supposed relationship with me, however fleeting, exemplify and figure into his life story of others provoking him to violence.

Dwight was deviant during our interview: he broke a rule against smoking inside the facility. Besides, he asked me to assist him in getting away with this by signaling to him if the house director returned from an errand. I suggested that we take the interview outside, where he *was* allowed to smoke, but Dwight was resolved to stay indoors because it had been raining and was damp outside:

> *Dwight:* See? Then I started uh—understandin'—under— Did he [halfway house director] come back? Did he come back?
> *Lo:* No. Why?
> *Dwight:* Did he come back?
> *Lo:* No.
> *Dwight:* S' anyway, 'scuse me, I got to have a cigarette.
> *Lo:* Oh.
> *Dwight:* You see a car comes, just say: "Y'all put it out!"
> *Lo:* Oh, 'cause you're not supposed to smoke?
> *Dwight:* Not here.
> *Lo:* Oh, you don't want to go out there?
> *Dwight:* No, it's too wet out there.
> *Lo:* It's too what?
> *Dwight:* Too wet.
> *Lo:* Oh.
> *Dwight:* Been rainin'! You been in here all—it been rainin'!
> *Lo:* Oh, it has been raining. Are you sure? Maybe you should.
> *Dwight:* No! I'm straight!
> *Lo:* Really? 'Cause if it's a rule, you know, and you just finished saying how you like people to keep you on the straight track.
> *Dwight:* Mm-mm!

Not only was Dwight breaking a rule: he solicited my assistance in doing so. I was initially surprised by such blatant deviance given Dwight's liberal use of reform talk. Yet my analysis revealed that Dwight's reform talk pertained specifically to desistance from drug use and crimes against women. In his elastic narrative, he neutralized transgressions committed in the context of struggle with a justice system he deemed unjust. Thus he had no self-critique concerning his participation in prison riots geared toward more humane treatment of inmates. Dwight claimed to have changed in some areas, but saw little need for change ("I'm straight!") in regard to violations that "only" subverted justice authority.

I was enlisted as a participant in struggle—I, a white, educated, female and otherwise circumscribed Other. There is every reason to believe that my statuses prompted some stories and suppressed others. The fact that various statuses the men ascribed to me all correlated with struggle suggests that that theme—along with that of moral decency—has cultural currency: I did not "cause" it. But a researcher with different ascribed characteristics would no doubt have elicited different stories of struggle.

Summary

Previous chapters set out the narratives of my research participants by focusing on two main themes, moral decency and heroic struggle. This chapter explored the situated nature of the narratives. Narrative themes emerged not just *in* the interview, but also *through* the interview. The men used the very fact of the interview, various constructions of who I am, and my supposed confirmation of their self-claims to shape and support their narratives. Thus, consistent with the interactionist proposition that meanings are socially and furthermore situationally constructed (see chap. 2), I discerned meanings of the self forged in the site of data collection.

In general, I have avoided analysis of the effects of my talk and demeanor. Instead, my analysis focused on active uses to which the narrator put the interview. By contrast, the scientific notion of "research effects" seems to invoke unagentive "subjects" whose actions are triggered by those of scientists.

I maintain that, without the discursive opportunities offered by the interview, *the men would have told different stories,* though I am not at all prepared to gauge *how* different. The study, then, suggests sociolinguistic mechanisms through which certain narratives about crime and violence get supported by other people, and not only interviewers, through symbolic interaction. To the extent that such "narrative support" ultimately has desirable (e.g., peaceful) or undesirable (e.g., neutralizing) consequences, further study is well warranted.

In accessing the interview for self-construction, my research participants constructed me as a certain sort of person. Michielsens (2000) observes that "mutual construction is inevitable." Kevin, Dwight, and others positioned me as female and heterosexual, thus somewhat vulnerable. Clarence positioned me in terms of social class, bristling at my middle-class bias. I had clinical expertise for some narrators (e.g., Ralph, Kevin) and inferior intellect for others (e.g., Oren). I was a social scientist who would disseminate what the men had shared with the public, thus helping them to do good (e.g., Dwight, José). I refused to take charge of my life, José alleged, by not learning to drive. In all of these cases, identifying the *other* (me) was a means to identifying the *self*. By chastising *me,* José redeemed himself and substantiated his future claim to an anti-criminal self.

Whereas my review in chapter 2 promoted the benefits (and perhaps the inevitability) of studying identity through narratives, this chapter's findings lead me to recommend that research on identity take the research setting into view. The men I interviewed did not so much *present* negative identities as *grapple* with negative identities. That they frequently presented the struggle proudly does not negate the fact that they presented struggle. My observation of struggle where others see static self-presentation, positive or negative (see, e.g., Chambliss 1964), owes largely to my research method. I solicited stories and I included my own part in the stories as data. The research context is part of the data insofar as the "how" of talk is part of the data (Holstein and Gubrium 2000). Critical and especially feminist researchers are eager to eliminate hierarchies of knowledge construction, hence their attempts to share jurisdiction over protocols and the like. These researchers try to give audience to speakers' "own" stories (e.g., Frankenberg 1993; Presser 2005; Wolf 1996). This study uncovered selves getting constructed in research settings in ways that the researcher could not possibly control.

THE POWER OF STORIES

In that, I think I did rape. In that—that night, that time, I think I did. But I'm not a rapist. You know, I never done it before, and I know in my heart it'll never happen again.

—Tim

I am led to the proposition that there is no fiction or nonfiction as we commonly understand the distinction; there is only narrative.

—E. L. Doctorow, "False Document," 1983

My research has demonstrated that story *telling* impacts stories. In this chapter I reconsider the impact of stories on violence, thus relating storytelling to violent behavior. The power of stories and storytelling leads me to recommend redirection for criminological research and for public policy and interventions, including correctional interventions. But first it is necessary to take another look at heroism as a key plot in the men's stories. The gendered nature of the heroic tale and the gender gap in violence signal the importance of cultural constructions of power, agency, and autonomy, to violence, which in turn suggests that narratives ought to play a central role in criminology.

Is Heroism Criminogenic?

Heroic struggle was the dominant plot with which the men in my study framed the decent self and endowed an incapacitated situation or degraded status with moral purpose. In some cases I was an unwitting partner in constructing stories of heroic struggle. A return to the literature on labeling, and especially the psychosocial processes that labeling instigates, leads me to the question: Might stories of heroic struggle be criminogenic?

Stigmatization and Heroism

Labeling theorists have long maintained that stigmatization leads to reoffending by reducing noncriminal opportunities and social experiences and by hardening one's criminal identity (H. Becker 1963; Kitsuse 1962; Lemert 1967; Schur 1971; Tannenbaum 1938). Contemporary writers have zeroed in on *affective* dimensions of being stigmatized, such as the experience of shame and injustice. These are said to mediate the effects of being stigmatized on criminal behavior.

James Gilligan (1997) believes that shame leads to violence as the shamed person seeks to get rid of shame and attain justice. The most ostensibly "irrational" acts of brutality that Gilligan witnessed and heard about as a prison psychiatrist were in fact directed toward that purpose. Gilligan (1997) writes that, "The most dangerous men on earth are those who are afraid that they are wimps" (66). Sherman (1993) theorizes that shame may lead to reoffending by stimulating pride in defying the justice system. Alternatively, sanctions may either provoke shame and thus deter future crime *or* have no effect. The outcome of sanctions depends on the offender's perception that they are either unfair or stigmatizing, the strength of bonds to the sanctioning agent and community, and the offender's own expressions of shame (Sherman 1993, 460).

According to Braithwaite (1989), shame that tags the individual as bad, as opposed to shame that seeks to reintegrate the individual into the law-abiding collective, leads to recidivism. Braithwaite therefore believes that we should take care in the way that we shame an offender if we are to reduce crime. We want the offender to identify him- or herself as a person who did harmful things but is still "one of us." Most of my interviewees spoke of the opposite experience. They said they did not do (much) harm yet they are treated as outcasts. My study does not weigh in on the effects of such a script, but it does suggest the value of reframing stigmatization as a *narrative* of being stigmatized, for theorizing and addressing harmful action.

The men I interviewed did not just lament and subsequently cope with their having been kicked to the margins of society. They *made meaning* of their perceived marginalization. In particular, they made much of being a lone hero, to the point of delighting in their heroism—most vividly seen in descriptions of one's deviance as sport—and enacting the heroic struggle in the interview with me. The view of stigmatization as criminogenic does not capture the creativity and satisfactions of managing stigmatization—of coming to terms with a "heavy life." Hence, the difference between conceptualizing the actual experience as criminogenic and conceptualizing the narrated experience as criminogenic is that the latter (1) recognizes the individual as an active maker of meaning of his or her own life and (2) problematizes the stigmatization story's more coveted and pervasive cousin; I speak here of the heroic tale (J. Campbell 1949).

The pervasive theme of heroism in the life stories I heard coheres with a culturally dominant model of Western masculinity. A man is a fighter who defies the odds to "make it." Popular stories of men pursuing their goals gain interest—the plot thickens—from obstacles standing in the way of the pursuit. According to this view, "masculinity challenges" (Messerschmidt 2000) are a necessary aspect of doing masculinity. The contest proves the character (Goffman 1967).

The men I interviewed reinterpreted both their criminal trajectory and their poor treatment by others as signifying a persona that is put-upon but takes it "like a man." Sometimes they overcame the obstacles in their way through the use of physical force. In those cases, the story has it that the protagonist did not do violence per se. The adversary's affront or obduracy demanded and justified the aggression; the battle was a noble one. In other narratives, fighting for a good cause—such as Tim's attempting to help his rape victim avoid revictimization—was highlighted even when the narrator acknowledged having done *some* "bad" violence. The bad violence was not the main event in the story. Notably, in all of the men's life stories, current battle against the criminal justice system was featured over other battles.

The Gender Gap in Violence and the Heroic Tale

Though much more research is needed on the question of gender and narrative in the area of criminology, female offenders do not seem to script their lives in the idiom of battle (Gaarder and Belknap 2002; Gilfus 1992; Girshick 1999). Carol Gilligan (1982) famously observed that girls make moral decisions based on interpersonal considerations, whereas males make more abstract moral decisions, conceptualizing more autonomous selves. Against Gilligan's psychodynamic theory, scholars like Hare-Mustin and Marecek (1988) insist that women prioritize relationship because of gender *oppression;* an ethic of care is necessary to survive. Bourgois' (2003) ethnographic work also suggests the necessity of contextualizing how women (and men) story their lives. All of these analyses share the same basic observation, however:

that today's women present a more relational and less adversarial perspective than today's men.[1]

Women and girls perpetrate far less violence than do men and boys. Violence seems to signify something different for females than it does for males (A. Campbell 1993). Bourgois (2003), for example, finds that a vocabulary of motives for Puerto Rican women's violence is mainly confined to jealousy over a husband's unfaithfulness (222–26). Having conducted interviews with active street offenders who had engaged in violent retaliation, Mullins et al. (2004) conclude: "The men in our sample typically talked about retaliatory events emanating from streetcorner disputes, and the women more frequently identified incidents stemming from domestically oriented interactions" (928). Jack (1999) observes that women's violence is about correcting a power imbalance, and thus "improving" a relationship: it is not about vanquishing the Other.

Nor is there evidence that women typically narrate themselves in opposition to the justice system. Girshick (1999) describes a lack of antagonism toward correctional officers among forty female prisoners in North Carolina: "Most prisoners reported getting along with a few guards and trying to avoid the others. Some were respected, and in general all were seen as just 'doing their job'" (93). In Gaarder and Belknap's (2002) research, incarcerated girls whose cases were transferred to adult prison described "mixed feelings about their time in prison" (504). They heard girls comment on the good that prison did them by removing them from destructive circumstances. They also heard girls critique the overuse of incarceration. They did not hear strong condemnation. "For many girls, the hardest part of prison was being separated from their families" (Gaarder and Belknap 2002, 504). Conceivably, the way that females in this culture script their lives helps to prohibit violence, and the way that males in this culture script their lives helps to enable it.

And, as Naffine (1997) reminds us, the gender gap is a signpost for a general theory of criminal behavior. That is, a theory that explains criminal behavior must account for men's disproportionate involvement as offenders and especially serious violent offenders. It is also time that, in theorizing criminal behavior, criminology take discourse and language seriously.

Narratives of Powerlessness and Difference

Powerlessness—vulnerability in the face of crime inducements and other people's crimes—and *difference*—self as distinct and autonomous agent—are elements of many of the heroic tales I heard. The protagonist is threatened and differs from other people and especially from one's victim. I propose that narratives of powerlessness and difference conduce to harmful action.

A narrative of powerlessness is discernible in other close studies of offenders' talk. Matza (1964) observes that depicting oneself as the subject of external influences spurs a "mood of fatalism"—of experiencing oneself as being "pushed around" (89). While in this mood, "dramatic reassurance that [one] can still make things happen is necessary" (ibid., 189). For Matza, such reassurance comes in the form of offending. Katz (1988a) is likewise attuned to criminal conduct as signifier of a self that can still make things happen. The precondition for use of crime in this way is the actor's insecurity about his or her power.

In her perceptive examination of contemporary American men, Faludi (1999) makes a similar point: "Violence stands in for action but is also an act of concealment, a threatening mask that hides a lack of purpose" (37). Faludi collected data on a diverse array of men in the United States, including participants in a batterers' group, avid football fans, Vietnam War veterans, actors in pornographic films, and astronauts. Her findings contradict conceptions of men brandishing power: "Many in the women's movement and in the mass media complain that men just 'don't want to give up the reins of power.' But that would seem to have little applicability to the situations of most men, who individually feel not the reins of power in their hands but its bit in their mouths. What's more likely is that they are clinging to a phantom status" (41).

For Faludi, men today are in crisis.[2] Her argument about men, power, and powerlessness echoes Gilligan's (1997) insistence that students of violence take seriously the violator's scripting, in the first instance, of vulnerability. Gilligan reports: "Murderers see themselves as literally having no other choice" (112). Scholars and the public have not believed such offenders because their talk (not coincidentally for Matza [1964]) resembles the legalistic discourses that might reduce sanctions. But the truth-value of such talk is a matter separate from its role in galvanizing action, whether it is one's own action or, in the case of collective violence, the actions of others. Mark Currie (1998) maintains that narratives that mobilize people to violence are not "inventions of the mind but political and ideological practices as much a part of the material texture of reality as bombs and factories, wars and revolutions" (90). It remains the task of scholars to examine how violence and narrated identity co-operate—that is, to identify the mechanisms for a causal relationship. Violence may confer general reassurance of agency in some cases, while in others, and especially in cases of collective violence, perpetrators may be avenging one or several (supposed) dominators in particular or eliminating their alleged threat (Mason 2002; Vetlesen 2005).

The second storyline that I propose as conducive to harmful action is a narrative of difference. It depicts would-be targets as qualitatively different from oneself. An autonomous self is presented in the heroic tales my research participants told, though foes varied—notably, as external or internal. The likelihood of their future violence might be associated with the adversary depicted, the degree to which the adversary is internalized/externalized, or the degree to which the heroic struggle is "alive" or especially self-defining. Weighing in on these alternate possibilities is, again, a matter for future research.

A narrative of difference is particularly evident where *collective* harms are concerned. Sternberg (2003) observes that genocide, massacres, and terrorism rest on a depiction of violence targets as violence *threats* who are qualitatively different kinds of people than the rest of us: "*The target is revealed to be anathema*" (319; emphasis in original). Black (2004) similarly proposes that high social distance between perpetrators and targets is typical of terrorist attacks.[3] Distinctions are not given in the nature of things (Zerubavel 1997); they are socially constructed, sometimes *for the sake of* inflicting harm, as seen in any number of genocidal atrocities (Vetlesen 2005). Differentiation in the case of group violence seems to involve the denial of individuality, and thus the location of the other in an out-*group* (Kelman 1973). Of Nazi propaganda, Sternberg (2003) writes: "The negation of intimacy was fostered by condensing the Jews into a single disgusting entity" (311). Vetlesen (2005) describes the process in the genocide in the former Yugoslavia the 1990s: "In Bosnia, even though the assaults often took place in conditions of proximity, on a person-to-person basis, the perpetrator would frequently attempt to *deindividualize* his particular victim. If known—and recognized—by his victim, the perpetrator would make an effort to deny that the person before him possessed the status of unique individual that till then had obtained between the two of them in a mutual and taken-for-granted manner" (260; emphasis in original). Narratives of difference may also widen the scope of in-group members, as in the case of pro-life killers who identify the virtuous living as including the unborn—represented, significantly, as unborn whites—in Mason's (2002) analysis. Narration is creative but tethered to existing arrangements.

Of course, distinguishing self from other is part and parcel of identity formation (Jenkins 2004). What appears to be at stake in harmful action is a radical demarcation of self from other—what some criminologists (unreflexively) term a lack of empathy (see Melossi 2000). Such extreme differentiation may be rooted in fundamental understandings of the world, even "prosocial" ones like the Judeo-Christian understanding of good and evil, as Judith Kay (2005) conceives it: "With such a split in the fundamental ontology of the world—good and bad, light and dark, armies of glory and armies of darkness—it is easy to think of humans as being similarly split. . . . It is not a question of a good person (ontologically) behaving badly (morally), but of some people becoming evil in their inherent nature" (Kay 2005, 133). The most normal of endeavors and the most virtuous of norms blur into violence. One of those endeavors is the scholarly effort to understand crime.

Toward a More Reflexive Criminology

Critical criminologists have long observed the contribution of criminology to penal harm through the discursive construction of dangerous and blameworthy criminal subjects. But the contribution must be viewed in its specificity: the alternative is nihilism. I view criminology as actively purveying narratives of powerlessness and difference.

Many of the dominant criminological theories locate crime in criminal natures or at least long-honed predilections. Some theories are more explicit in this depiction than others. Gottfredson and Hirschi's (1990) "general theory of crime" is one of the more dramatic examples of a theory that features offenders whose dispositions are different from those of the rest of us. By a young age, offenders' antisocial predilections are so firmly established that incapacitation is the only strategy we have for controlling them. Yet, as Garland (2001) points out, contemporary criminology generally orients to the control of persons who are unlike the rest of us.

In the history of the discipline, few criminologists have considered their role in constructing the problem of crime and those problem persons we call offenders. Naffine (1997) writes: "Often [criminologists] have been quite oblivious of the fact that they have been constituting a body of facts and theory all along, selecting certain objects to include in their studies (and in the same moment defining the meaning of those objects), and selecting others to exclude. Instead, there has been a tendency simply to treat crime and the criminal as brutal facts, as phenomena which are naturally occurring out in the world, demanding the criminologist's attention" (9). I too am guilty of reifying "offenders" simply by using that term. My study proceeds as if there is such a being as "an offender." By asking participants if they had met evil people in prison, I implied that evil people exist and that the problem of evil is a problem of individuals. (And now I address the reader as though he or she is *not* this type of being.) There is additional (and inestimable) trouble with what I did *not* do: for example, I did not (and do not now) refer to other actors in my study that do harm, such as prison officials, as "offenders." At the outset of my study, I was not especially mindful of my role in the stories of violent men. Now that I have analyzed my data, including data on my interactions with research participants, the metanarratives of my research and thus my place in my findings are more clear. Reviewing my interview transcripts, I see how I communicated features of mainstream discourses on offenders.

Criminologists *must* become more reflexive. To the extent that we can, we must reveal our contributions to "crime," "criminals," and "criminogenic variables," because what goes unrecognized cannot be changed. To begin to reveal such contributions requires another analytical step and a measure of humility. Much as criminologists have deconstructed mass media depictions of crime, we can deconstruct our own depictions, acknowledging all the while that we cannot help but frame our subject matter in some way—and that way will inevitably be influenced by the larger culture. I am optimistic. Such disparate developments in the discipline as peacemaking criminology (Pepinsky and Quinney 1991), constitutive criminology (Henry and Milovanovic 1996), and convict criminology (Ross and Richards 2002) thematize the discursive construction of offenders. I am encouraged by these developments and by other work that is reflexive (e.g., Cohn 1987; Maher 1997; Woolford 2006), that resists the reification of causes and effects (e.g., Halsey 2006), that theorizes tolerance for harmful action as well as the active doing of it (e.g., Crelinsten 2003; Huggins, Haritos-Fatouros, and Zimbardo 2002; Vetlesen 2005), and that looks to systemic bases for harmful action (e.g., Bourgois 2003; Matthews and Kauzlarich 2000).

The call for reflexivity can easily be construed narrowly and not sociologically—say, as a minor fad—just as my study may be taken as a demonstration in data corruption. My main finding, however, is not that I biased the stories by conveying hegemonic understandings of crime and criminals. My main finding is that I played a role in the stories, one co-designated by my research participants. The inventiveness of the research participant and the dynamism of "the offender" suggest nothing short of the need for a new social policy agenda than is currently being followed in the United States.

Redirection for Policy

Several prominent theorists recognize that American culture, and specifically its values, shapes offending (E. Currie 1997; Matza and Sykes 1961; Merton

1938; Messner and Rosenfeld 2006). In the perspective advanced here, mainstream American culture shapes offending *narratives*. Polanyi (1985) derives elements of "the American story," a few of which include:

- "Not having" is proof of the fact of not being an adult since an adult has what he needs and can do what he must do in order to satisfy those needs (134)
- Each individual is alone and must satisfy his own needs because he cannot depend on another person to satisfy his needs in all circumstances (ibid.)
- Causing pain is wrong and wrongdoing should be punished with pain (136)
- Not working hurts everyone because all must work if life is to continue (139)
- "Proper people" have power over other people (140)

Analogous story elements that conduce to harmful action include: humans advance through struggle; ends justify means; and humans, especially men, *should* be in control of their circumstances. Hence the envisaging of struggle across social space; the legitimation of harm-causing means for just ends; and the practical intolerability of threats to control, or threats to the future satisfaction of needs. These story elements are conveyed through both criminal justice and more general social policies.

Criminal Justice Practice

If ends justify means, then violence is a legitimate tool for stopping violence (Kay 2005). And so it is perceived to be, at least in the United States, where the death penalty is available in a majority of states and the killing of innocent suspects—unintended violence—for the sake of a larger program of control is condoned. The notion that government violence is more acceptable than other forms of violence is both fertilizer for neutralization and a model for narrating difference. Larry said he has no remorse for killing a man while intoxicated because he didn't "mean to do it." Arnell remarked that "fightin' ain't violence . . . when it's street." These remarks serve the same classificatory and responsibility-reducing functions as the vocabularies of nuclear war scientists Cohn (1987) studied.

In the United States, terms like "war" and "battle" are commonplace in criminal justice policy discussions, as they are in our judicial system (Zehr 1995). Elliott Currie (1998) refers to the "myth that there are no credible alternatives" as guiding the contemporary get-tough mandate (78). Adversarial processes both animate and emerge from stories of powerlessness and difference. We must change criminal justice processes so that perpetrators are not exiled or branded or, more fundamentally, pitted against other people, including victims. Change these processes, and the heroic tales of offenders and would-be offenders lose some of their grounding.

Dialogue is an essential tool for changing stories, yet it is all but absent from standard criminal justice practices in both the courts and in corrections. Restorative justice encounters, including victim-offender mediation and truth-telling commissions (Minow 1998; Van Ness and Strong 2001; Zehr 1995), feature talk and especially stories. In these encounters, victims and offenders meet, often with support persons and always with a facilitator, to share their perspectives on the crime. Victims and offenders, as well as communities, have needs that led to the crime and that resulted from the crime. A major focus of restorative justice talk is addressing these needs.

I have found that restorative justice encounters create space for examining social injustices as well as those injustices we call crime, and problematize victim and offender positions (Presser and Hamilton 2006). At the same time, I appreciate critical evaluations that share my concern with the repression of participants through the discourses of restorative justice or criminal law, which in many cases restorative justice has not altered (Arrigo and Schehr 1998; Cook 2006). In the 1970s, a similarly critical gaze was cast on correctional rehabilitation (Cullen and Gilbert 1982). More recently Fox (1999) has applied Foucault's theory of power/knowledge to cognitive correctional interventions in particular. Cognitive skills programs help offenders to modify their criminal "thinking errors," in part by verbally articulating new thinking patterns (Van Voorhis et al. 2000). I question whether cognitive interventions *as currently designed and implemented* achieve justice—both in the sense of reducing long-term reoffending among participants, which is their explicit objective, and in the sense of offering a vision of peaceful relations generally.

Most immediately, cognitive interventions for offenders discourage creative deliberation about one's crimes. Fox (1999) found that male inmates in a Vermont prison who resisted the rhetoric of cognitive treatment—emphasizing their ability to make choices and control the self but not others—were seen as evidencing criminogenic pathology. To use Loseke's (2003) constructionist terms, participants' resistance was taken to be proof that the inmates are *problem persons*. The basis for this diagnosis is made plain in typologies of thinking "errors" and "distortions" that, for example, place blame for one's actions on other people (see, e.g., Ross and Fabiano 1985; Yochelson and

Samenow 1976). Informed by neo-liberalism, the dominant story of violence posits a private, not a public problem. Elliott Currie (1998) maintains that "many programs that purport to offer 'rehabilitation' for offenders have tried to 'treat' them in isolation from the broader social environment which surrounds them" (105). Currie is mainly concerned to view crime in ecological context. My concern is with the conventional sources of violent *stories*, which the cognitive correctional interventions ignore.

In the cognitive treatment literature, the problematic attitudes of offenders are their own (see, e.g., Andrews and Bonta 2006). They are not considered as conventional. At a minimum, then, these programs do nothing to change the stories of "the rest of us." But even with their intended clientele, in privatizing "their" violence and its cognitive foundations, these programs deny the co-construction of cognitions at all times, including in treatment—in those spoken forums where the cognitions are targeted. One implication of my research is that counselors (as well as fellow group participants) will inevitably be cast in particular roles in a story—say, as an authority figure with whom one is locked in battle—and thus ought to heed just how they engage with that story. *Authorizing* a different pattern of thought stands to backfire. Another implication of my research is that people who have perpetrated violence voluntarily grapple with why they did it. In telling their stories, they strive to establish agency (McKendy 2006; O'Connor 2000). Increasing agency is a project to be taken on conjointly, through storytelling and more tangible strategies of empowerment (discussed below).

Correctional interventions (as well as restorative justice encounters) can and should be grounded in critical criminology. Such critical interventions would encourage participants to become cultural critics (Presser 2003, 820), appraising the story forms they have adopted and contemplating how these story forms are supported by and reproduce material inequalities. Active engagement with the "treatment" protocol would be welcome, much as we (should) welcome active learning in college courses. These programs' focus on harmful thinking need not be disposed of per se, but the view of such thinking as residing in the few and as requiring governance from the expert other is counterproductive. Denying as it does the prevalence of harmful thinking among citizens and state agents alike, it will prompt defiance, and it will leave justifications for harmful action intact in the culture.

Social Policies

Beyond the criminal justice system, but inextricably tied to it, the structural foundations of narratives of powerlessness and difference for individual harm-doers such as the men I interviewed include the concrete, interrelated injustices we find in the contemporary United States: among other things, joblessness and the scarcity of basic income supports, economic inequality and exploitation, and racist discrimination. Add to these the hardships heaped especially on ex-convicts, such as obstacles to getting decent jobs, higher education, and housing (Olivares et al. 1996). These injustices and hardships provide substance for criminogenic stories.

More compassionate and just social arrangements that would universalize basic income and health care eliminate some of the tangible resources for narrating victimhood and alienation. Such policies are advised for their own sake, but they are probably not enough to alter dominant models of personhood—at least not in the short run. As Fine (1993a) puts it, we use "whatever is handy to construct our own selves" (76). Many powerful offenders, apparently high on the global ladder of status and wealth, depict themselves as having come precipitously close to losing it all. Privileged youth engage in destructive activities when they "fail" to achieve perfection in their every endeavor, so acculturated are they in zero-tolerance of failure (E. Currie 2005). Never mind that these are not "really" underdogs: the story of the underdog coming from behind to win may still guide their actions.

In that regard, I am reminded of Tim recounting his rape. He shared that he "felt victimized" because the victim had agreed to sexual activity but changed her mind midway through. He also deployed hypothetical scenarios of the victim intimidating *him* that had him running scared from the scene. Power deficits (Tittle 1995) are scripted. The script matters. The script changes. Tim condemned the man he was who had raped, but he also struggled to redefine the act as not a rape. He spoke critically of that old Tim who interpreted the woman's behavior as an affront that necessitated his raping her, but he also urged me—the actual, specific me—to consider that interpretation as accurate. As a researcher my goal was to understand the story and storyteller. If my goal were more directly peacemaking, with the understandings I have gained from the research, I would respectfully and empathetically help Tim continue to interrogate his own story.

Notes

Chapter 1: Self and Story

1. What is violence? I define it here as direct, intended bodily harm—more narrowly than alternative conceptions in which nonbodily action, including language, may constitute violence (e.g., Henry and Milovanovic 1996; van Dijk 1995). Note, though, that my definition maintains the requirement, characteristic of the legal conception, of *intent* to do bodily harm.

2. The word "story" is reserved for an account of a particular episode in one's life. Gergen and Gergen (1988) have usefully referred to such episodic accounts as "nested narratives," meaning "narratives within narratives" (34).

3. I refer to all but two research participants by a pseudonym, also referring to other identifiers (e.g., interview location, family members' names) with made-up terms. Clarence and Vaughan were the two exceptions. Both rejected such contrivances. Clarence insisted that I use his real name (see chap. 9 for details). So too did Vaughan, who shared full details of his story in a published book (Booker and Phillips 1994).

4. Polkinghorne (1988), summarizing Ricoeur's position on the relationship between narrative and experience, presents these three perspectives as follows: "The relationship can be defined in any of three ways. The first two ways assume that life, as lived, is independent of narrative description. If this separation is accepted, then one can hold either that narrative gives an accurate description of the way the world really is or that it is descriptively discontinuous with the real world it depicts. The third position, advocated here, is that aspects of experience itself are presented originally as they appear in the narration and that narrative form is not simply imposed on preexistent real experiences but helps to give them form" (67–68).

5. In addition, the researcher makes choices concerning what to analyze and highlight as important: data, variables, and findings. For this reason as well, an under-

standing of the world "is necessarily partial and is always hermeneutic" (Scheper-Hughes 1992, 23).

6. This despite classic sociological work positing verbalizations about behavior (Mills 1940) and about the self (Foote 1951) as motivating behavior.

7. Elsewhere (e.g., Presser 2004) I refer to these as return narratives—a more precise but less elegant expression.

Chapter 2: Offender Identities, Offender Narratives

1. What I call labeling theorists constitutes a group with its own complex issues of identity, for labeling theory was largely defined from without. To quote Best (2004), it "was not, in fact, a theory, but rather a more-or-less shared orientation to issues of deviance and social control" (20)—one that saw social control as a precondition of most deviance.

2. See Gilgun and McLeod (1999) for a comparable argument about male violence and hegemonic masculinity; they do not stress structural deprivation.

3. Toch's (1993) work suggests the close relation between identity and narrative. The telling of "war stories" constitutes the "dragon-slaying" identities of violent men who justify their violence as morally right.

4. Such interpretations fit the definition of narrative offered by Gergen and Gergen (1988)—that it concern an event but also say something in value terms about the narrator (20–21). My definition of narrative is broader, however.

5. In addition, so-called cultural deviance theories explain community-level violence as a function of subcultural values or codes, which may be considered shared narratives (W. Miller 1958; Wolfgang and Feracutti 1967; cf. Anderson 1999).

Chapter 3: Thinking about Research Effects

1. In Goffman's (1959) words: "Life may not be much of a gamble, but interaction is" (243). Strauss (1997) refers to face-to-face interaction as "a fluid, moving, 'running' process" (57), the course of which "is due in considerable part to unwitting responses made by each participant" (60).

2. Psychoanalytic thinkers are an exception. They consider how processes situated in the clinical encounter (e.g., transference and counter-transference) shape personalities. Furthermore, to quote Rosenwald (1992), they have "taken self-formation through narrative especially seriously" (267). In that their chief concern is not in generating social theory, I treat them separately.

3. In general, conversation analysts study conversation that takes place in "naturally occurring interactional settings" and not research settings (Boden 1990, 248). The exclusion of research talk is problematic as interviewing "has become a routine procedure in everyday life" (Cicourel 1964, 99).

4. In addition, I concur with Athens (1994), who states that "The people in whose company we find ourselves undergoing a social experience are not our only interlocutors. We also converse with *phantom others*, who are not present, but whose impact

upon us is no less than the people who are present during our social experiences" (525).

Chapter 4: Research Methods When Research Is Being Researched

1. All four states in which interviews were conducted—New Jersey, New York, Ohio, and Pennsylvania—had the death penalty during the study period.

2. Others who have interviewed convicted offenders have likewise rarely come across outright denial of misconduct (e.g., Benson 1985).

3. The topic of class that day was "The Offender's Experience." Seven students, a colleague (who had arranged the meeting), and I engaged in a very rich discussion with James. Some weeks after the class meeting/discussion, James and I scheduled a formal interview, to include just the two of us. James did not appear for our interview and did not contact me; I learned later that he had violated his parole. I have only the polyphonic talk from that classroom appearance available as data.

4. The author/researcher goes by "Lo."

5. The view of "event time" as preexisting "story time" is itself an artifact of drawing lines between events and representations of events (B. Smith 1981), and between doing and speaking (Atkinson and Coffey 2002; Austin 1962; J. Bruner 1990; van Dijk 1995). My study problematizes those dichotomies. To define relational statements or any other present-oriented statements as *necessarily* extraneous to the narrative is no doubt related to the idea that research (reporting) activity is extricable from "the data."

6. N5 (and similar software in the NUD*IST series) involves hierarchical structuring. The structure created by the user can be reorganized as analysis proceeds.

Chapter 5: Reform Narratives

1. Reform narratives and stability narratives map onto the three generic forms identified by Gergen and Gergen (1988, 24): (1) the stability narrative, suggesting a steady state, (2) the progressive narrative, suggesting change in a more favorable direction, and (3) the regressive narrative, suggesting change in a less favorable direction. My reform narrative is a combination of (2) and (3)—a regressive-to-progressive combination—in that it describes a moral fall followed by moral renewal.

Chapter 6: Stability Narratives

1. Matza has called attention to the extensive overlap that exists between subcultural and conventional values (Matza 1964; Matza and Sykes 1961). Others have drawn useful distinctions between these "codes" (Anderson 1999; Wieder 1983). For the men I interviewed, the codes were not mutually exclusive. That is, they did not reject mainstream values (e.g., murder is wrong), even when they extolled some subcultural value (e.g., violence may be necessary), a finding consistent with Matza's argument.

2. These three forms of gendered violence are historically and ideologically related, based on a worldview about masculinity and femininity underpinning all three (Kimmel 2004).

3. I only heard about "being beat" and "buggin'" from African American participants, but the narration of crime as uncharacteristic of self was not race specific.

4. Klapp (1954) distinguishes three deviant person types, the hero, villain, and fool. Many of my research participants channeled that distinction to dispute being positioned as villainous.

Chapter 7: Elastic Narratives

1. A fatalistic attitude about one's future was evident in stability narratives as well. What is distinctive about elastic narratives is inclusion of talk about reform, hence the joint appearance of fatalism and desistance references.

Chapter 8: Tales of Heroic Struggle

1. Nelson was of Indian descent. He was born and raised in Guyana.

2. I include the juvenile justice system here as well. The narrators spoke as though the systems were of a piece.

Chapter 9: The Situated Construction of Narratives

1. Other men *rejected* supposed evaluation on my part, a phenomenon I discuss in terms of enacting one's self, in the next section.

2. The researcher's ignorance about her impact on the narratives may be considered a technique to avoid purposely biasing the data.

Chapter 10: The Power of Stories

1. Feminist criminological and legal discourses that minimize the agency of violent women (H. Allen 1998; Kruttschnitt and Carbone-Lopez 2006; Morrissey 2003) might shape violent women's narratives in ways that understate autonomy and overstate connection. My argument that gender conditions narratives does not dispute that possibility. Indeed, my research is partly a demonstration of the patterning of individual narratives after societal discourses.

2. Faludi "genders" and circumscribes historically the dilemma that Ernest Becker (1973) calls a "crisis of heroism" (see also Mason 2002). Faludi observes that in popular and especially feminist discussions of problems among men, "what gets discussed is how men are exercising or abusing their control and power, not whether a lack of mooring, a lack of context, is causing their anguish" (13).

3. The two storylines—powerlessness and difference—"meet" where the differentiated Other is depicted as threatening the actor in a way that reduces his or her agency. For example, Alvarez (1997) summarizes analyses of Nazi propaganda: "This propaganda drove home three messages: the Jews were subhuman vermin; they threatened the racial purity of Aryans; and they threatened the German state" (163). Conceivably, violent action entails a marked "othering," whereas nonviolent action does not.

References

Agar, Michael, and Jerry R. Hobbs. 1982. "Interpreting Discourse: Coherence and the Analysis of Ethnographic Interviews." *Discourse Processes* 5:1–32.

Agnew, Robert. 1992. "Foundation for a General Strain Theory of Crime and Delinquency." *Criminology* 30:47–87.

Akers, Ronald L. 1998. *Social Learning and Social Structure: A General Theory of Crime and Deviance.* Boston: Northeastern University Press.

Allen, Hilary. 1998. "Rendering Them Harmless: The Professional Portrayal of Women Charged with Serious Violent Crimes." In Kathleen Daly and Lisa Maher, eds., *Criminology at the Crossroads: Feminist Readings in Crime and Justice.* New York: Oxford University Press. 54–68.

Allen, Judith. 1989. "Men, Crime and Criminology: Recasting the Questions." *International Journal of the Sociology of Law* 17:19–39.

Alvarez, Alexander. 1997. "Adjusting to Genocide: The Techniques of Neutralization and the Holocaust." *Social Science History* 21 (2): 139–78.

Anderson, Elijah. 1999. *Code of the Street: Decency, Violence, and the Moral Life of the Inner City.* New York: W. W. Norton and Co.

Andrews, D. A., and James Bonta. 2006. *The Psychology of Criminal Conduct,* 4th ed. Cincinnati: Anderson.

Arendell, Terry. 1997. "Reflections on the Researcher-Researched Relationship: A Woman Interviewing Men." *Qualitative Sociology* 20 (3): 341–68.

Armitage, Susan H. 1983. "The Next Step." *Frontiers: A Journal of Women Studies* 7 (1): 3–8.

Arrigo, Bruce A., Dragan Milovanovic, and Robert C. Schehr. 2005. *The French Connection in Criminology: Rediscovering Crime, Law, and Social Change.* Albany: State University of New York Press.

Arrigo, Bruce A., and Robert C. Schehr. 1998. "Restoring Justice for Juveniles: A Critical Analysis of Victim-Offender Mediation." *Justice Quarterly* 15 (4): 629–66.

Athens, Lonnie. 1997. *Violent Criminal Acts and Actors Revisited.* Urbana: University of Illinois Press.

———. 1994. "The Self As a Soliloquy." *Sociological Quarterly* 35 (3): 521–32.

Atkinson, Paul, and Amanda Coffey. 2002. "Revisiting the Relationship between Participant Observation and Interviewing." In Jaber F. Gubrium and James A. Holstein, eds., *Handbook of Interview Research: Context and Method.* Thousand Oaks, Calif.: Sage. 801–14.

Atkinson, Paul, and David Silverman. 1997. "Kundera's *Immortality:* The Interview Society and the Invention of the Self." *Qualitative Inquiry* 3 (3): 304–25.

Austin, J. L. 1962. *How to Do Things with Words.* Cambridge, Mass.: Harvard University Press.

Bachman, Ronet, and Russell K. Schutt. 2001. *The Practice of Research in Criminology and Criminal Justice.* Thousand Oaks, Calif.: Pine Forge.

Bandura, Albert. 1973. *Aggression: A Social Learning Analysis.* Englewood Cliffs, N.J.: Prentice-Hall.

Barthes, Roland. 1977. *Image, Music, Text.* Selected and translated by Stephen Heath. New York: Hill and Wang.

Becker, Ernest. 1973. *The Denial of Death.* New York: Free Press.

Becker, Howard S. 1963. *Outsiders: Studies in the Sociology of Deviance.* New York: Free Press.

———. 1958. "Problems of Inference and Proof in Participant Observation." *American Sociological Review* 23 (6): 652–60.

Belknap, Joanne. 2001. *The Invisible Woman: Gender, Crime, and Justice,* 2nd ed. Belmont, Calif.: Wadsworth.

Bem, Daryl J. 1967. "Self-Perception: An Alternative Interpretation of Cognitive Dissonance Phenomena." *Psychological Review* 74:183–200.

Benson, Michael L. 1985. "Denying the Guilty Mind: Accounting for Involvement in a White-Collar Crime." *Criminology* 23 (4): 583–607.

Benveniste, Emile. 1971. *Problems in General Linguistics.* Trans. Mary Elizabeth Meek. Coral Gables, Fla.: University of Miami Press.

Berger, Peter L., and Thomas Luckmann. 1966. *The Social Construction of Reality: A Treatise in the Sociology of Power.* New York: Anchor Books.

Berkowitz, Leonard. 1989. "Frustration-Aggression Hypothesis: Examination and Reformulation." *Psychological Bulletin* 106 (1): 59–73.

Best, Joel. 2004. *Deviance: Career of a Concept.* Belmont, Calif.: Wadsworth.

Black, Donald. 2004. "The Geometry of Terrorism." *Sociological Theory* 22 (1): 14–25.

Bloom, Barbara, Barbara Owen, and Stephanie Covington. 2003. *Gender-Responsive Strategies: Research, Practice, and Guiding Principles for Women Offenders.* Washington, D.C.: National Institute of Corrections.

Blumer, Herbert. 1969. *Symbolic Interactionism: Perspective and Method*. Berkeley: University of California Press.

Blumstein, Philip. 1991. "The Production of Selves in Personal Relationships." In Judith Howard and Peter Callero, eds., *The Self-Society Dynamic*. New York: Cambridge University Press. 305–22.

Boden, Deirdre. 1990. "People Are Talking: Conversation Analysis and Symbolic Interaction." In Howard S. Becker and Michal M. McCall, eds., *Symbolic Interaction and Cultural Studies*. Chicago: University of Chicago Press. 244–74.

Booker, Vaughan, with David Phillips. 1994. *From Prison to Pulpit: My Road to Redemption*. New York: Cadell and Davies.

Bortner, M. A., and Linda M. Williams. 1997. *Youth in Prison: We the People of Unit Four*. New York: Routledge.

Bosworth, Mary. 1999. *Engendering Resistance: Agency and Power in Women's Prisons*. Sydney: Ashgate.

Bourdieu, Pierre, and Loic Wacquant. 1992. *An Invitation to Reflexive Sociology*. Chicago: University of Chicago Press.

Bourgois, Philippe. 2003. *In Search of Respect*, 2nd ed. Cambridge, UK: Cambridge University Press.

Braithwaite, John. 1989. *Crime, Shame and Reintegration*. Cambridge, UK: Cambridge University Press.

Bruner, Edward M. 1986. "Ethnography as Narrative." In Victor W. Turner and Edward M. Bruner, eds., *The Anthropology of Experience*. Urbana: University of Illinois Press. 139–55.

Bruner, Jerome. 1990. *Acts of Meaning*. Cambridge, Mass.: Harvard University Press.

———. 1987. *Actual Minds, Possible Worlds*. Cambridge, Mass.: Harvard University Press.

Burgess, Ernest W. 1966. "Discussion." In Clifford R. Shaw, *The Jack-Roller: A Delinquent Boy's Own Story*. Chicago: University of Chicago Press. 184–97.

Burke, Peter J. 1991. "Identity Processes and Social Stress." *American Sociological Review* 56 (6): 836–49.

———, and Stephen L. Franzoi. 1988. "Studying Situations and Identities Using Experiential Sampling Methodology." *American Sociological Review* 53 (4): 559–68.

Campbell, Anne. 1993. *Men, Women, and Aggression*. New York: Basic Books.

Campbell, Joseph. 1949. *The Hero with a Thousand Faces*. New York: Pantheon.

Caspi, Avshalom, Daryl J. Bem, and Glen H. Elder Jr. 1989. "Continuities and Consequences of Interactional Styles across the Life Course." *Journal of Personality* 57 (2): 375–405.

Chambliss, William. 1964. "The Negative Self: An Empirical Assessment of a Theoretical Assumption." *Sociological Inquiry* 35:108–12.

Chanfrault-Duchet, Marie-Françoise. 2000. "Textualisation of the Self and Gender Identity in the Life-Story." In Tess Cosslett, Celia Lury, and Penny Summerfield, eds., *Feminism and Autobiography: Texts, Theories, Methods.* London: Routledge.

Charmaz, Kathy. 2002. "Qualitative Interviewing and Grounded Theory Analysis." In Jaber F. Gubrium and James A. Holstein, eds., *Handbook of Interview Research: Context and Method.* Thousand Oaks, Calif.: Sage. 675–710.

Christie, Nils. 1993. *Crime Control as Industry: Toward Gulags, Western Style.* London: Routledge.

Cicourel, Aaron Victor. 1964. *Method and Measurement in Sociology.* New York: Free Press of Glencoe.

Clear, Todd R. 1994. *Harm in American Penology.* Albany: State University of New York Press.

————. 2007. *Imprisoning Communities: How Mass Incarceration Makes Disadvantaged Neighborhoods Worse.* New York: Oxford University Press.

Clemmer, Donald. 1958. *The Prison Community.* New York: Holt, Rinehart, and Winston.

Cohen, Albert K. 1955. *Delinquent Boys.* New York: Free Press of Glencoe.

Cohn, Carol. 1987. "Sex and Death in the Rational World of Defense Intellectuals." *Signs: Journal of Women in Culture and Society* 12 (4): 687–718.

Collins, Randall. 1987. "Interaction Ritual Chains, Power and Property: The Micro-Macro Connection as an Empirically Based Theoretical Problem." In Jeffrey C. Alexander, Bernhard Giesen, Richard Münch, and Neil J. Smelser, eds., *The Micro-Macro Link.* Berkeley: University of California Press. 193–206.

Connell, R. W. 1995. *Masculinities.* Berkeley: University of California Press.

Cook, Kimberly J. 2006. "Doing Difference and Accountability in Restorative Justice Conferences." *Theoretical Criminology* 10 (1): 107–24.

Cooley, Charles Horton. 1902. *Human Nature and the Social Order.* New York: Scribner's.

Crelinsten, Ronald D. 2003. "The World of Torture: A Constructed Reality." *Theoretical Criminology* 7 (3): 293–318.

Cressey, Donald R. 1953. *Other People's Money: A Study in the Social Psychology of Embezzlement.* Glencoe, Ill.: Free Press.

Cullen, Francis T., and Karen E. Gilbert. 1982. *Reaffirming Rehabilitation.* Cincinnati: Anderson.

Currie, Elliott. 2005. *The Road to Whatever: Middle-Class Culture and the Crisis of Adolescence.* New York: Metropolitan Books.

————. 1998. *Crime and Punishment in America.* New York: Metropolitan Books.

————. 1997. "Market, Crime and Community." *Theoretical Criminology* 1 (2): 147–72.

Currie, Mark. 1998. *Postmodern Narrative Theory.* New York: St. Martin's Press.

Dean, John P., and William Foote Whyte. 1958. "'How Do You Know If the Informant Is Telling the Truth?'" *Human Organization* 17 (2): 34–38.

de Certeau, Michel. 1980. "On the Oppositional Practices of Everyday Life." *Social Text* 3:3–43.

Delgado, Richard. 1989. "Storytelling for Oppositionists and Others: A Plea for Narrative." *Michigan Law Review* 87 (8): 2411–41.

Denzin, Norman K. 1987. *The Alcoholic Self.* Newbury Park, Calif.: Sage.

Doctorow, E. L. 1983. "False Document." *E. L. Doctorow: Essays and Conversations.* Ed. Richard Trenner. Princeton, N.J.: Ontario Review Press. 16–27.

Dollard, John, Leonard W. Doob, Neal E. Miller, O. H. Mowrer, and Robert R. Sears. 1939. *Frustration and Aggression.* New Haven, Conn.: Yale University Press.

Dudley, Kathryn Marie. 1994. *The End of the Line: Lost Jobs, New Lives in Postindustrial America.* Chicago: University of Chicago Press.

Ebaugh, Helen Rose Fuchs. 1988. *Becoming an Ex: The Process of Role Exit.* Chicago: University of Chicago Press.

Ellis, Albert. 1973. *Humanistic Psychotherapy.* Secaucus, N.J.: Lyle Stuart.

Erdrich, Louise. 2001. "The Butcher's Wife." *New Yorker,* October 15, 188–200.

Faludi, Susan. 1999. *Stiffed: The Betrayal of the American Man.* New York: Harper-Collins.

Fine, Gary Alan. 1993a. "The Sad Demise, Mysterious Disappearance, and Glorious Triumph of Symbolic Interactionism." In Judith Blake and John Hagen, eds., *Annual Review of Sociology,* vol. 19. Palo Alto, Calif.: Annual Reviews.

———. 1993b. "Ten Lies of Ethnography: Moral Dilemmas of Field Research." *Journal of Contemporary Ethnography* 22 (3): 267–94.

Fontana, Andrea, and James H. Frey. 2000. "The Interview: From Structured Questions to Negotiated Text." In Norman K. Denzin and Yvonna Lincoln, eds., *Handbook of Qualitative Research.* Thousand Oaks, Calif.: Sage. 645–72.

Foote, Nelson N. 1951. "Identification as the Basis for a Theory of Motivation." *American Sociological Review* 16 (1): 14–21.

Foucault, Michel. 1980. *Power/Knowledge: Selected Interviews and Other Writings, 1972–1977.* New York: Pantheon.

Fox, Kathryn J. 1999. "Changing Violent Minds: Discursive Correction and Resistance in the Cognitive Treatment of Violent Offenders in Prison." *Social Problems* 46:88–103.

Frankenberg, Ruth. 1993. *White Women, Race Matters: The Social Construction of Whiteness.* Minneapolis: University of Minnesota Press.

Fromm, Erich. 1994. *Escape from Freedom.* New York: Holt & Company.

Gaarder, Emily, and Joanne Belknap. 2002. "Tenuous Borders: Girls Transferred to Adult Court." *Criminology* 40 (3): 481–517.

Gadd, David. 2004. "Making Sense of Interviewee-Interviewer Dynamics in Narratives about Violence in Intimate Relationships." *International Journal of Social Research Methodology* 7 (5): 383–401.

———. 2003. "Reading between the Lines: Subjectivity and Men's Violence." *Men and Masculinities* 5 (3): 1–22.

Garfinkel, Harold. 1967. "What Is Ethnomethodology?" In Harold Garfinkel, ed., *Studies in Ethnomethodology.* Englewood Cliffs, N.J.: Prentice Hall. 1–34.

———. 1956. "Conditions of Successful Degradation Ceremonies." *American Journal of Sociology* 61 (5): 420–24.

Garland, David W., ed. 2004. *Mass Imprisonment: Social Causes and Consequences.* Thousand Oaks, Calif.: Sage.

———. 2001. *The Culture of Control: Crime and Social Order in Contemporary Society.* Chicago: University of Chicago Press.

Gecas, Viktor, and Peter J. Burke. 1995. "Self and Identity." In Karen S. Cook, Gary Alan Fine, and James S. House, eds., *Sociological Perspectives on Social Psychology.* Boston: Allyn and Bacon. 41–67.

Gergen, Kenneth J. 1971. *The Concept of Self.* New York: Holt, Rinehart and Winston.

———, and Mary M. Gergen. 1988. "Narrative and the Self as Relationship." In Leonard Berkowitz, ed., Advances in Experimental Social Psychology, vol. 21. San Diego: Academic Press.

———. 1986. "Narrative Form and the Construction of Psychological Science." In Theodore R. Sarbin, ed., *Narrative Psychology: The Storied Nature of Human Conduct.* New York: Praeger. 22–44.

Gergen, Mary. 1992. "Life Stories: Pieces of a Dream." In George C. Rosenwald and Richard L. Ochberg, eds., *Storied Lives: The Cultural Politics of Self-Understanding.* New Haven, Conn.: Yale University Press. 127–44.

Gilfus, Mary E. 1992. "From Victims to Survivors to Offenders: Women's Routes of Entry and Immersion into Street Crime." *Women and Criminal Justice* 4 (1): 63–89.

Gilgun, Jane F., and Laura McLeod. 1999. "Gendering Violence." *Studies in Symbolic Interactionism* 22:167–93.

Gilligan, Carol. 1982. *In a Different Voice: Psychological Theory and Women's Development.* Cambridge, Mass.: Harvard University Press.

Gilligan, James. 1997. *Violence: Reflections on a National Epidemic.* New York: Vintage Books.

Girshick, Lori B. 1999. *No Safe Haven: Stories of Women in Prison.* Boston: Northeastern University Press.

Glaser, Barney G., and Anselm L. Strauss. 1967. *The Discovery of Grounded Theory: Strategies for Qualitative Research.* Hawthorne, N.Y.: Aldine de Gruyter.

Goffman, Erving. 1971. *Relations in Public: Microstudies of the Public Order.* New York: Basic Books.

———. 1967. *Interaction Ritual.* New York: Pantheon.

———. 1963a. *Stigma: Notes on the Management of Spoiled Identity.* Englewood Cliffs, N.J.: Prentice-Hall.

———. 1963b. *Behavior in Public Places: Notes on the Social Organization of Gatherings.* New York: Free Press of Glencoe.

———. 1961. *Asylums: Essays on the Social Situation of Mental Patients and Other Inmates.* New York: Anchor.

———. 1959. *The Presentation of Self in Everyday Life.* Garden City, N.Y.: Doubleday.

Gordon, Avery. 1997. *Ghostly Matters: Haunting and the Sociological Imagination.* Minneapolis: University of Minnesota Press.

Gordon, Chad. 1968. "Self-Conceptions: Configurations of Content." In Chad Gordon and Kenneth J. Gergen, eds., *The Self in Social Interaction.* New York: John Wiley and Sons. 115–36.

Gottfredson, Michael R., and Travis Hirschi. 1990. *A General Theory of Crime.* Stanford, Calif.: Stanford University Press.

Greenspoon, Joel. 1955. "The Reinforcing Effect of Two Spoken Sounds on the Frequency of Two Responses." *American Journal of Psychology* 68:409–16.

Griffin, John Howard. 1960. *Black Like Me.* New York: Signet.

Gubrium, Jaber F., and James A. Holstein. 2000. "Analyzing Interpretive Practice." In Norman K. Denzin and Yvonna Lincoln, eds., *Handbook of Qualitative Research.* Thousand Oaks, Calif.: Sage. 487–508.

Guerra, Nancy G. 1993. "Cognitive Development." In Patrick H. Tolan and Bertram J. Cohler, eds., *Handbook of Clinical Research and Practice with Adolescents.* 45–62.

Halsey, Mark J. 2006. "Negotiating Conditional Release: Juvenile Narratives of Repeat Incarceration." *Punishment & Society* 8 (2): 147–81.

Hammersley, Martyn, and Paul Atkinson. 1995. *Ethnography: Principles in Practice,* 2nd ed. New York: Routledge.

Haney, Craig. 2006. *Reforming Punishment: Psychological Limitations to the Pains of Imprisonment.* Washington, D.C.: American Psychological Association.

Harding, Sandra. 1987. "Introduction: Is There a Feminist Method?" In Sandra Harding, ed., *Feminism and Methodology.* Bloomington: Indiana University Press. 1–14.

Harding, Susan. 1992. "The Afterlife of Stories: Genesis of a Man of God." In George C. Rosenwald and Richard L. Ochberg, eds., *Storied Lives: The Cultural Politics of Self-Understanding.* New Haven, Conn.: Yale University Press. 60–75.

Hare-Mustin, Rachel T., and Jeanne Marecek. 1988. "The Meaning of Difference: Gender Theory, Postmodernism and Psychology." *American Psychologist* 43 (6): 455–64.

Harris, M. Kay. 1991. "Moving into the New Millennium: Toward a Feminist Vision of Justice." In Harold E. Pepinsky and Richard Quinney, eds., *Criminology as Peacemaking.* Bloomington: Indiana University Press. 83–97.

Harter, Susan. 1996. "Historical Roots of Contemporary Issues Involving Self-Concept." In Bruce A. Bracken, ed., *Handbook of Self-Concept: Developmental, Social, and Clinical Considerations.* New York: Wiley. 1–37.

Hassine, Victor. 2007. *Life Without Parole: Living in Prison Today,* 3rd ed. Ed. Robert Johnson and Thomas J. Bernard New York: Oxford University Press.

Hayes, Terrell A. 2000. "Stigmatizing Indebtedness: Implications for Labeling Theory." *Symbolic Interaction* 23 (1): 29–46.

Hearn, Jeff. 1998. *The Violences of Men: How Men Talk About and How Agencies Respond to Men's Violence to Women.* London: Sage.

Henry, Stuart, and Dragan Milovanovic. 1996. *Constitutive Criminology: Beyond Postmodernism.* London: Sage.

Herman, Nancy J. 1994. "Interactionist Research Methods: An Overview." In Nancy J. Herman and Larry T. Reynolds, eds., *Symbolic Interaction: An Introduction to Social Psychology.* Dix Hills, N.Y.: General Hall. 90–111.

———. 1993. "Return to Sender: Reintegrative Stigma-Management Strategies of Ex-Psychiatric Patients." *Journal of Contemporary Ethnography* 22 (3): 295–330.

Hertz, Rosanna. 1997. "Introduction: Reflexivity and Voice." In Rosanna Hertz, ed., *Reflexivity and Voice.* Thousand Oaks, Calif.: Sage. vii–xviii.

Hirschi, Travis. 1969. *Causes of Delinquency.* Berkeley: University of California Press.

Holbert, Fred, and N. Prabha Unnithan. 1990. "Free Will, Determinism, and Criminality: The Self-Perception of Prison Inmates." *Journal of Criminal Justice* 18:43–53.

Hollway, Wendy, and Tony Jefferson. 2000. *Doing Qualitative Research Differently: Free Association, Narrative and the Interview Method.* London: Sage.

Holstein, James A., and Jaber F. Gubrium. 2000. *The Self We Live By: Narrative Identity in a Postmodern World.* New York: Oxford University Press.

———. 1995. *The Active Interview.* Thousand Oaks, Calif.: Sage.

Huggins, Martha K., Mika Haritos-Fatouros, and Philip G. Zimbardo. 2002. *Violence Workers: Police Torturers and Murderers Reconstruct Brazilian Atrocities.* Berkeley: University of California Press.

Husserl, Edmund. 1964. *The Phenomenology of Internal Time-Consciousness.* Bloomington: Indiana University Press.

Ickes, William, and Richard Gonzalez. 1996. "'Social' Cognition and Social Cognition: From the Subjective to the Intersubjective." In Judith L. Nye and Aaron M. Brower, eds., *What's Social About Social Cognition?: Research on Socially Shared Cognition in Small Groups.* Thousand Oaks, Calif.: Sage. 285–310.

Irwin, John. 1985. *The Jail: Managing the Underclass in American Society.* Berkeley: University of California Press.

———. 1970. *The Felon.* Berkeley: University of California Press.

Iser, Wolfgang. 1989. "The Play of the Text." In Stanford Budick and Wolfgang Iser, eds., *Languages of the Unsayable: The Play of Negativity in Literature and Literary Theory.* New York: Columbia University Press. 325–39.

———. 1978. *The Act of Reading: A Theory of Aesthetic Response.* Baltimore: Johns Hopkins University Press.

Ives, Edward D. 1980. *The Tape-Recorded Interview: A Manual for Field Workers in Folklore and Oral History.* Knoxville: University of Tennessee Press.

Jack, Dana Crowley. 1999. *Behind the Mask: Destruction and Creativity in Women's Aggression.* Cambridge, Mass.: Harvard University Press.

Jacobs, James B. 1978. *Statesville: The Penitentiary in Mass Society.* Chicago: University of Chicago Press.

Jenkins, Richard. 2004. *Social Identity,* 2nd ed. London: Routledge.

Jordan, Pat. 2001. "The Outcast: Conversations with O. J. Simpson." *New Yorker,* July 9, 42–47.

Katz, Jack. 1988a. *Seductions of Crime: The Moral and Sensual Attractions of Doing Evil.* New York: Basic Books.

———. 1988b. "A Theory of Qualitative Methodology: The Social System of Analytic Fieldwork." In Robert M. Emerson, ed., *Contemporary Field Research: A Collection of Readings.* Prospect Heights, Ill.: Waveland Press. 127–48.

Kay, Judith W. 2005. *Murdering Myths: The Story Behind the Death Penalty.* Lanham, Md.: Rowman and Littlefield.

Kelman, Herbert C. 1973. "Violence Without Moral Restraint." *Journal of Social Issues* 29 (4): 25–61.

Kerby, Anthony Paul. 1991. *Narrative and the Self.* Bloomington: Indiana University Press.

Kimmel, Michael S. 2004. *The Gendered Society,* 2nd ed. New York: Oxford University Press.

Kinch, John W. 1963. "A Formalized Theory of the Self-Concept." *American Journal of Sociology* 68 (4): 481–86.

Kitsuse, John I. 1962. "Social Reaction to Deviant Behavior." *Social Problems* 9:247–56.

Klapp, Orrin E. 1954. "Heroes, Villains and Fools, as Agents of Social Control." *American Sociological Review* 19 (1): 56–62.

Kruttschnitt, Candace, and Kristin Carbone-Lopez. 2006. "Moving Beyond the Stereotypes: Women's Subjective Accounts of Their Violent Crime." *Criminology* 44 (2): 321–51.

Kuhn, Manford H. 1962. "The Interview and the Professional Relationship." In Arnold M. Rose, ed., *Human Behavior and Social Processes: An Interactionist Approach.* Boston: Houghton Mifflin. 193–206.

———, and Thomas S. McPartland. 1954. "An Empirical Investigation of Self-Attitudes." *American Sociological Review* 19 (1): 68–76.

Labov, William. 1982. "Speech Actions and Reactions in Personal Narrative." In Deborah Tannen, ed., *Analyzing Discourse: Text and Talk.* Washington, D.C.: Georgetown University Press. 219–47.

———, and Joshua Waletzky. 1967. "Narrative Analysis: Oral Versions of Personal Experience." In June Helms, ed., *Essays on the Verbal and Visual Arts.* Seattle: University of Washington Press. 12–44.

Leary, Mark. 1995. "The Private Self." In *Self-Presentation: Impression Management and Interpersonal Behavior.* Madison, Wis.: WCB Brown and Benchmark. 156–78.

Lecky, Prescott. 1945. *Self-Consistency: A Theory of Personality.* New York: Island Press.

Lemert, Edwin M. 1974. "Beyond Mead: The Societal Reaction to Deviance." *Social Problems* 21:457–68.

———. 1967. *Human Deviance, Social Problems, and Social Control.* Englewood Cliffs, N.J.: Prentice-Hall.

Levi, Ken. 1981. "Becoming a Hit Man: Neutralization in a Very Deviant Career." *Urban Life* 10 (1): 47–63.

Liebow, Elliot. 1967. *Talley's Corner: A Study of Negro Street Corner Men.* Boston: Little, Brown.

Linde, Charlotte. 1993. *Life Stories: The Creation of Coherence.* New York: Oxford University Press.

Lindesmith, Alfred R. 1981. "Symbolic Interactionism and Causality." *Symbolic Interaction* 4 (1): 87–96.

Loseke, Donileen R. 2003. *Thinking About Social Problems: An Introduction to Constructionist Perspectives,* 2nd ed. New York: Aldine de Gruyter.

Lynch, Michael. 1991a. "Laboratory Space and the Technological Complex: An Investigation of Topical Contextures." *Science in Context* 4 (1): 51–78.

———. 1991b. "Method: Measurement—Ordinary and Scientific Measurement as Ethnomethodological Phenomena." In Graham Button, ed., *Ethnomethodology and the Human Sciences.* Cambridge, UK: Cambridge University Press. 77–108.

Maher, Lisa. 1997. *Sexed Work: Gender, Race, and Resistance in a Brooklyn Drug Market.* New York: Oxford University Press.

Maines, David R., Noreen M. Sugrue, and Michael A. Katovich. 1983. "The Sociological Import of G. H. Mead's Theory of the Past." *American Sociological Review* 48 (2): 161–73.

Manis, Jerome G., and Bernard N. Meltzer, eds. 1978. *Symbolic Interaction: A Reader in Social Psychology.* Boston: Allyn and Bacon.

Manning, Peter K. 1995. "The Challenges of Postmodernism." In John Van Maanen, ed., *Representation in Ethnography.* Thousand Oaks, Calif.: Sage. 245–72.

Markus, Hazel, and Susan Cross. 1990. "The Interpersonal Self." In Lawrence A. Pervin, ed., *Handbook of Personality: Theory and Research.* New York: Guilford Press. 576–608.

Markus, Hazel, and Shinobu Kitayama. 1991. "Culture and the Self: Implications for Cognition, Emotion, and Motivation." *Psychological Review* 98 (2): 224–53.

Marquart, James W. 2001. "Doing Research in Prison: The Strengths and Weaknesses of Full Participation as a Guard." In J. Mitchell Miller and Richard Tewksbury, eds., *Extreme Methods: Innovative Approaches to Social Science Research.* Boston: Allyn and Bacon. 35–47.

Maruna, Shadd. 2001. *Making Good: How Ex-Convicts Reform and Rebuild Their Lives.* Washington, D.C.: American Psychological Association.

———, and Heith Copes. 2005. "What Have We Learned from Five Decades of Neutralization Research?" *Crime and Justice: A Review of Research* 32:221–320.

Mason, Carol. 2002. *Killing for Life: The Apocalyptic Narrative of Pro-Life Politics.* Ithaca, N.Y.: Cornell University Press.

Matsueda, Ross L. 1997. "'Cultural Deviance Theory': The Remarkable Persistence of a Flawed Term." *Theoretical Criminology* 1 (4): 429–52.

———. 1992. "Reflected Appraisals, Parental Labeling, and Delinquency: Specifying a Symbolic Interactionist Theory." *American Journal of Sociology* 97 (6): 1577–1611.

Matthews, Rick A., and David Kauzlarich. 2000. "The Crash of Valujet 592: A Case Study in State-Corporate Crime." *Sociological Focus* 3 (3): 281–98.

Matza, David. 1969. *Becoming Deviant.* Englewood Cliffs, N.J.: Prentice-Hall.

———. 1964. *Delinquency and Drift.* New York: Wiley.

———, and Gresham M. Sykes. 1961. "Juvenile Delinquency and Subterranean Values." *American Sociological Review* 26 (5): 712–19.

Mauer, Marc. 2006. *Race to Incarcerate.* New York: New Press.

———, and Meda Chesney-Lind, eds. 2003. *Invisible Punishment: The Collateral Consequences of Mass Imprisonment.* New York: New Press.

Maxfield, Michael G., and Earl Babbie. 2001. *Research Methods for Criminal Justice and Criminology.* 3rd ed. Belmont, Calif.: Wadsworth.

Maynard, Douglas W., and Marilyn R. Whalen. 1995. "Language, Action, and Social Interaction." In Karen S. Cook, Gary Alan Fine, and James S. House, eds., *Sociological Perspectives on Social Psychology.* Boston: Allyn and Bacon. 149–75.

McAdams, Dan P. 1999. "Personal Narratives and the Life Story." In Lawrence A. Pervin and Oliver P. John, eds., *Handbook of Personality: Theory and Research,* 2nd ed. New York: Guilford.

McCall, Michal M., and Judith Wittner. 1990. "The Good News about Life History." In Howard S. Becker and Michal M. McCall, eds., *Symbolic Interaction and Cultural Studies.* Chicago: University of Chicago Press. 46–89.

McKendy, John P. 2006. "'I'm Very Careful about That': Narrative and Agency of Men in Prison." *Discourse & Society* 17 (4): 473–502.

Mead, George Herbert. 1934. *Mind, Self, and Society from the Standpoint of a Social Behaviorist.* Chicago: University of Chicago Press.

Melossi, Dario. 2000. "Changing Representations of the Criminal." *British Journal of Criminology* 40:296–320.

———. 1985. "Overcoming the Crisis in Critical Criminology: Toward a Grounded Labeling Theory." *Criminology* 23 (2): 193–208.

Merleau-Ponty, Maurice. 1978. *Phenomenology of Perception.* Trans. Colin Smith. London: Humanities Press.

Merton, Robert K. 1938. "Social Structure and Anomie." *American Sociological Review* 3 (5): 672–82.

Messerschmidt, James W. 2000. *Nine Lives: Adolescent Masculinities, the Body, and Violence*. Boulder: Westview.

———. 1997. *Crime as Structured Action: Gender, Race, Class, and Crime in the Making*. Thousand Oaks, Calif.: Sage.

———. 1993. *Masculinities and Crime: Critique and Reconceptualization of Theory*. Lanham, Md.: Rowman and Littlefield.

Messner, Steven F., and Richard Rosenfeld. 2006. *Crime and the American Dream*, 3rd ed. Belmont, Calif.: Wadsworth.

Michielsens, Magda. 2000. "Memory Frames: The Role of Concepts and Cognitions in Telling Life-Stories." In Tess Cosslett, Celia Lury, and Penny Summerfield, eds., *Feminism and Autobiography: Texts, Theories, Methods*. London: Routledge. 183–200.

Miles, Miranda, and Jonathan Crush. 1993. "Personal Narratives as Interactive Texts: Collecting and Interpreting Migrant Life-Histories. *Professional Geographer* 45 (1): 84–94.

Miller, David L. 1973. *George Herbert Mead: Self, Language, and the World*. Austin: University of Texas Press.

Miller, Walter B. 1958. "Lower Class Culture as a Generating Milieu of Gang Delinquency." *Journal of Social Issues* 14 (3): 5–19.

Mills, C. Wright. 1959. *The Sociological Imagination*. New York: Oxford University Press.

———. 1940. "Situated Actions and Vocabularies of Motive." *American Sociological Review* 5 (6): 904–13.

Minow, Martha. 1998. *Between Vengeance and Forgiveness: Facing History after Genocide and Mass Violence*. Boston: Beacon Press.

Mishler, Elliot G. 1992. "Work, Identity, and Narrative: An Artist-Craftsman's Story." In George C. Rosenwald and Richard L. Ochberg, eds., *Storied Lives: The Cultural Politics of Self-Understanding*. New Haven, Conn.: Yale University Press. 21–40.

———. 1986a. "The Analysis of Interview-Narratives." In Theodore R. Sarbin, ed., *Narrative Psychology: The Storied Nature of Human Conduct*. New York: Praeger. 233–55.

———. 1986b. *Research Interviewing: Context and Narrative*. Cambridge, Mass.: Harvard University Press.

Modell, Judith. 1992. "'How Do You Introduce Yourself as a Childless Mother?': Birthparent Interpretations of Parenthood." In George C. Rosenwald and Richard L. Ochberg, eds., *Storied Lives: The Cultural Politics of Self-Understanding*. New Haven, Conn.: Yale University Press. 76–94.

Molotch, Harvey L., and Deirdre Boden. 1985. "Talking Social Structure: Discourse, Domination, and the Watergate Hearings." *American Sociological Review* 50 (3): 273–88.

Morrissey, Belinda. 2003. *When Women Kill: Questions of Agency and Subjectivity*. London: Routledge.

Mullins, Christopher W., Richard Wright, and Bruce A. Jacobs. 2004. "Gender, Streetlife and Criminal Retaliation." *Criminology* 42 (4): 911–40.

Naffine, Ngaire. 1997. *Feminism and Criminology.* Cambridge, UK: Polity Press.

Nietzsche, Friedrich W. 2006. *Human, All Too Human, parts 1 and 2.* Mineola, N.Y.: Dover.

———. 1968. *The Will to Power.* Ed. Walter Kaufmann. New York: Vintage.

Norum, Karen E. 2000. "Black (w)Holes: A Researcher's Place in Her Research." *Qualitative Sociology* 23 (3): 319–39.

O'Connor, Patricia E. 2000. *Speaking of Crime: Narratives of Prisoners.* Lincoln: University of Nebraska Press.

Olivares, Kathleen M., Velmer S. Burton, and Francis T. Cullen. 1996. "The Collateral Consequences of a Felony Conviction: A National Study of State Legal Codes Ten Years Later." *Federal Probation* 60 (3): 10–17.

Paternoster, Raymond, and Leeann Iovanni. 1989. "The Labeling Perspective and Delinquency: An Elaboration of the Theory and an Assessment of the Evidence." *Justice Quarterly* 6 (3): 359–94.

Pepinsky, Harold E., and Richard Quinney, eds. 1991. *Criminology as Peacemaking.* Bloomington: Indiana University Press.

Polanyi, Livia. 1985. *Telling the American Story: A Structural and Cultural Analysis of Conversational Storytelling.* Norwood, N.J.: Ablex.

Polkinghorne, Donald E. 1988. *Narrative Knowing and the Human Sciences.* Albany: State University of New York Press.

Polletta, Francesca, and John Lee. 2006. "Is Telling Stories Good for Democracy? Rhetoric in Public Deliberation after 9/11." *American Sociological Review* 71 (5): 699–723.

Polonoff, David. 1987. "Self-Deception." *Social Research* 54 (1): 45–53.

Pool, Ithiel de Sola. 1957. "A Critique of the Twentieth Anniversary Issue." *Public Opinion Quarterly* 21 (1): 190–98.

Presser, Lois. 2005. "Negotiating Power and Narrative in Research: Implications for Feminist Methodology." *Signs: Journal of Women in Culture and Society* 30 (4): 2067–90.

———. 2004. "Violent Offenders, Moral Selves: Constructing Identities and Accounts in the Research Interview." *Social Problems* 51 (1): 82–101.

———. 2003. "Remorse and Neutralization among Violent Male Offenders." *Justice Quarterly* 20 (4): 801–25.

———, and Cynthia A. Hamilton. 2006. "The Micro-Politics of Victim Offender Mediation." *Sociological Inquiry* 76 (3): 316–42.

Prus, Robert C. 1996. *Symbolic Interaction and Ethnographic Research: Intersubjectivity and the Study of Human Lived Experience.* Albany: State University of New York Press.

Reinharz, Shulamit. 1997. "Who Am I? The Need for a Variety of Selves in the Field." In Rosanna Hertz, ed., *Reflexivity and Voice.* Thousand Oaks, Calif.: Sage. 3–20.

Rhodes, Lorna A. 2004. *Total Confinement: Madness and Reason in the Maximum Security Prison.* Berkeley: University of California Press.

Richardson, Laurel. 1995. "Narrative and Sociology." In John Van Maanen, ed., *Representation in Ethnography.* Thousand Oaks, Calif.: Sage.

Ricoeur, Paul. 1985. "History as Narrative and Practice." Trans. Robert Lechner. *Philosophy Today* (Fall): 198–221.

———. 1984. *Time and Narrative.* Trans. Kathleen McLaughlin and David Pellauer. Chicago: University of Chicago Press.

Rosenberg, Morris, and Howard Kaplan. 1982. *Social Psychology of the Self-Concept.* Arlington Heights, Ill.: Harlan Davidson.

Rosenblatt, Louise M. 1978. *The Reader, the Text, the Poem.* Carbondale: Southern Illinois University Press.

Rosenwald, George C. 1992. "Conclusion: Reflections on Narrative Self-Understanding." In George C. Rosenwald and Richard L. Ochberg, eds., *Storied Lives: The Cultural Politics of Self-Understanding.* New Haven, Conn.: Yale University Press. 265–89.

———, and Richard L. Ochberg. 1992. "Introduction: Life Stories, Cultural Politics, and Self-Understanding." In George C. Rosenwald and Richard L. Ochberg, eds., *Storied Lives: The Cultural Politics of Self-Understanding.* New Haven, Conn.: Yale University Press. 1–18.

Ross, Jeffrey Ian, and Stephen C. Richards, eds. 2002. *Convict Criminology.* Belmont, Calif.: Wadsworth.

Ross, Robert R., and Elizabeth A. Fabiano. 1985. *Time to Think: A Cognitive Model of Delinquency Prevention and Offender Rehabilitation.* Johnson City, Tenn.: Institute of Social Science and Arts.

Rubin, Herbert J., and Irene S. Rubin. 1995. *Qualitative Interviewing: The Art of Hearing Data.* Thousand Oaks, CA: Sage.

Samenow, Stanton E. 1984. *Inside the Criminal Mind.* New York: Times Books.

Sampson, Robert J., and John H. Laub. 1993. *Crime in the Making: Pathways and Turning Points through Life.* Cambridge, Mass.: Harvard University Press.

Santos, Michael G. 2006. *Inside: Life Behind Bars in America.* New York: St. Martin's Press.

Sarbin, Theodore R. 1986. "The Narrative as a Root Metaphor for Psychology." In Theodore R. Sarbin, ed., *Narrative Psychology: The Storied Nature of Human Conduct.* New York: Praeger. 265–89.

Schegloff, Emanuel A. 1982. "Discourses as an Interactional Achievement: Some Uses of 'Uh Huh' and Other Things That Come between Sentences." In D. Tannen, ed., *Analyzing Discourse: Text and Talk.* Washington, D.C.: Georgetown University Press. 71–93.

Schenkein, Jim. 1978. "Identity Negotiations in Conversation." In Jim Schenkein, ed., *Studies in the Organization of Conversational Interaction.* New York: Academic Press. 57–78.

Scheper-Hughes, Nancy. 1992. *Death Without Weeping: The Violence of Everyday Life in Brazil.* Berkeley: University of California Press.

Schiffrin, Deborah. 1996. "Narrative as Self-Portrait: Sociolinguistic Constructions of Identity." *Language in Society* 25 (2): 167–203.

Schlenker, Barry R., Michael F. Weigold, and Kevin Doherty. 1991. "Coping with Accountability: Self-Identification and Evaluative Reckonings." In C. R. Snyder and Donelson R. Forsyth, eds., *Handbook of Social and Clinical Psychology: The Health Perspective.* New York: Pergamon Press. 96–115.

Schuman, Howard. 1982. "Artifacts Are in the Mind of the Beholder." *American Sociologist* 17:21–28.

Schur, Edwin M. 1971. *Labeling Deviant Behavior: Its Sociological Implications.* New York: Harper & Row.

Schutz, Alfred. 1967. *The Phenomenology of the Social World.* Trans. George Walsh and Frederick Lehnert. Evanston, Ill.: Northwestern University Press.

Schwartz, Michael, and Sheldon Stryker. 1970. *Deviance, Selves and Others.* Washington, D.C.: American Sociological Association.

Scott, Marvin B., and Stanford M. Lyman. 1968. "Accounts." *American Sociological Review* 33 (1): 46–62.

Shaw, Clifford R. 1930. *The Jack-Roller: A Delinquent Boy's Own Story.* Chicago: University of Chicago Press.

Sherman, Lawrence W. 1993. "Defiance, Deterrence, and Irrelevance: A Theory of the Criminal Sanction." *Journal of Research in Crime and Delinquency* 30 (4): 445–73.

Shover, Neal. 1996. *Great Pretenders: Pursuits and Careers of Persistent Thieves.* Boulder: Westview Press.

Smith, Barbara Herrnstein. 1981. "Narrative Versions, Narrative Theories." In Ira Konigsberg, ed., *American Criticism in the Post-Structuralist Age.* Ann Arbor: Michigan Studies in the Humanities. 162–86.

Smith, Dorothy E. 1987. *The Everyday World as Problematic: A Feminist Sociology.* Boston: Northeastern University Press.

Somers, Margaret R. 1994. "The Narrative Constitution of Identity: A Relational and Network Approach." *Theory and Society* 23 (5): 605–49.

Spence, Donald P. 1982. *Narrative Truth and Historical Truth: Meaning and Interpretation in Psychoanalysis.* New York: W. W. Norton and Co.

Sternberg, Robert J. 2003. "A Duplex Theory of Hate: Development and Application to Terrorism, Massacres, and Genocide." *Review of General Psychology* 7 (3): 299–328.

Stone, Albert. 1982. *Autobiographical Occasions and Original Acts.* Philadelphia: University of Pennsylvania Press.

Stone, Gregory P. 1962. "Appearance and the Self." In Arnold M. Rose, ed., *Human Behavior and Social Processes.* Boston: Houghton Mifflin. 86–118.

Strauss, Anselm L. 1997 (1959). *Mirrors and Masks: The Search for Identity.* New Brunswick, N.J.: Transaction.

Stryker, Sheldon. 1980. *Symbolic Interactionism: A Social Structural Version*. Menlo Park, Calif.: Benjamin Cummings.

———, and Elizabeth A. Craft. 1982. "Deviance, Selves and Others Revisited." *Youth and Society* 14:159–83.

Stryker, Sheldon, and Anne Statham. 1985. "Symbolic Interaction and Role Theory." In Gardner Lindzey and Elliot Aronson, eds., *Handbook of Social Psychology*, vol. 1, 3rd ed. New York: Random House. 311–78.

Suchman, Lucy, and Brigitte Jordan. 1990. "Interactional Troubles in Face-to-Face Survey Interviews." *Journal of the American Statistical Association* 85 (409): 232–41.

Sullivan, Mercer L. 1998. "Integrating Qualitative and Quantitative Methods in the Study of Developmental Psychopathology in Context." *Development and Psychopathology* 10 (2): 377–93.

Swora, Maria G. 2002. "Narrating Community: The Creation of Social Structure in Alcoholics Anonymous through the Performance of Autobiography." *Narrative Inquiry* 11:363–84.

Sykes, Gresham M. 1971. *The Society of Captives: The Study of a Maximum Security Facility*. Princeton, N.J.: Princeton University Press.

———, and David Matza. 1957. "Techniques of Neutralization: A Theory of Delinquency." *American Sociological Review* 22 (Dec.): 664–70.

Tajfel, Henri. 1981. *Human Groups and Social Categories*. Cambridge, UK: Cambridge University Press.

Tannenbaum, Frank. 1938. *Crime and the Community*. New York: Ginn and Co.

Taylor, Charles. 1985. *Human Agency and Language: Philosophical Papers I*. Cambridge, UK: Cambridge University Press.

Tedlock, Barbara. 1991. "From Participant Observation to the Observation of Participation: The Emergence of Narrative Ethnography." *Journal of Anthropological Research* 47 (1): 69–94.

Thomas, Charles W., and Donna M. Bishop. 1984. "The Effect of Formal and Informal Sanctions on Delinquency: A Longitudinal Comparison of Labeling and Deterrence Theories." *Journal of Criminal Law and Criminology* 75 (4): 1222–45.

Thomas, William I., and Dorothy Swain Thomas. 1928. *The Child in America: Behavior Problems and Programs*. New York: Knopf.

Tittle, Charles R. 1995. *Control Balance: Toward a General Theory of Deviance*. Boulder: Westview.

Toch, Hans. 1993. "Good Violence and Bad Violence: Self-Presentations of Aggressors through Accounts and War Stories." In Richard B. Felson and James T. Tedeschi, eds., *Aggression and Violence: Social Interactionist Perspectives*. Washington, D.C.: American Psychological Association. 193–206.

———. 1977. *Living in Prison: The Ecology of Survival*. Washington, D.C.: American Psychological Association.

———. 1969. *Violent Men: An Inquiry into the Psychology of Violence*. Washington, D.C.: American Psychological Association.

Turner, John C. 1999. "Some Current Issues in Research on Social Identity and Self-Categorization Theories." In Naomi Ellemers, Russell Spears, and Bertjan Doosje, eds., *Social Identity: Context, Commitment, Content*. Oxford, U.K.: Blackwell.

———. 1987. *Rediscovering the Social Group: A Self-Categorization Theory*. Oxford, UK: Basil Blackwell.

Turner, Ralph H. 1976. "The Real Self: From Institution to Impulse." *American Journal of Sociology* 81 (5): 989–1016.

Ulmer, Jeffery T., and J. William Spencer. 1999. "The Contributions of an Interactionist Approach to Research and Theory on Criminal Careers." *Theoretical Criminology* 3 (1): 95–124.

U.S. Department of Justice, Bureau of Justice Statistics. 1999. *Women Offenders*. (Report NCJ 175688). Washington, D.C.: Bureau of Justice Statistics.

van Dijk, Teun A. 1995. "The Violence of Text and Talk." *Discourse and Society* 6 (3): 307–8.

Van Maanen, John. 1995. "An End to Innocence: The Ethnography of Ethnography." In John Van Maanen, ed., *Representation in Ethnography*. Thousand Oaks, Calif.: Sage. 1–35.

Van Ness, Daniel W., and Karen Heetderks Strong. 2001. *Restoring Justice*, 2nd ed. Cincinnati: Anderson.

Van Voorhis, Patricia, Michael Braswell, and David Lester, eds. 2000. *Correctional Counseling and Rehabilitation*, 4th ed. Cincinnati: Anderson.

Vetlesen, Arne Johan. 2005. *Evil and Human Agency: Understanding Collective Evildoing*. Cambridge, UK: Cambridge University Press.

Watson, Rodney. 1992. "The Understanding of Language Use in Everyday Life: Is There a Common Ground?" In Graham Watson and Robert M. Seiler, eds., *Text in Context: Contributions to Ethnomethodology*. Newbury Park, Calif.: Sage. 1–19.

West, Candace, and Don H. Zimmerman. 1987. "Doing Gender." *Gender and Society* 1 (2): 125–51.

Whorf, Benjamin Lee. 1956. *Language, Thought, and Reality: Selected Writings*. Cambridge: Technology Press of Massachusetts Institute of Technology.

Wieder, D. Lawrence. 1983. "Telling the Convict Code." In Robert M. Emerson, ed., *Contemporary Field Research: A Collection of Readings*. Boston: Little, Brown. 78–90.

———. 1977. "Ethnomethodology and Ethnosociology." *Mid-American Review of Sociology* 2 (2): 1–18.

———. 1974. *Language and Social Reality: The Case of Telling the Convict Code*. The Hague: Mouton.

Wiersma, Jacquelyn. 1988. "The Press Release: Symbolic Communication in Life History Interviewing." *Journal of Personality* 56 (1): 205–38.

Williams, Frank P. III. 1999. *Imagining Criminology: An Alternative Paradigm*. New York: Garland.

Willott, Sara, Christine Griffin, and Mark Torrance. 2001. "Snakes and Ladders: Upper-Middle Class Male Offenders Talk about Economic Crime." *Criminology* 39 (2): 441–66.

Wolf, Diane L. 1996. "Situating Feminist Dilemmas in Fieldwork." In Diane L. Wolf, ed., *Feminist Dilemmas in Fieldwork*. Boulder: Westview. 1–55.

Wolfgang, Marvin E., and Franco Feracutti. 1967. *The Subculture of Violence: Toward an Integrated Theory in Criminology*. Beverly Hills, Calif.: Sage.

Woolford, Andrew. 2006. "Making Genocide Unthinkable: Three Guidelines for a Critical Criminology of Genocide." *Critical Criminology* 14 (1): 87–106.

Yochelson, Samuel, and Stanton E. Samenow. 1976. *The Criminal Personality: A Profile for Change*. New York: Jason Aronson.

Zajdow, Graznya. 1999. "Al-Anon Stories: Transformations in an Emotional Culture." In Norman K. Denzin, ed., *Studies in Symbolic Interaction* 22. Stamford, Conn.: JAI Press. 103–37.

Zehr, Howard. 1995. *Changing Lenses: A New Focus for Crime and Justice*. Scottdale, Penn.: Herald Press.

Zerubavel, Eviatar. 1997. *Social Mindscapes: An Invitation to Cognitive Sociology*. Cambridge, Mass.: Harvard University Press.

Index

Note: First names in *italics* refer to specific offenders interviewed.

addiction, 111–12. *See also* twelve-step philosophy
Agar, Michael, 24, 43, 53, 56, 132
Anderson, Elijah, 114
antisocial attitudes, 108–10
archetypes, 62
Arendell, Terry, 39
Arnell: codes of honor, 74; defiance of conventional authority, 137–38; environment, 113; identity negotiations, 14; negative referents, 93; offender status protest, 126; offense justification, 153; reform rejection, 59
Athens, Lonnie, 23, 27–28
Atkinson, Paul, 38–39, 40

bad seed critiques, 94–95
Barthes, Roland, 5
Benson, Michael L., 25–26
biases, 33
Blumstein, Philip, 44
Boden, Deirdre, 26, 38, 41
Bourgois, Philippe, 147
Braithwaite, John, 146
Bruner, Jerome, 6, 39–40
Burke, Peter J., 43

Campbell, Joseph, 107
Chanfrault-Duchet, Marie-Françoise, 19, 23, 43
chivalry, 75, 76, 141. *See also* codes of honor; masculinity
Cicourel, Aaron Victor, 33
Clarence, 66, 84–85, 114, 119, 135–36, 140
codes of honor, 73–74
Coffey, Amanda, 40
cognitive intervention, 154–55
coherence system, 23–24, 132
Cohn, Carol, 153
conventional authority. *See* criminal justice system; defiance of conventional authority
conversation analysis, 41, 158n3 (chap. 3)
Cooley, Charles Horton, 30
co-production of data, 38–44. *See also* interview mechanism
cost-benefit analysis, 104–5
Craft, Elizabeth A., 2–3
criminal justice system: as enemy, 116–21; practices, 153–55; reflexivity need, 151–53; social policy relationship, 155–56; violent nature, 153–55
criminal record length, 120
critical criminology, 155
Currie, Elliott, 153–54, 155
Currie, Mark, 149
Cyrus, 100–102, 111, 113, 126–27

LOIS PRESSER is an associate professor of sociology at the University of Tennessee. Her research concerns narratives, violence, restorative justice, and criminological theory. She is currently developing a theory of harm based on the stories individuals and groups tell about themselves.

The University of Illinois Press
is a founding member of the
Association of American University Presses.

Composed in 10.5/13 Minion Pro
with Helvetica Neue LT Std display
at the University of Illinois Press
Designed by Kelly Gray
Manufactured by Cushing-Malloy, Inc.

University of Illinois Press
1325 South Oak Street
Champaign, IL 61820-6903
www.press.uillinois.edu